James!

CW00545287

stiffkey 1991.

BUSH PATHS

BUSH PATHS

BY

Keith Arrowsmith

THE PENTLAND PRESS
EDINBURGH · CAMBRIDGE · DURHAM

Typeset by Spire Origination, Norwich.
Printed and bound by Antony Rowe Ltd., Chippenham, Wiltshire SN14 6LH.

To my former friends and colleagues,
both Nigerian and British.

*"Whosoever will be chief among you,
let him be your servant"*

CONTENTS

Chapter 1

"Have a look at Africa"

In January 1949, after steaming for several hours up the New Calabar river through mile after mile of mangrove swamp, we docked at Port Harcourt, the headquarters of Rivers Province, the Province to which I had been posted. Some hours later I was installed in a room at the Catering Rest-House with my tin trunk, tin bath, chop box, one crate and a couple of suitcases stacked beside my bed. I had not been there long before I was approached by a small man with an egg-shaped head, wearing a white shirt, khaki shorts and white canvas shoes. After reading the tattered testimonials, which he produced from a grubby envelope, I engaged him as my steward. His name was Philip Ajoku, and he proved to be a very good choice. He remained my "Man Friday" until the day I left Nigeria. I soon had another caller. This was a well-built, middle-aged Englishman wearing in his case a blue shirt, khaki shorts and white canvas shoes.

"Arrowsmith? How do you do? Good, you have arrived safely. My name is Chubb. I am the Resident of Rivers Province. I should be very glad if you would have dinner with me this evening. On my own at present so don't expect anything much. My wife will be coming out in a month or two."

He then explained to me how to reach the Residency. With a twirl of his walking stick he was on the point of leaving when he appeared suddenly to recall a question he had been meaning to ask.

"By the way, Arrowsmith," he said, "do you play hockey?"

I was glad to be able to answer that I did.

I was accompanied to the Residency by two other new recruits, who had arrived on the same ship as I had. Chubb's first words when he met us were "coats off". He himself was wearing grey flannels, white shirt and a tie. We took seats in the spacious drawing-room. The chairs were ranged along the walls and consequently

1

we had the disadvantage of being seated at some distance from each other. The absence of Mrs. Chubb was evidenced by the bareness of the room, which was plainly furnished with Public Works Department furniture. In the centre of the highly polished wooden floor there was a single carpet. Hanging on the white walls were one or two small passe-partouted prints. There were no cushions for the chairs nor curtains for the long French windows. I was surprised when before going in to dinner Chubb suggested that we should "have a look at Africa" and led us into the garden. We soon learned that there was a very practical reason for this excursion.

In due course after dining, the only other member of the party apart from us new boys, an Administrative Officer on his third tour and therefore worthy of considerable respect, murmured the words "Well, it's a working day tomorrow" and we took our leave. Earlier in the evening Chubb had told me that I was to remain in Port Harcourt for a few months in order to give him a hand in his office which, he said, was in a hell of a mess and needed sorting out.

During the weeks which followed I systematically rearranged the Resident's collection of maps and plans; I filed an accumulation of secret and confidential correspondence, and taught myself to type. As a result of sitting in the same office as Chubb I gleaned a lot of useful general knowledge and made the acquaintance of a wide cross-section of people. A memorable visit was that of a Nigerian merchant seaman and his young Liverpudlian wife, who arrived at the office on a bicycle-made-for-two, a sight not previously seen in the Rivers Province. The seaman did all the talking, the burden of which was that he wanted a good Government job; and it was very evident that he felt he was fully entitled to one on the strength of the marriage he had contracted. In spite of the fatherly remarks which the Resident addressed to her his wife remained silent throughout, and it was with real concern that he said goodbye to her. The same day they left by launch for a village in the creeks.

On my first Saturday evening I went to the cinema. This amounted to little more than a walled-in enclosure, half of which was cement-floored. The best seats were tatty upholstered armchairs and the less expensive ones folding camp chairs. The extreme end of the concrete flooring by the entrance was used as a cycle park. In the uncemented half of the enclosure low bushes and shrubs were growing, and at the far end was a white-painted screen. Apart from some corrugated iron which partially covered the sitting area the cinema was open to the heavens.

Before the programme began the first verse of the National Anthem was played, but so much noise was going on that it was some time before I realised what it was. The young lads about town occupying the benches at the sides appeared to get much satisfaction out of remaining seated and talking loudly while the record was played. I was soon to discover that it was their practice to talk equally loudly throughout the entire performance, sometimes breaking into derisive cries and at other times into shouts of approval. The main film starred Veronica Lake, whose charms were clearly appreciated by the audience.

While in Port Harcourt I saw something of the work of a number of different government departments, and I was particularly interested to visit the Prison. When I arrived, the Superintendent was seated beneath a swinging punkah in his office interviewing a prisoner. He looked very smart in his white drill shorts and bush shirt with its brass buttons and pips. He took me on a conducted tour, and I was surprised to find that the prison was enclosed by a very flimsy fence consisting of only a few strands of barbed wire, and I had previously noticed the very limited supervision of gangs of prisoners working here and there about the town. I remarked on this to the Superintendent and enquired whether there were many attempted escapes. He replied that there were not as on the whole prisoners were quite happy where they were. I was able to appreciate the reason for this when I glanced at the ration-scale posted on a board in the cook-house. Rations per man per day amounted in bulk to three to four pounds.

The warders looked smart in their uniform: khaki-drill shirt and shorts, navy-blue peak hat, whistle chain, stockings and prisoner-made leather sandals. The convicts wore only knickers and a sack-like shirt made of drab white calico. Wherever we went, warders kept springing to attention, saluting and reporting, "Twenty men. All correct, sah," but the Superintendent never gave any indication of having heard. On our tour around the premises we were dogged by two uniformed African Officers. One was the grizzled old Chief Warder. The other was an unattractive young man, whose dull bleary eyes behind the thick lenses of his spectacles looked like two chunks of cucumber inside a pickle jar. He wore a white band around his hat, and was styled a cadet.

Prisoner strength was 1,044, of which number about 300 were criminal lunatics. Except for the latter and those undergoing punishment, prisoners enjoyed a high degree of liberty. The prison grounds themselves were spacious and attractive. A series of red brick, windowless, single-storeyed buildings were ranged round a grass square. Here and there were beds of flowers, and low hedges bordered the trim gravel paths. On the other side of the wire fence were clumps of palm trees, which gently fanned their feathery fronds in the breeze.

We looked inside one of the empty red brick cells. The bare concrete floor had been washed down. In the centre wooden bed boards and blankets were stacked in two piles. The only other thing in the room was a small wooden screen in one corner. We visited the blacksmith's forge and the carpenter's, mat-maker's, tailor's and bootmaker's shops, in all of which prisoners were busy at work. The tailor's shop was producing green shirts for Forestry Department staff and the bootmaker's shop was turning out sandals for prison warders.

There were seven men in the condemned cells, two of whom were to be hanged in three days' time. There was also one condemned female prisoner. The entrance to the women's part of the prison was opened by a smart young wardress, who spoilt the effect by collapsing into giggles when asked a question by the Superintendent. After various other doors had been unlocked we reached the cell where the condemned woman was housed. The door was thrown open, and a poor old creature stood up and looked fearfully and bewilderedly at us. There she stood blinking in the doorway, while the buxom young wardress, interpreting for the Superintendent, told her that her appeal had been rejected. The old woman's lips faltered and her eyes looked uncomprehendingly. We heard the short story of her crime: she was being chased by a man in the village; to escape him she hid; the man's child discovered her hiding place and told his father; the woman killed the child with a panga (i.e. a matchet). We left; and the prisoner was locked up again by her young custodian.

Finally we visited the part of the prison which served as a lunatic asylum. I have no very clear impression of the many drooling, gibbering bodies which we saw therein. I do, however, recall one old woman. She was squatting crosslegged on the floor like some wizened undersized Buddha. Her arms and legs were as thin as walking sticks; and I had the impression that propped up against the wall she would not have been more than four feet high. She was only identifiable as a woman by the two straps of loose skin that stretched down to the navel in the pit of her wrinkled stomach. Her hair was tinged with white; her eyes watered; her toothless mouth gaped open into one vacuous grin after another; and from time to time she made queer, unintelligible noises. The Superintendent deplored the lot of the lunatics whom he had in his charge, and complained of his inability to do anything for them.

At Easter I was invited by Newington, one of the District Officers in the Province, to go with him and his wife to Bonny, situated at the mouth of the New Calabar river. We travelled on the District Officer's somewhat antiquated coal-fired launch, and we had not been steaming downstream from Port Harcourt long before it began to blow strongly and pour with rain. Tarpaulins flapped madly, and the crew appeared powerless to make them fast. Water cascaded into the cabin through the slatted wooden window frames. Thunder boomed; the water grew rougher and visibility less. The Quartermaster decided to run for shelter up a side creek, and we dropped anchor close to the edge of the mangrove swamp. While we waited for the worst of the storm to pass we ate an excellent lunch, which to my amazement the Newingtons' cook had been able to produce outside in the open galley.

Bonny was first famous as a slave-trading centre, and later as a prosperous palm-oil trading station and the Headquarters of the British Consul to the Bights of Benin and Biafra. But at the time of this visit of mine in 1949 it had for many years been in a state of stagnation and decay. The founding of Port Harcourt up the river in the earlier part of this century had doomed Bonny's days as a trading station. None of the many ships which crossed the bar at the mouth of the New Calabar river ever stopped to trade at Bonny, and all that the Chiefs could hope for was an occasional fiver, being the fee levied on ships that lay offshore overnight to wait for the tide.

Walking around the "town" all I saw as evidence of its earlier history and prosperity were the sixty-five graves of British traders and seamen in the over-grown cemetery, a few elaborately carved marble memorials to former Kings of Bonny and a quantity of old cannon.

The day after our arrival we loaded the dinghy with food boxes, bottles and bathing gear, and rowed to a nearby sandy beach. As we approached we disturbed a great flock of curlews paddling at the water's edge. As one bird they took to flight, and dividing wheeled off in two formations towards the far bank of the river. After bathing and eating we lay in the sun. As soon as we were quiet crabs, the colour of the sand and almost transparent, furtively emerged from their holes and like children playing "Grandmother's footsteps" advanced with great circumspection towards our encampment. A wave of the hand sent them all scuttling back in hasty retreat. Various people passed by from time to time. One man, who had told us that he was "taking stroll" and who had insisted on washing our dirty cups and plates in a nearby stream, later returned with a bag of mangoes for Madam. He then sat down on the sand nearby and almost became a member of the party. A young girl, naked except for a string of beads across her buttocks, stood and looked at us in apparent astonishment for some minutes before continuing her leisurely way.

On Easter Monday a dance was held in the town to celebrate the emergence of a local beauty from the "Fattening Chamber", it being customary there for girls to be fattened up before marriage. From the Rest-House I heard the sound of drumming begin at 3.00 p.m., and later I went round to see the fun. On an open patch between the houses a small circular enclosure was stringed off. In the centre of this sat a huddle of men drinking. They were, I was told, all members of the Club which was organising the proceedings. A few faded and tattered Union Jacks were the only attempt at decoration. The band, which squatted beneath an awning, consisted of a "drummer", who struck with a sort of brush the mouths of three or four large flagons sunk into the ground and filled with water to different levels, and a bevy of women armed with wooden instruments very similar to Dutch-hands. These they beat together in time, maintaining the while a frenzied vocal accompaniment. The dancers shuffled incessantly in an anticlockwise direction inside the string enclosure. Girls were on the inside and men on the outside. The former maintained a certain uniformity of movement. Bending low, and dangling a handkerchief in each hand which brushed the ground, they advanced jerkily forwards, their backsides constantly a-twitch. The men were individualistic in their movements except when they joined up from time to time for a sort of "Follow-my-leader".

The "Belle of the Ball" had a small palm-frond shelter to herself, the shape of which reminded me very much of a Punch and Judy stand. Periodically she came out and joined in the dancing, which in her fattened state she must have found very exhausting. There were of course many onlookers; and frisking around on the edge of the throng was the local Juju. He cut a rather ludicrous figure and certainly appeared to cause no one any concern. He wore anklets of shells, padded breeches and a cloth over his face with a couple of slits for his eyes. On his head he had a certain amount of foliage superimposed on a rough wooden carving of a crocodile.

Despite the fact that festivities had begun in the heat of the afternoon the band continued its drumming and the dancers their shuffling far into the night. It had been a hot day and I was glad of a bathe from the rickety jetty in front of the Rest-House before going to bed. The water was warm and caressingly soft, and the undulating lift of the incoming swell had the gentle motion of a rocking chair. Facing the open sea, and swimming just sufficiently to hold my own against the pull of the tide, I was able to see the curve of the palm-fringed shore and the two tall silk-cotton trees by the Cathedral looming in the distance. Nearer at hand were the dancing lights of countless fireflies. Above was a twinkling star-dusty sky, and as I swam I scattered handfuls of phosphorescent gems around me in the water. I would not have exchanged my lot with anyone.

Chapter 2

"Defendant's son still at school conceived my daughter"

Soon after Easter Chubb decided that it was time for me to leave Provincial Headquarters and go to a Division. I packed my few belongings, bade farewell to the staff of the Resident's Office and accompanied by Philip set forth in my recently acquired Morris Minor for Bori, the Headquarters of Ogoni Division, forty miles away. Bonniface, my newly engaged cook, followed behind in the lorry carrying my loads and a supply of provisions.

Reviewing Native Court cases was one of the many jobs performed by District Officers and Assistant District Officers. For two days I sat beside Ollard, the District Officer in charge of Ogoni, while he reviewed cases, and strove with only moderate success to pay attention. At the end of the second day Ollard wished me luck and drove away, leaving me for the first time since my arrival in Nigeria to fend for myself alone amongst the local inhabitants.

The following morning at 8.20 a.m. I entered the Court to continue the hearing of reviews. In a manner that would have done credit to a Guards' sergeant-major a Court Messenger ordered those present to stand. I took my seat behind a table on a raised concrete platform at one end of the building. Two formidable piles of judgement books were stacked on the table, in front of which were two wooden docks. The one on my left accommodated the defendant, and the one on my right the plaintiff. Beside me stood Wikina, the District Interpreter, and behind me sat the Court Clerk. Chief Ndeema, the Head of the Local Clan, was seated in a chair on my left, and on two benches on either side of my table sat the village Elders. The body of the hall was filled with those who had received summonses, and interested spectators. Five uniformed Court Messengers kept order peremptorily quelling any expressions of merriment, expostulation or approval, and they also roused any who appeared to be sleeping.

7

My first review case was a criminal one and somewhat complicated. It involved a husband and wife, the former being the complainant and the latter the accused. She was charged with desertion, theft and unlawful possession of children. The Native Court had found the accused guilty and had sentenced her to three months' imprisonment with hard labour, at the same time ordering the return of the children to the husband. This judgement had been upheld by the Appeal Court. I listened to the stories of the two parties. The accused admitted that she had left her husband to go "harloting" in Port Harcourt. It was there that she had met the man with whom she was now living, one Harrison by name and of unprepossessing appearance. After some forty-five minutes' talk by the parties I decided it was time to bring my first case to an end, and I confirmed the judgement of the Native Court. Harrison took a poor view of this decision, and informed me that he intended to apply for review by the Resident. I told him he was at liberty to do so. He also applied for bail, and this I agreed to. The other cases I dealt with that day with Wikina's unofficial assistance were fortunately more straightforward. I ordered the divorce of one young woman, and rejected a claim for divorce made by another. I allowed various claims for damages for adultery. I declared ownership in respect of a matchet and some goats, and settled sundry claims for "brushing", i.e. trespass on land. One case was rather different. In this one woman had sued another for £10 damages for defamation of character. Judgement had been given for the plaintiff in both the Native and Appeal Courts. I gathered from the earlier proceedings that the defendant had explained that she had accused the plaintiff of stealing because the plaintiff had come to her with a story about her servant having accidentally dug up three of the defendant's yams. When I asked the plaintiff if this were so she hotly denied that her servant had at any time dug up any of the defendant's yams. The plaintiff had, however, unwisely seen fit to hand to me in Court a letter written by her husband on her behalf. This contained the statement: "I told defendant that my boy had dug up three of her yams by mistake, whereupon she asked me to come and see the damage. I strongly refused ...". The plaintiff was most put out when I reversed the Native Court judgement and said I considered that the defendant had had every cause to feel some dissatisfaction and that in the circumstances her imputations could be considered neither unreasonable nor defamatory.

I used to enjoy my defamation of character cases because of the insight into human nature which they afforded. One day I had had a dreary succession of cases to deal with when I came to one, Jane Obadiah versus Abel Jambo, in which the claim was for damages of £10 for defamation of the plaintiff's character. On my right was Jane Obadiah, the defamed, and on my left Abel Jambo, the alleged villain of the piece. I restrained myself from shouting "seconds out of the ring", and eagerly scanned the proceedings recorded in the Native Court judgement book, keen to plumb the depths to which Abel had sunk in his abuse of Jane. While I did so brawny Jane's features bore the imprint of righteous indignation, and she kept her face averted from the man who had cast a wanton slur upon her fair name. For his part the defendant looked with bitter rancour at his implacable opponent. It was with a feeling of foreboding that I read in the plaintiff's statement these few words terse and to the point: "Defendant's son still at school conceived my daughter". Prelude to what awful scene was this, I wondered, and reading on I learned that Abel Jambo, incensed by this accusation, had averred in public that the lady's head was "rotten". This might well have been considered unpardonable but for the fact that Jane had on her side so forgotten her maidenly delicacy as to cast aspersions on the quality and quantity of Abel's spittle and had declared that he had "a watering mouth". This utterance had caused him to institute an action for defamation against her in return. When questioned Jane Obadiah, with face no longer averted, glared defiance. The solution was easy. I ordered each to pay the other fifty shillings damages and to share the costs.

"Wakey, wakey, Massah," said Philip pulling at my mosquito net. It seemed much too early to get up, and then I remembered that this was Empire Day. After breakfasting I went to the District Officer's house. Ollard was in the process of donning his uniform. There was a hush within the white-washed walls, broken now and again by muted oaths from the bedroom. Expectancy filled the air, because there was something moving and symbolical about the annual robing of a District Officer – the Sovereign's representative – in his white uniform. For 363 days in the year a District Officer's uniform remained fallow and gathering mould in the bottom of his tin trunk; on the 364th it was cleaned and starched preparatory to its wearing on the following day. A figure entered the room and for a moment I thought I beheld the resurrection of an officer of the former East India Company. In his white tunic buttoning to the neck with georgettes at the throat, his drainpipe trousers, sword and white Bombay bowler, Ollard's appearance evoked thoughts of chota pegs and pig-sticking. I was sorry that no spurs embellished his black boots; and I was surprised to see that his sword transfixed his tunic, so that only the hilt and the tip of the scabbard were visible. This arrangement coupled with the narrowness of his trousers made it almost impossible for him to bend an inch, and it was with the greatest difficulty that he succeeded in inserting himself into the front seat of my small car. I drove him to the sports ground, and a little later he was standing braced (a stance which the confines of his uniform made inevitable) beside a limp Union

Jack, hanging from a bent bamboo. Having read the King's Message to the assembled schoolchildren, there followed a march-past, carried out to the accompaniment of a babel of noise. Half a dozen school bands struck up different tunes, and one squad of children singing one song vied with the next in the line singing another. Until I was informed that the bands were rendering "Rule Britannia", "John Brown's Body" and similar imported refrains I had imagined that they were playing traditional African jungle airs. The different schools taking part had different uniforms. The boys were for the most part wearing khaki shorts and white shirts. The dress of the girls was more variegated. Some sported pink blouses and blue skirts; others had dresses of alternate green and grey bands; and others wore green dresses with white hems. The teachers, who seemed to be even more full of spirits than their charges, were dressed in their smartest clothes. In many cases these resembled their school uniform in colour. A young teacher leading his contingent of boys, who were clad in white shorts and blue shirts, was himself wearing long blue trousers of the same shade and a white jacket. While the march-past was going on I sat in the shade of a hut with Mrs. Ollard and her baby son. An effusive African woman forcibly gathered Martin to her ample bosom. One breast overflowed from her blouse. Martin pinched this and then gave vocal indication of his disapproval.

Interschool sports began at 11.00 a.m. and were conducted in a state of seemingly utter confusion. However, the children appeared happy enough; and the spectators enjoyed themselves gossiping, joking and adjourning periodically to the palm-wine sellers for liquid refreshment. Only the teachers seemed dissatisfied and went around accusing the judges of partiality. Acrimony reached such a pitch while the girls' races were being run that I intervened, and promptly found myself in the position of chief judge of all remaining events. The bulk of the work of organising the races seemed to fall on the District Clerk, Mr. Fineface. He was the starter, and as a symbol of office he carried a .22 rifle, which he used for prodding small feet which failed to toe the starting line. Before each race a policeman carrying an instrument like a T-square three and a half feet long went along the line of runners checking their heights and sorting out juniors from seniors. I am glad to say that Mr. Fineface's weapon was never loaded, and as a signal to start a race there was only the click of the trigger. Many children failed to wait for the click before beginning and had to be called back. Occasionally, however, the trigger clicked unexpectedly, and it was then that those who had their wits about them got off to a good start.

With bands playing continuously and constant hubbub reigning the sports seemed to drag on interminably, but by 5.00 p.m. they had run their weary length.

The competitors gathered in a close circle around Mrs. Ollard, who first presented the coveted shield to the winning school amidst the jubilant shouts of its staff and pupils, and then disbursed the prizes: three shillings for the first, two shillings for the second and one shilling for the third in each event. As the children made their way home the sun set on this small outpost; but for some of the older generation Empire Day was not yet over. They adjourned to the local hall for a dance. A notice outside stated that admission was sixpence for men but free for ladies and that the band of the Roman Catholic Mission School would "discuss the latest musical hits". Later I fell asleep on my camp bed to the distant sounds of revelry by night.

More court work followed this interlude. One case concerned a certain Na-eru who laid claim to the headship of the village of Berah in place of the existing title holder. To resolve this issue I decided to hold a meeting in the village in question. We assembled beneath the spreading branches of a large tree in an open space between the huts, and I seated myself behind a table facing a semicircle of men. In the background there were innumerable children and a few women. I explained that the purpose of the meeting was to enable the villagers to decide for themselves which man had a better claim to the Headship. I called the village elders and the two claimants forward. Then I let those present have their say. Wikina and two Court Messengers strove to keep order, but from time to time uproar broke out. Having allowed both sides ample time to express their views I announced that I was going to allow the head of each household to vote in favour either of Na-eru or Tona-dane, the other claimant. When it came to the point the latter decided not to stake his success on a vote and shewed himself amenable to a compromise. Finally I decided that Na-eru should pay Tona-dane 4,800 manillas, being a refund of pledge money paid by the latter's forefathers, in return for his renunciation of all claims to the Headship of the village. Sustained uproar broke out on this decision being made known, which I hoped could be interpreted as evidence of the enthusiasm with which the village was acclaiming its new Head. As Wikina and I were leaving Na-eru presented me with two yams, a fowl and a bag of oranges, and we departed to the rousing cheers of the populace.

Pledging was a practice much indulged in. When in need of cash a person would pledge a piece of land or some article to someone else in return for an advance. This often led to complications, and many of the cases dealt with in the Native Courts concerned or were connected with pledging. This was so in an action brought by a man against a woman for damages of £25 for having locked him into his house. The woman had taken a basket to the man to be repaired at a cost of seven shillings and sixpence. Having repaired it, the man who was in need of cash to pay his tax pledged it for ten shillings and sixpence. All was well for a time because the woman

11

could not raise the necessary repair fee. However, in due course she paid the agreed sum of seven shillings and sixpence and asked for her basket. The man said that he could not give it to her there and then because he had pledged it. There followed an ugly scene during which, according to the woman, the man somewhat improbably in the circumstances loosened his clothes and tried to have sexual intercourse with her. Be that as it may, she eluded him, and escaping out of the house she turned the lock of the front door. A few moments later the man also gained the street having found the kitchen door open. He was very put out about the indignity he had suffered. So much so that not only had he taken a civil action for damages but also a criminal one for false imprisonment, as a result of which the woman had been fined ten shillings. It was a relief to have a straightforward case to deal with, involving no juju or oath-swearing. In rejecting the plaintiff's claim I pointed out to him that he was not blameless as he had pledged something which did not belong to him, and that in any event he had not suffered in any way as a result of the defendant's action in locking his front door. He appeared hurt that I did not regard his short-lived incarceration with the same horror as he did. As regards the alleged indecent exposure and attempted intercourse, as they were not relevant to reaching a decision I did not probe into their authenticity. My belief was that these allegations were fabrications by the defendant made with the mistaken idea that they would lend weight to her side of the case.

The complications which could arise out of the pledging of land came to light in a case in which the plaintiff sued the defendant for damages for having planted yams on some of his land. The plaintiff admitted that five years earlier he had pledged the land in question to a certain Nwikirikiwa, but said that six months ago he had redeemed the land by refunding the necessary sum to Nwikirikiwa. As far as the plaintiff was aware the defendant had no right to the land at all. However, Nwikirikiwa after receiving the land on pledge from the plaintiff had himself pledged it to one Nwitunglo. Nwitunglo had in his turn pledged it to the defendant. When the plaintiff refunded the pledge money to Nwikirikiwa, he refunded Nwitunglo, who tried to refund the defendant. The latter had by then, however, cleared the land prior to planting crops on it, and he would not agree to Nwitunglo redeeming it from him. The plaintiff, unaware of the ramifications, imagined that since Nwikirikiwa had accepted the return of his pledge money the land was once again his. The defendant, also unaware of the ramifications, imagined that since he had not accepted the return of his pledge money from Nwitunglo the land was still his. Native law and custom did not prevent a man holding land on pledge from pledging it himself. Furthermore, it permitted a man holding land on pledge to refuse to accept its redemption, if he had already cleared it, until after the ensuing harvest. The defendant was therefore within his rights in refusing to quit the land when Nwitunglo sought to redeem it; and the plaintiff's claim against him accordingly failed. I upheld the judgement of the Appeal Court but made an order that after the coming harvest the defendant must accept the refund of his pledge money and quit the land. At the end of the proceedings the defendant popped up and said that the plaintiff had also planted yams on the land in question. To the amusement of those present apart from the plaintiff I said that in that case he could sue him for damages.

Many of the cases I dealt with concerned dowry. Possession of a wife and the children she bore was established by payment of dowry. Native law and custom did not recognise a marriage unless dowry had been paid by the man to the woman's family. In the event of the husband's death a wife was inherited by some other male member of his family. However, if dowry were refunded by them the parents of a woman could then re-marry her to another man. A Chief, a wizened old man with a mean look in his eyes, was plaintiff in an action for the return of a woman and her child. She had been married to the Chief's son and dowry had been paid for her. Later the son had died, and the woman had married the defendant. According to the Chief himself it was three years since his daughter-in-law first went to live with the defendant; and he failed to give any reason why he had allowed so long to elapse before suing for her return. The defendant maintained that he had paid dowry for his wife; and he produced as a witness the man to whom he had paid it. This individual acknowledged that he had received the dowry and explained that it had been handed over to him because he was a close relative of the Chief and was living with him at the time. This was, however, vehemently denied by the plaintiff. In view of the corroboration of the defendant's statement and in the absence of any evidence to disprove it I was able to assume that he had in fact paid dowry for the woman. This then made him her indisputable husband, and the father-in-law was not entitled to her return. As regards the child, whereas the Chief assured me that he was his son's and was born three years ago, I noticed in the Native Court proceedings an admission by him that the child had been born only a few months previously. Even if the child had been his son's it is most improbable that I would have ordered him to be taken from his mother and handed over to the keeping of the ancient and vituperative plaintiff.

Sometimes the Native Court was needlessly harsh in the sentences it awarded. A young man was accused of stealing two manillas (worth sixpence). He was the member of a Club, which had a meeting following the burial ceremony of one of its members. At the gathering two members, whose subscriptions were due, deposited a manilla apiece on a table. The accused admitted that later in the evening, being annoyed with the Head of the Club, he had pocketed the two manillas, which were found in his possession. He was sentenced to three months' imprisonment. When reviewing his case I learned that he had never been in trouble before, and I therefore reduced the sentence to a fine of five shillings. While I was eating my sandwiches later I saw him setting off home with a couple of friends. He was chatting excitedly with them, while he twirled a stick and held his head high. I was glad he was going home and not to prison – the five shillings had already been handed over to the Court Clerk.

Another action for damages for defamation of character concerned a plump good-looking woman called Paula. She stated that the defendant, Fubara, had called her a harlot. On reading through the Native Court proceedings I came to the conclusion that he had had good grounds for having done so. The plaintiff had admitted that she had left her husband and for a time had lived with Fubara as his lover. Over a year ago she had left him too. Thereafter she lived on her own, and she traded – she told me – in singlets and sun helmets. Paula spoke pigeon English, but the assistance of Wikina, the interpreter, was nevertheless necessary. When I asked whether she had divorced her husband, Wikina put my question as follows: ''The man you go leave for good, him what you call husband, did him go pay you back money for head (i.e. dowry)?''

My enquiry as to whether she had ever received payment from the defendant for her services was rendered as: ''A.D.O. say what time you go give him body this man, he make you present money or not?'' and accompanied by appropriate gestures.

Paula replied with feeling, ''I no time take him money: he go be my lover.''

The defendant alleged that others besides himself had enjoyed Paula's favours. She faltered when asked about a man called Moses, but hotly denied knowing anything about a man from Lagos or another from Benin. In dismissing her claim I expressed the hope that her trading in singlets and sun helmets would prosper in the future; but these words were probably lost on Paula who had already broken into angry expostulations. On returning home in the car I gathered that Wikina had some knowledge of this lady. I did not press for details. He confirmed that her annoyance with Fubara, which caused her to take this case against him, was on account of some unsettled debt.

The next time I sat in Court was not in order to hear reviews but to attend a Reception given by the Bori Recreational Club in honour of the Ollards who had only recently arrived in Ogoni. The Reception was held in the sombre surroundings of the octagonal-shaped Appeal Court building. I noticed that the juju relics – a battered skull, a few feathers and other less identifiable matter – which normally adorned the floor as a warning to litigants to speak the truth had been removed for the occasion. The fourteen members of the Club were resplendent in white suits, spotlessly cleaned and rigidly pressed, and despite the evening hour they wore or carried white sun-helmets. Ollard had squeezed himself into a cotton jacket, much shrunken after innumerable washings, and his tie seemed to be slowly throttling him. We took our seats at small tables draped with white cloths. Mr. Fineface began the proceedings by making a fulsome speech in which he testified to the noble qualities of Mr. Ollard, the new District Officer, and his wife. With commendable adroitness he went on to draw attention to the difficulties confronting the Bori Recreation Club. He expressed his conviction that the District Officer would do all within his power to provide them with premises of their own and a tennis court. Loud applause by members of the Club. Fineface then proposed a toast to the Guests of Honour, but this was apparently only a figure of speech because at that stage of the proceedings nothing had been provided in which to drink it. Ollard made a somewhat non-committal speech in reply. We then reached item 3, "Refreshments", on the typewritten agenda. Beer, whisky and palm wine were produced in turn from the Chiefs' Retiring Room. Justice having been done to the refreshments, and Mrs. Ollard having left, the members of the Club and their guests got down to a game of Housey-housey, in the art of playing which they were instructed by Mr. Fineface, self- appointed Master of Ceremonies. Darkness fell; lamps were lit; further refreshment was imbibed; and play continued until a late hour.

A few days later, as I was on the point of leaving the office shortly after 2.00 p.m., I received an urgent message that the Native Administration lorry with the District Officer's touring loads on board had had a crash. My informant indicated with expressive hand movements that the lorry had over-turned. I learned that the only load-carrying vehicle available in the station was the newly acquired ambulance. Accordingly I instructed Fineface to collect a band of labourers and take them in the "juju car" to the scene of the accident. I then sought the assistance of our local engineer, and armed with thirty yards of rope and a five-ton jack we set forth in my Morris Minor. We were accompanied by Macauley, the office messenger. For some reason best known to himself Macauley, who was conventionally clad in other respects, wore on his head a yellow, white-spotted, lady's bathing cap. On arrival we found the lorry already righted and surrounded by the greater part of the inhabitants of a nearby village. The lorry had crashed over a bank on the side of the road and down a four-foot drop. The villagers had borne it bodily from its resting place among the yams to where we found it back on the road. The only damage was a crumpled right wing. The jack was brought into play and the wheel was removed.

Our audience followed every movement with the closest attention. The circle round the lorry edged constantly nearer and nearer until we were left with so little room that I had to drive them back. Thereafter we enjoyed a breathing space for a few moments before the contraction recommenced. Two small boys had a bird's eye view of the proceedings from a nearby tree and four more watched in a recumbent position beneath the lorry. Fresh excitement was afforded by the arrival of the ambulance in all its pristine whiteness. It was only that morning that it had performed its first errand of mercy in taking a man bitten by a snake to the dispensary. The entire staff from District Headquarters, or so it seemed, emerged from it. Finding there was nothing to be done and affected no doubt by the general holiday spirit they adjourned to a nearby shack to drink palm wine. After an hour and a half the necessary repairs were completed, and the lorry left with – I hoped – a somewhat chastened driver at the wheel. It was followed by the ambulance loaded with local inhabitants all ready to walk the eight miles back from Bori for the sake of a ride in the "juju car". My small car brought up the rear; and as we left we were given a rousing send-off.

At 2.30 a.m. one night I was awakened by the onslaught of a violent storm. First came very heavy rain, the noise of which was like the roar of angry waves breaking on a rocky shore. Following the thrashing rain, and while it was still beating down, came violent squalls of wind which buffeted the house and even shook my bed. I feared the matting roof would be carried away; and I wrestled to close those wooden window shutters which had not already been slammed to. Back beneath my mosquito net I lay awake waiting for the storm to pass. During the holocaust I seemed to lose my individuality and to become part and parcel of the wood and concrete of the house and the land on which it stood. Lightning flashed almost without a break. The gruff rumbling of thunder approached and increased immeasurably in volume as it passed ponderously overhead. The whole impressive performance struck me not so much as a battle of the elements but as a combined operation of the elements against the earth; and it seemed to me that it was only thanks to a merciful Providence that we frail mortals cowering in our flimsy abodes were not all blasted into oblivion.

Some nights later I was staying at the Rest-House in Port Harcourt. About midnight I was woken by a great hullaballoo: cries, running footsteps, one or two thuds, a babel of excited voices, followed by whistles as the first constable arrived belatedly on the scene. It was evident that a thief-man had been caught, but I did not consider it to be any concern of mine. Time went by and the racket continued. Eventually, more keen on ending the din than on discharging my responsibilities as a Justice of the Peace, I got up and sallied forth armed with a torch. In the centre of a cluster of excited Rest-House boys I found a stricken and gory body lying prostrate on the ground. A proud watch-night told me that he had found the man attempting to break into one of the servants' quarters. I considered he had made an unnecessary mess of the felon. I stretched the body out on some grass and sent someone for some water, and dispersed the onlookers with injunctions to be quiet. By now a Police Sergeant had appeared and I told him to ring up the station for a kit-car in which to remove the offending object. At this stage of the proceedings a kindly but tough District Officer, Bill Newington, arrived on the scenes dressed in a mackintosh. It seemed that I had been guilty of too much clemency, and Bill congratulated the watch-night on the damage he had inflicted. A kit-car was deemed an unnecessary luxury, and the thief-man suddenly became very alive when two constables began twisting his arms. He leapt shrieking to his feet, and was propelled towards the Police Station two miles distant.

At 3.30 p.m. the following day, a Sunday, all Administrative Officers of the Rivers Province and Heads of Departments gathered in the Resident's Office at the request of Hugh Foot (later Lord Caradon), the Officer administering the Government in the absence of the Governor who was on leave. He looked very smart in his fawn, double-breasted palm beach suit and cream-coloured shirt. At the outset he apologised for having called us together at such an hour on such a day, and explained that he had had to do so because he would be leaving Port Harcourt early the following morning. He said that he was in the process of visiting a number of provincial headquarters throughout the country, his intention being to try to establish direct contact between the centre and the men in the field. He stressed the need for new thinking at all levels of the Service, and while acknowledging that great work had been done in Nigeria he said that one could not hope profitably and indefinitely to carry on with old methods. Times were changing, and it was vital that the Service should adapt itself to them. The good sense of his remarks was indisputable, but I felt that they left one with nothing very concrete to work on. Having spoken for half an hour Foot then invited us to raise any matter whether connected with what he had been saying or not. The ensuing two hours were taken up with discussion on a wide variety of subjects which included: the attitude to be adopted towards a hostile and vituperative local press; conditions of service; the financial difficulties confronting married officers with children; and the probable future duration of the Service in Nigeria. Foot dealt with all the points without hesitation and in a forthright manner. That evening he visited the Port Harcourt Club where he mingled and chatted freely with members.

Chapter 3

"The Groans of the Ogu taxpayers"

After six months in Nigeria the time arrived for me to sit the Ibo language examination. I had already taken and passed the law examination. The Ibo exam took place in Umuahea, the headquarters of the neighbouring Owerri Province. At 9.00 a.m. one morning nine Assistant District Officers assembled at the Resident's Office there. We did three written papers that day; and the following day we had our orals, in the course of which we had to make polite conversation with two of the station labourers. For some obscure reason we had to wait four months before learning the results of our efforts.

After the exam on my way back to Port Harcourt I planned to spend a night with a friend in a nearby Rest-House at Itu. I had difficulty in finding the place. Fortunately, however, I chanced upon a Roman Catholic establishment. I motored up a drive to a well-built, two-storeyed house where I was met by an Irish Father, who invited me in for a drink and introduced me to two more Irish Fathers, each with a two-day growth of beard. All three wore open-necked shirts and shorts and no clerical garb of any kind. An attempt had been made to brighten the room in which we were seated. There were flowers on a table, cretonne covers on the chair cushions and curtains of the same material. Through the open doorway of a bedroom I saw on a small table a pair of brass candlesticks flanking the picture of a saint. The Fathers talked mainly about a forthcoming rugger match between the Roman Catholic Mission and a Government team.

The Rest-House at Itu was a well-built structure consisting of an outer room open to the four winds with an inner and enclosed room behind. A small garden separated it from the bush which encompassed it on three sides. The ground sloped away in front, and there was a distant view of tree-clad undulations with the Residency at Umuahea just discernible some ten miles away. To the south the Rest-House was

18

flanked by a line of cashew nut trees. That evening it was very windy and the rain came down in torrents. Ron and I retreated to the inner room. The camp beds were pushed to one side, and the dining table and two armchairs were brought in. The wind and rain made the evening cool and refreshing; and by the pleasant light of a shaded Aladdin lamp we had an excellent meal which we consumed to the accompaniment of a "Ring up the Curtain" programme from the B.B.C. London.

Chubb considered that the time had come for me to move to another Division in order to further my training as an Assistant District Officer. He decided that I should do a spell at Degema in the creeks as Newington's assistant. Leaving my car in Port Harcourt I travelled by launch with Philip, Bonniface, my personal belongings and the inevitable fowl or two to my new station. A crocodile of prisoners met us on arrival to carry my loads to my house and then to re-coal *Dorothy*, the launch on which I had travelled.

Compared with Bori, Degema was a sizeable place. In addition to the Newingtons and me there was a Medical Officer (a Nigerian) and a Sierra Leonian Magistrate married to an English woman. There were also five European trading company officials, two of whom had their wives with them. Degema was a pleasing little enclave in a vast wilderness of mangrove swamp and creeks on the eastern fringe of the enormous Niger delta. The golf course occupied a considerable part of the station, and the general effect was a park-like one of cut grass and tall trees. Backing onto the golf-course and facing the Sombrero river were the government and commercial houses. The three government houses were stalwart structures of red brick built about fifty years earlier. In the days when there was a Consultate in Degema two officers occupied the outside houses and used the smaller one in the centre – in which I was living – as their Mess. In front of all three houses attractive gardens extended to the bank at the water's edge. The District Officer's was graced with a very fine flagstaff with a couple of old cannons at its base. My garden boasted only a single cannon, which pointed out across the river. Hedges of hibiscus divided the gardens and some casuerina trees lined the water's edge. Scattered here and there were frangipanis, pawpaws, coconut palms and clumps of bougainvillea. The flowerbeds, which lacked variety, were filled for the most part with cannas, African marigolds and bachelor's buttons. Apart from the District Office and the Magistrate's Court there was a small hospital, a post and telegraph office and a prison. There was also a Club, the total membership of which at any one time did not exceed ten or eleven persons. Because of the recalcitrant attitude of the European traders neither the Nigerian medical officer nor the Sierra Leonian magistrate and his wife belonged to the Club (I am glad to say that they were granted honorary membership a little later). The Club enjoyed the refinement of electric lighting.

19

Two bulbs powered by the United Africa Company Manager's generator glowed somewhat dimly as long as the generator was working. The Club was equipped with a ping-pong table, full-size billiard table and a bar. At one end of this stood a life-size wooden man. Glimpsing him out of the corner of an eye I frequently mistook him for a fellow member; and in a sense I suppose he was in fact our one honorary inanimate life member. He was the figure head off the "George Shotton", one of the last of the old trading hulks at Degema. After one lunch-time Club party Newington conceived the idea that George would like to participate in a game of golf. A gang of prisoners was summoned, and somewhat to their mystification they were required to hump George's heavy frame around the course.

Members tended to foregather in the Club on Wednesday and Saturday evenings. The Club building was low and squat. Its corrugated-iron roof and walls were painted a drab green. It had no proper windows, just flaps which were held in an upright position by bamboos and looked like great eyelids propped open with giant matchsticks. The pride of the Club was the billiard table, which beneath its over-head lamps looked like a vast operating table. The players played their shots with quite as much concentration as a surgeon making his incision. When a ball dropped into a pocket, Titus, the one and only Club boy, adjusted the score on the score-board. The massive table stood as immutable as the Sphinx, and seemed to me to epitomise the inviolability and permanence of the English Club. In the front part of the building four bridge players sat in the patch of light afforded by one of the two electric light bulbs. What an infinitesimal small pinpoint of light that was, I thought, in the enormous dark mantle of the mangrove swamps which extended around us for thousands of square miles. Moths and winged insects flitted around the naked bulb. Outside could be heard the motor providing the necessary power. A great flying beetle thudded into the room, and one of the ladies gave a scream. A man crunched it with the sole of his mosquito boot as it lay writhing on its back on the floor. In between hands Titus moved softly around the bridge table taking orders for drinks. Two dogs lay prone beneath it as inert as a couple of hassocks. Outside the fire flies danced, but we in the Club did not see them.

Degema, being almost entirely surrounded by swamp and water, had very much the atmosphere of a small island. Only a single path led out of Degema station past the overgrown European Cemetery. One morning I set off along this path on a bicycle accompanied by an interpreter, a police constable and a court messenger. Our destination was Buguma, about ten miles away. For the first seven miles we cycled through thick bush along a bumpy track. The last part of the journey lay for the most part over mangrove swamp, a poor attempt having been made to bank up the path. From time to time by means of rickety footbridges we crossed creeks of muddy water and ooze, the colour and consistency of over-used engine oil; and at one point we had to transfer ourselves and cycles to a canoe. It rained off and on and we reached Buguma in a sodden state.

My purpose in making the journey was twofold. I wished to make a surprise check on the registration of men for tax payment, and I wished also to reconnoitre the proposed route for a new "road". Before beginning to do either of these things I made my way between the congestion of corrugated-iron roofed shacks to the two-storeyed house of Mr. David-West, a retired government chief clerk. He welcomed me warmly and I ate my picnic lunch in the shelter of his "parlour". This was the sitting half of a large room, the other half being dining-room. A large number of solid wooden armchairs were ranged side by side around the walls, and were adorned with a multifarious collection of clashing-coloured cushions. There were no curtains and only a small piece of worn-out carpeting on the floor. Apart from these modest furnishings the room was bare of everything except photographs, which were there in profusion – hanging on the walls and propped up on tables and shelves. I noticed that everybody in them was wearing English-style clothes: little boys in peak school caps, bigger boys in blazers and young men in butterfly collars and drainpipe trousers. As befitted a man in his position Mr. David-West had portraits of the King and Queen gracing his walls and also a group photo of the Royal Family shewing the Princesses aged twelve and eight.

After lunching I sallied forth with my small cortège through the streets of Buguma on our quest for tax defaulters. I checked the name of every man we found against the Tax Register, a copy of which I had with me. If his name was not recorded he was arrested. Surprisingly few men seemed to be in town that day, and we made a disappointingly small bag. Later in the afternoon I inspected the route of the proposed new road. This entailed struggling for two and a half miles through thick bush with two men in front hacking a way through the undergrowth, followed by a mile of floundering up to our knees through mangrove swamp. It rained heavily during this excursion and throughout our return journey to Degema.

One Sunday I was about to sit down to a belated lunch of palm oil chop when three blasts on the *Dorothy's* hooter announced the Newingtons' arrival home from tour. On going to meet them I found Bill making arrangements for the return of the corpse of the District Interpreter of Brass Division, which adjoined Degema. In the course of his tour Bill had come across this man festering with improperly treated abscesses. He had sent him forthwith to the hospital at Degema on board the *Vampire*, but he had died that morning a day or two after being admitted. Members of his family who had followed on the *Dorothy* refused to allow him to be buried in foreign soil. After much questing they had found a canoe and paddlers who were willing to take them to Brass, ninety-one miles distant, for £6 each way. While dangling a hook from the end of the government jetty I watched the relations load their dead kinsman onto the canoe. He was borne to the water's edge on a stretcher covered with a red hospital blanket. The floorboards from the centre of the canoe were removed, and the body was bedded on some sacks while a woman screamed unrestrainedly in a torment of grief. The paddlers dipped their blades, and started off on their long journey through the fast approaching night.

As Assistant District Officer I was in charge of the prison at Degema. This occupied an area of about sixty by forty yards, and was encompassed by a few strands of barbed wire. It normally accommodated about ninety men and three or four women. The warders paraded at 7.00 a.m. Ten of them, including two ward-resses, lined up in two ranks and were marched by a corporal warder to the Senior Warder's office. The Senior Warder, Sergeant Odiachi, made a perfunctory inspection of the warders' turn-out, and then notified them of the numbers of prisoners in and the duties of their respective gangs. The work of the day then began. Some prisoners went to draw water, some to chop firewood, some to cut grass and others resumed work on my path-draining operations. Another gang under the direction of a mason-warder continued the building of a chimney inside the prison cook-house. Two of the women prisoners set about sweeping out the cells, and the third assisted a male prisoner who was plying a sewing machine and mending uniforms. Apart from those in the gangs a number of prisoners worked unsupervised at various jobs. Two worked in the District Officer's compound and one in mine. Another rolled and marked out the tennis court. Another worked as office boy in the prison office and acted as my interpreter when interviewing prisoners or persons awaiting trial. He was an obliging and apart from his stammer a well-spoken lad. As a whole the inmates of the prison were a docile, deferential and easy-going crowd. One of the male prisoners, however, suffered from bouts of madness. I was seated in the prison office one morning when I heard a rumpus at the gate and saw someone struggling. It was the mad man being brought back after a visit to the hospital. I visited him in his cell later in the day. He had quietened down by then, and I found a pitiable form lying huddled on a blanket on the floor. He stood up when I entered and I asked him a few simple questions to which he made hesitant though in the main intelligent replies. When I asked him if there was anything he wished to tell me, he mumbled that Ede, the corporal-warder, was his enemy. He then asked if he might "take breeze" to which I agreed. Because of the leg irons he was wearing he was only able to take short steps; and he moved forward into the sunshine jerkily like a child learning to walk. Once outside his gaunt frame subsided onto the edge of the gutter. Before leaving the prison I had a word with Ede.

One of the many roles filled by the District Officer was that of Officer in charge of the local police detachment. In Degema the total establishment was about twenty. One morning the Sergeant came to the District Office to report some trouble in Buguma. A couple of days earlier I had signed search warrants for two constables as a result of information having been received that certain persons had illicit gin and drugs in their possession. On arriving in Buguma the constables had met with opposition and the search warrants had been seized and destroyed. On hearing this Newington seethed with righteous indignation, and his first reaction was to lead a sortie to Buguma that night. However, a little later he decided against a nocturnal visit and said we would leave at 2.00 p.m. instead. He was afraid that if we delayed our departure for more than an hour or two warning of our coming would reach Buguma before we did, and thereby the element of surprise would be lost. In due course Newington and I together with a corporal and nine constables boarded a launch specially chartered for the occasion. The police looked very businesslike in their blue steel helmets, with rolled capes slung over their right shoulders and armed with riot batons. In the course of the one-hour launch trip it began to pour with rain. Newington and I had come unprepared but two constables kindly lent us their capes. Inside mine I felt like a cross between Sherlock Holmes and Friar Tuck.

On arrival at Buguma we jumped smartly off the launch and went at the double through the town to the Horsefall compound, where the trouble with the police had occurred. Unfortunately our sudden appearance on the scene was a little spoilt because in our eagerness we overshot the compound we were making for, and had to turn about and retrace some of our steps. However, we eventually arrived in the Horsefall locality, and the "winkling-out" process began. Newington, looking like Napoleon with his cape gathered about him, stood in the centre of the compound and directed operations. Police were sent scuttling into all the various shacks and hovels in the neighbourhood with orders to haul out all and sundry. A few moments later constables brandishing rather than plying their truncheons reappeared with a mixed bag of men, women and youths. Nearby there was a small corrugated-iron shed, into which Newington told the constables to herd their captives. I looked into the shed and to my surprise saw that it was a juju house. Confronting me was a wooden stand, to which were attached six carved wooden heads, all with entirely expressionless features. The whole contraption including the heads was brightly painted. Inside the shed there was bustle and shouting as policemen handcuffed various people together. Outside the hunt continued. Constables went scurrying hither and thither, and each and every person they found was rounded up. Anyone espied by Newington even in the far distance was pointed out to the nearest available constable who brought him protesting to the juju house. One man who had been seized complained that he had only arrived in Buguma that very day. Others complained that they were students, fondly imagining that that in itself would be sufficient to secure their release. A young trio picked up in one of the houses said that their father was a policeman, but notwithstanding they were borne off to the shed. From afar one old man unwisely stood watching what was going on. He too was rounded up. The neighbourhood soon appeared to be completely devoid of human life; and Newington, the police and I joined the press of wet steamy bodies inside the shed. While the men protested and gesticulated, the women remained impassive. A young mother standing near me hitched up her blouse and suckled a podgy infant perched on her hip. When Newington began to speak, the infant began to cry, whereupon the woman was told to leave. She did so almost reluctantly as if she were afraid of missing some of the fun. The wickedness of Buguma was made known by Newington in no uncertain fashion to the fifty or so of its inhabitants who were packed inside the small building. After his harangue there followed the upheaval of sorting the sheep from the goats. Throughout the noise and confusion the six painted wooden heads gazed inscrutably ahead, and the rain poured steadily down.

That evening a dejected little crocodile of "goats", handcuffed two by two, wended its way down the main street of Buguma – which had become a river – on its way to durance vile in Degema prison.

Every weekday the District Office was the scene of much activity. The Sergeant of Police brought arrested persons to be charged; the Senior Warder produced prisoners to be remanded; members of the public called in order to apply for or to renew licences; station labourers came to draw tools; Chiefs and Councillors came to attend meetings; and a heterogeneous collection of people, classified as "complainants", appeared daily in order to voice disgruntlement, seek advice or ask favours. On the day when Newington went off on tour I had to deal with the various callers. The clerical warder brought me some payment vouchers in connection with the construction of the Prison cook house chimney to sign: "to cost of 2 lb of nails 1s. 10d., to blacksmith for cutting iron 2s., etc.". A constable in plain clothes (very plain, only an unbuttoned shirt and a pair of navy blue shorts) brought in a letter requiring the District Officer's signature in his capacity as Deputy Sheriff. Two men appeared who introduced themselves as the President and Vice-President of the Degema Native Court. The former was a large, well-built man, who wore white shorts very long in the leg. His dark face seemed to have an almost rubicund hue. His companion was short and sombrely clad in black coat and trousers, Wellington boots and a black felt hat. Their purpose was to enquire when they could expect to have an assistant Court Clerk. Next a smooth-spoken individual produced a letter in which he applied for a loan of £1,000 to develop his farmlands. He was unable to offer any acceptable security, and I turned his application down without more ado. I was surprised to see that the next to enter my office was a Lagos policeman. He produced both a letter and a small boy. The letter was from the Probation Officer, Lagos, and it informed me that the P.C. was acting as escort to the boy, Amiomimi, who had been committed by the Court to the care of his grandfather who resided in Degema Division. I learned that the grandfather lived in Bonny; and as I was leaving for Bonny the following day I sent the boy round to my house to be looked after by Philip and to be taken with us. A seedy-looking little man wearing a grey rope-stitched pullover over his white shirt and clasping an off-white topi told me that his name was Hutchinson Bob Manuel. I was glad to see him because a few days earlier I had been visited by a man who had complained that Hutchinson would not pay him some wages he owed him. I questioned Hutchinson about this, and he assured me that an amicable arrangement had been made. The purpose of his visit was naturally not to talk about his debts but to put out a feeler for a building contract. On that score I had nothing to say to him except that he was at liberty to submit a tender at the appropriate time. A station labourer came in very deferentially and asked permission to be excused from work as his sister had just come and told him that his grandmother had fainted in the latrine. I hastily granted this. White, a local African contractor, looked in to enquire about the possibility of buying worn-out railway sleepers. He was then kind enough to shew me a photograph of his cousin, who was studying in London, and the English typist with whom he was living. Owiya, formerly a station labourer, whom I had recently sacked for idling, begged to be given another chance. In spite of his pitiful protestations I did not relent, although I felt some sympathy for him. Many more came and went. My final visitor on that particular day was massive Mrs. Cole, whose fleshy arms bulged like sausage balloons beneath the short sleeves of her cotton frock. Mrs. Cole, formerly a midwife, was an enterprising woman and was endeavouring to establish her reputation as a contractor. She wished me to go and inspect two quarters whitewashed by her. I did so and found them satisfactory.

District Officers and Assistant District Officers spent a large part of their time touring their Divisions, sometimes being away from District Headquarters for a fortnight on end. Touring in Degema Division was done by launch. One day after the *Eveline* had been coaled and watered by a gang of prisoners I set off for Bonny accompanied by Philip and Bonniface, also Mr. Horsefall (the Supervisor of Native Administration Treasuries in the Division), two police constables, one warder and the small boy, Amiomimi.

En route we called at Okrika, where Horsefall handed over £500 to the local Treasurer. I left one of the constables there. He was not keen about this, being a Kalabari, as there was much bad blood between the Okrikans and the Kalabaris. However, I would not agree to him turning tail, and I saw him safely installed in the Court Messengers' lines.

We dropped anchor at Bonny at 5.15 p.m. For some reason Major, the Quarter-master of the launch, was reluctant to go alongside the jetty. Because of this we and our loads were ferried ashore in the dinghy. My chattels made quite a pile on the sandy foreshore, from where half a dozen station labourers leisurely transported them to the Rest-House; and I did not remain entirely unmoved by the sight of my newly acquired wireless balanced unsupported on a round black head. At the Rest-House I interviewed Chief Tofogiri and handed his grandson, Amiomimi, over to him. The small boy stood with downcast eyes looking at his bare feet. His tattered shirt stretched just low enough to hide his private parts. The Chief smiled affectionately when he saw him; and a few moments later the small boy was following the old man down the steps of the Rest-House.

Domestic arrangements not being organised I decided to take my bath in the sea and not in my tin tub. I walked to the end of the jetty in the moonlight wearing a dressing gown and sandals, and then plunged into the warm water. By the time I returned to the Rest-House my various belongings had been sorted out, and I sat down to a good dinner of pork chops followed by rice pudding. Afterwards I relaxed in my folding camp chair and listened to my wireless, while a few yards away the incoming tide lapped gently on the sand.

At 8.00 a.m. the following day Horsefall and I were seated in the Bonny Native Court hall, ready to make a start with the Executive Committee of the Clan Council on preparing the Bonny Native Administration Estimates for the coming 1950–1951 financial year. While waiting for the members to arrive I transacted such business as I could. I spoke a few sober words to Chief Francis Jumbo on the need for him to pay into the Treasury without more delay the outstanding tax due from his House for the year 1948–1949. One of the many Williams in Bonny gave me some information I required about the administrators of the disputed estate of a certain Johnson Ben Stowe. I was somewhat relieved to learn that, since the argument about the estate had begun five years earlier, two of the three persons claiming to be beneficiaries had died because this seemed to put the possibility of a solution within sight. Chief Josiah Hart gave me details of alleged unauthorised settlement by Okrika fishermen on Bonny Island. Finally Mrs. Grave Williams and another woman confirmed the genuineness of their thumbprints on a document which acknowledged one E.D. Harry's ownership of a 12-bore shotgun formerly the property of their late Father.

By about 10.00 a.m. three of the four Executive Committee members had arrived, a number sufficient to form a quorum. Chiefs Josiah Hart, Wilcox and Claude Manilla Pepple sat on a bench in front of me. Chief Josiah in a sports coat and Wellington boots looked like an English farmer. Chief Claude wore khaki shorts and a khaki bush jacket, of which the upper two buttons only were done up. Chief Wilcox wore a thick navy blue "shirt" of voluminous native cut.

I had little idea as to what Estimates were and had never in my life had anything to do with their preparation before. However, with a little prompting from Horsefall I made a start, and as I progressed I found it was a simpler business than I had expected. Fortunately for me I could not have been working with a less obstructive committee. Josiah studiously and laboriously took notes; Claude reclined – as far as that was possible on a wooden bench – and smiled a most engaging smile whenever I happened to catch his eye; and Wilcox leant forward, looking rather serious but saying little. Estimated revenue for the year amounted to only £1,280, a sum which when necessities had been provided for left only £50 to play with. I made various suggestions as to how this balance might be best utilised in the interests of the local taxpayers: in starting a Native Administration nursery garden, in contributing towards a mass-education drive, in providing a couple of scholarships, or in paying for the training of a girl as a midwife. It was the last suggestion which appealed most to the Committee; however, a damper was placed on their enthusiasm when they recalled the need to carry out repairs to the public latrine for women. As none of the three Chiefs was able to give any estimate of the cost of the repairs required it was necessary for us to adjourn and inspect the latrine in question. As we approached the tin structure, perched on wooden piles over the drab waters of a muddy creek, Chief Josiah had the forethought to call out a warning of our approach, and an old woman hastily scuttled out of the building. We entered the corrugated-iron shack via a wooden gangplank. Running the length of it was a sort of trough without a bottom. Twists of coconut fibre served in lieu of toilet paper. The corrugated iron had rusted away in many places and the piles on which the latrine was supported were rotting. We decided that £40 ought to cover the cost of repair. However, not wishing to cut the provision for the training of a midwife out of the Estimates we agreed that the latrine should be considered as a work extraordinary, which would enable the cost to be met out of the reserve fund. No further complications arose, and my first Estimates' exercise came to an end by lunchtime.

Sunday morning was wet, but I decided nevertheless to go to the morning service in Bonny's C.M.S. Cathedral. The Pastor-in-charge had told me that the service would begin at 9.00 a.m. I arrived a few minutes after the hour to find the place completely deserted. Somewhat disgruntled I went to the Pastor's house, which was close by. He remained quite unperturbed when I told him that I had not seen a single person inside the church. He merely gave me a chair, wiped the mud off my Wellingtons, and said that they would be coming later. He continued dressing slowly. Having finished robing himself he led me over to the vestry where we sat and waited while the rain continued to pour down. At 9.30 a.m. three girls and a youth entered. They comprised the choir. The Reverend Jumbo shewed me to a chair in the chancel next to the stall occupied by the lay reader. The harmonium struck up a funeral march, and the choir shuffled in with bowed heads. Behind the choir stalls I espied three girls and one old woman. The rest of the congregation consisted of another old woman, a man and two boys.

The Cathedral, which was associated with the name of Bishop Crowther, was sixty years old. Inside it was well equipped with wooden pews, choir stalls and pulpit. The lectern was a brazen eagle. Oil lamps were affixed to the walls in brass brackets, and in addition clusters of oil lamps were suspended at intervals from the roof. The altar cloth bore the words "NSO, NSO, NSO" (Holy, Holy, Holy). An attempt at imparting a stained-glass window effect had been made by the introduction of squares of bright-coloured glass in the tops of the side windows. Looking through the open door at the west end I could see a line of coconut palms standing between the churchyard and the sea.

With the aid of an Ibo prayer book I was able to follow the service which kept to the normal form of Matins. During the sermon I caught from time to time the names of Shadrach, Meshak and Abednego – but little else. Service over I trudged back through the rain to the Rest-House.

A day or two later I left Bonny on the *Eveline*. At Okrika Newington joined me on board, and we steamed through the creeks to a place called Ogu, which had not been visited by D.O. or A.D.O. for a year or more. On arrival at this remote settlement we dropped anchor and went ashore in the dinghy. Waiting to greet us on the edge of a stinking bank of mud, refuse and old seashells was a bevy of local chiefs. I was interested in the variety of headgear they were sporting. Some had spotlessly white topis; one had a khaki one which he wore sideways on his head, while someone else had a khaki one enclosed in a protective mackintosh covering. One chief was wearing a black circular ecclesiastical hat, and another a wide-brimmed cowboy hat. There were also some elaborate slouch caps to be seen, including a woofy orange-coloured one and another made of simulated leopard skin material. The robe of one of the chiefs in particular caught my eye. The motif of its pattern was the crossed flags of Great Britain and France.

We went first to visit the site where the local people wished to have a footbridge built to connect Ogu island with the mainland. To do this we had to traverse the town, which was the most congested settlement I had ever seen. Making our way in and out along the narrow alleys, which twisted between the squalid backs of jostling houses, reminded me of those puzzle pages in children's Annuals where one is required to trace a route from A to B without crossing any lines. In due course we all clambered into a canoe, which because of the number on board was all but submerged beneath the muddy waters of the creek. The single paddler had to work hard to make headway against the ebbing tide. Having completed our reconnaissance of the position suggested for the bridge, we visited St. Martin's C.M.S. School. By that time many more persons had attached themselves to our party, and it was quite a crowd which filed through the classrooms. As we emerged from the school building we saw a troop of Boy Scouts lining our route ahead. One of them held a Union Jack. Newington halted. I halted, and the cortège perforce followed suit. There was a brief pause, and then the troop-leader began popping forth orders: "Stand at ease! Attenshun! About turn! Lay down staves! Pick up staves! Sit on staves! ..." They ended up in a position of attention with an expectant look on their faces. I wondered how Newington was going to disperse them. He did so most effectively.

"I want to see the first man up that tree," he said, pointing to one nearby; and he gave a shilling to the one who climbed the highest in the shortest time.

Our next port of call was the village hall, this being the most convenient place in which to assemble. Newington and I were given chairs behind a small table covered with a white cloth. Knowing the low regard in which Newington held the people of this outpost in his Division I was rather amused to see that immediately in front of him embroidered in alternating blue and red letters were the words *"Honi soit qui mal y pense"*! After some appropriate words of welcome, a sixteen-page petition was placed in front of Newington which was headed "The Groans of the Ogu Taxpayers". He was unimpressed by this title, and when he rose to speak he told his expectant hearers that they were in no position to groan about tax unless they had paid tax, and that having now thoroughly inspected the village it was more than evident to him that countless men of Ogu had for years evaded payment. This state of affairs, he assured them, he was looking forward to remedying immediately. Instead of breaking into groans on receiving this news those present smiled benignly, appreciating that their District Officer had spoken as a District Officer should. General discussion followed. The hall was packed. The Boy Scouts tried to prevent further bodies from infiltrating inside by barring the entrances with their staves. Small naked children peered through their elders' legs. Others were perched on the shoulders of their parents outside in order to be able to get a glimpse of the two visiting white men, the first representatives of this mysterious species whom they had ever seen. The formal proceedings finished, we were regaled with beer and petit beurre biscuits.

Okrika was one of the largest settlements in Degema Division. It was situated on an island of reclaimed mangrove swamp in the middle of the creeks fanning out from the New Calabar river. Two or three inches of rubbish, soil and putrefying matter covered the glutinous swamp mud. On this thin veneer of "dry" land, which had an area of barely 100 acres, lived, laboured and died a vigorous community numbering several thousands. At Newington's request I spent a week in Okrika in order to make a map of the place which it was thought would be helpful in deciding where to site some wells to improve the town's water supply. On arrival I had to arm myself with a mapping board. As a makeshift I used the back of one of the hard wooden chairs from the public Reading Room which I had dismantled for the purpose. Having drawn a skeleton outline map of the island, which I was able to do fairly easily by enlarging an ancient Survey Department map which I found in the Native Administration Treasury Office, I then systematically worked my way from one end of the island to the other, entering on my map as I did so paths, houses and any other features of significance. In this undertaking I was accompanied by two sanitary labourers, and Nathaniel, the Head Court Messenger from Degema. One labourer carried my folding camp table, and the other the mapping board, my raincape and haversack. Nathaniel insisted on carrying my umbrella, which I think he regarded as a status symbol.

My progress through the town excited a good deal of interest. Swarms of people young and old clustered round my table whenever I halted. When moving, innumerable children followed in our wake, shrilling and darting hither and thither like seagulls behind a fishing smack.

Except for the cemetery, the compound of St. Peter's Church and the playing field of a school, every square foot of the island which was not positive swamp was built on. The houses were densely concentrated, some in twisting lines and some in higgledy-piggledy clusters. Only a few paths of any size traversed the labyrinths of mud and thatch and corrugated iron. Usually we had to make erratic progress along alley ways only two or three feet wide between the houses – from time to time emerging into an open space a few yards square. Many women and some old men lurked within the dark interiors of their homes. Infants with protruding navels the size and shape of door-knobs tottered on unsteady legs with a look of wonder in their eyes, or were carried uncomplaining on the hips of their only slightly older and rather more pot-bellied brothers and sisters. Here and there a goat, an emaciated dog or a vulture – its ugly head protruding above its collar of white feathers like a gargoyle in a choirboy's ruffle – scavenged for food. Occasionally I passed houses made of brick or concrete blocks, some of which had the distinction of a second floor. Despite their better construction, however, these stood cheek by jowl with the humble dwellings of sticks and mud. In open spaces between houses I frequently came upon elaborate concrete tombstones and memorial slabs bearing the name of some former chief in roughly carved letters.

At the water's edge there were great heaps of shells and rotting corn-cobs to be used in due course to reclaim a few more square feet of mangrove swamp for human habitation. At intervals, perched on wooden stumps driven into the black mud of the swamp and approached by single planks extending from the banks of shells, there were public latrines made of sheets of corrugated iron. In the creeks and inlets along the waterfront canoes of varying sizes were moored, and between the houses cone-shaped fishing nets, dangling from the end of bamboos like outlandish maypoles, were drying.

A garish effect to the squalid scene was given by the large number of naked children and partly clad women who had covered their bodies with white chalk. I was told that chalk kept the body healthy and made the skin smooth. I was also informed that it was thought to be a cure for measles, a person suffering from that disease having chalk circles drawn round his eyes. I did in fact see some children who had chalk spectacles, and one who had a circle round his right ear. Some of those I saw had tried to enhance their appearance by adopting fancy hairstyles. Many of the women had their hair gathered into little plaits two or three inches long which stood out from their round heads like the conventional rays of the sun drawn by a child. Some of the children had had their hair shaved in irregular patches, giving the effect of a jigsaw puzzle.

Okrika was distinguished by possessing one of the largest and finest churches in the whole of Eastern Nigeria. In the centre of the squalid settlement the tower of St. Peter's Church, substantially built of concrete blocks, rose high above all the surrounding buildings. St. Peter's was the size of a large parish church in England. On the Sunday of my stay in Okrika I went to the morning service which began at 9.00 a.m. A choir, thirty or more strong, filed sedately into the church, followed by two clergy, two vergers, a sexton and a lay reader. The congregation, sparse to begin with, increased as the service proceeded. People wore their Sunday best. Clothes were clean and for the most part of gay hue, and the brightly coloured headscarves worn by the women in the congregation gave the effect of a field of exotic flowers.

31

The service adhered to the prayer-book form of morning service. The psalms were spoken; the lessons were excessively long; hymns were sung with great lustiness. In such a setting I found it hard to believe that the place where I was attending divine worship was located in the midst of the mangrove swamps of Southern Nigeria. Archdeacon Spiff, an Ijaw, with a truly episcopal embonpoint, delivered his sermon in English, a member of the choir acting as interpreter. He reminded the congregation of the good example set sixty-eight years earlier by the first Okrika Christian convert, a Juju doctor. He went on to bewail the sad decline in Christian living by the Okrikans of the present day. He referred in plain terms to the "war" with the Kalabaris and the eight Okrika men convicted of murder awaiting hanging in Port Harcourt prison. The sermon over the congregation rose and sang the hymn "When I survey the wondrous Cross" with great fervour, while the two vergers, two men and two young women, took the collection. The service came to an end 130 minutes after it began!

During the course of the service a little man seated in the front pew caught my attention. His legs were wasted away to the width of cricket stumps, and because his knees and feet jutted out at curious angles they reminded me of a pair of motor car cranking handles. During the prayers he lowered himself from his seat and crouched on the floor completely hidden by the pew. During the hymns he some-how managed to lever himself into an upright position, and, sharing a book with his neighbour, sang with zest. His white shirt though old and frayed was clean; and he had clearly been at pains to make himself as presentable as possible. When the collection was taken he made his contribution, and I was minded of the widow's mite. However, in this case the all was not cast in because in return for the penny which he put in the plate the little man took out change of a halfpenny.

I was to make the acquaintance of the Pastor of the splendid Okrika Church the following day. The previous week when out mapping I had met an emaciated girl with one of her legs bandaged with leaves. Through Nathaniel I had learned that she had not been to the dispensary because she lacked the necessary penny. I had supplied this and had been pleased to note later in the day that the horrible ulcer which she had had for eight years had been well and truly bandaged. On Monday I met the girl, Derefakama by name, again because she came and asked me for money to buy chop. As a result of making enquiries I gathered that her parents had died several years previously, and that although the pastor of St. Peter's was her next of kin she lived on her own with no one to look after her.

I made a Court Messenger cut a staff for her, and with the aid of this the girl tottered off on her matchstick legs. A little later accompanied by Nathaniel I set out to see the place in which she lived. I found her squatting in the corner of a room of a partially built house, construction of which had long since been abandoned. There were neither doors, windows nor roof. A few sheets of rusty and smoke-begrimed corrugated iron partially covered the corner in which she lived. There was no floor, only wet earth covered with weeds. The girl's possessions comprised one wooden plank, one small earthenware pot, two tins and the single dirty rag which she wore. A few twigs on the ground indicated where she had made her fire, and the smell from the adjoining shell of a room was evidence that it served as a latrine. A fly buzzed hungrily around the bandage on her leg. Neighbours, inquisitive about my appearance, gathered round and confirmed that the Reverend was "a son of the same Father as Derefakama". Their remarks betrayed no vestige of regret about her plight.

I called upon the pastor who was evasive and full of excuses for neglecting his niece. However, the upshot of our meeting was that he agreed that I should take Derefakama to Degema hospital and that he would remit thirty shillings a month for her maintenance.

When the *Eveline* arrived to take me back to Degema I sent a station labourer to carry Derefakama down to the jetty. A gaggle of small children watched with curiosity as she was brought on board, but no one was there to say goodbye to her.

On my return to Degema I learned that Newington was being detained for a short time in hospital in Lagos, and a telegram from the Resident informed me that during his absence I was in charge on the Division. I spent the next week or two at Headquarters. Every day I had a large number of callers. One morning I was visited by a deputation of ten station labourers, who were afraid that because of being paid on the 26th of every month they were losing some of their rightful earnings. With the aid of an office calendar and a paperknife as a pointer I demonstrated to them that there were as many days between the 26th of one month and the 26th of the next as there were between the 30th of one and the 30th of the next. They left still, I thought, not entirely convinced.

The next to enter was Mr. White, the contractor. He gave me the keys of a government quarter which he had finally completed. Then with a furtive grin on his face he told me that he had a personal favour to ask. Undaunted by my reply he proceeded with his request. It was for a note to the Manager of the United Africa Company in Abonnema asking him to sell White a Raleigh bicycle (new bicycles – particularly Raleighs – were limited in number and there was keen competition amongst the Eastern Nigerians to obtain them). As a bicycle would be of use to him in supervising his government contract work, I advised him to send in a written application. He then produced a further request, to wit that I should recommend him to the Manager of the Bulk Oil Plant in Abonnema as a reliable contractor for the supply of firewood. I told him that he should write to the manager and that he could quote me as a reference. Finally in tones of great humility White enquired whether I would regard sympathetically an application for a loan of £200 for the purpose of starting a poultry farm in a patch of mangrove swamp. I said this was possible but queried the suitability of the site he proposed. Mr. White, beaming happily, left my office seemingly well satisfied with the success he had achieved.

I received a further request for a note about a bicycle, this time from the assistant district clerk. In his case I refused because I knew he already owned a new bicycle, having noticed on the payroll which I had signed the previous day that he was that month paying back the second instalment of an advance made to him for the purchase of one.

Four more applicants came to see me in quick succession. Chief Dappa requested that the Court Members' chairs in the Native Court be repaired. A recently discharged soldier came with a query about payment of tax and a request for a job. A woman applied for permission to visit a prisoner called Saturday Cotterell. And then entered Mohd Sulla, most imposing of them all. With the customary courtesy of Moslems from the North he bowed low while his face which looked almost circular, framed as it was by the elaborate turban he was wearing, creased into a great toothy smile, and his black eyes twinkled brightly. When he had finished enquiring solicitously after the well being of the District Officer and myself he broached the matter about which he had come to see me. Having heard that I was shortly to be transferred to the neighbouring Division of Ahoada he wished to impress on me in advance the desirability of building a slaughterhouse there so that he would be able to extend his meat-trading business. I said that on reaching Ahoada I would look into the matter. Mohd Sulla beamed with pleasure. He was a tall man and also one of ample girth. His whole generous being emanated goodwill. Still murmuring soft persuasive words, he again inclined his black bearded face. Then with a hoist of his long loose sleeves, and flinging a cloth like a table-runner over his shoulder he smiled his way out of the room.

I was visited too by several people with complaints to make. A certain Bob Manuel (a member of Chief Limejuice Bob Manuel's House), who was the headman of the Native Administration ferrymen, brought along an erring member of his gang who refused to obey instructions. A duly chastened ferryman left the office a few moments later.

Next I found myself facing three men. One was wearing an old jungle-green army uniform; another was poorly clad in old shorts and a shirt; the third, who was older, was sprucely dressed in white. The two younger men complained that they had gone up country to work for the dapper little man, having agreed on a wage of

34

one shilling and sixpence a day. They said they had worked for three months and had not received their due. The dapper little man insisted that he had paid them in full for three months. A little later in refuting the young men he declared that he had paid one of them £3 and the other £1. 15s. 0d. This was a blunder on his part. I pointed out to him that at one shilling and sixpence a day for three months each man's entitlement was £6 odd. I advised him to come speedily to an amicable arrangement with his former employees, because otherwise he might find himself let in for more than he had ever bargained for as a result of Court proceedings.

A man accompanied by a comely young woman, whom he introduced as his sister, came in next. Woefully he told the tale of an *enfant terrible* in the family, another and younger sister. Apparently this erring but energetic young girl was breaking up a happy home. The man confirmed that their father having died he was responsible for her. I suggested that he should beat her, but he did not regard this proposal with enthusiasm, and displaying a calloused thumb he complained that it had never been the same since his young sister had bitten it on his attempting to chastise her. I next suggested that they should give her in marriage to some unsuspecting male as rapidly as possible. They laughed forlornly at this idea, and I was led to understand that there was no immediate likelihood of such a welcome release being achieved. Unable to tame the girl themselves they wanted the assistance of the strong arm of the Law. I had to explain that, tiresome though it was for them, the matter was a domestic one and that there were no grounds for intervention by the police.

My last visitor that morning was a Court Messenger from one of the Courts in the neighbouring Division of Brass, situated in the heart of the huge Niger delta. He handed me a note from his Court Clerk which read, "Here is the corps of a woman who is reported to have been murdered by Nelson Ogu, her husband". The "corps", which was four days old, had been deposited in the mortuary to await a post-mortem.

There was a single sandy track which led out of Degema. It was the path to Buguma and Harry's Town. Except for an occasional cyclist, people only passed along it on foot. One evening I went for a stroll along this track. Leaving the clerks' houses and the group of newly completed junior government staff quarters behind, I passed through land that had previously been cleared but which was rapidly reverting to bush. Here and there lofty trees towered above their ground defences of undergrowth. Behind me the sky loured with grey-blue clouds, which betokened an approaching storm. The shadows cast across the track by the trees were lengthening fast. It was very quiet; and bird calls sounded clear and loud in the silent wilderness of leaves.

After walking for a few more minutes I came to a lane cleared through the bush; and about 100 yards away at the end of it I could glimpse an iron railing. I walked down this green aisle and came to Degema's European Cemetery. A rectangular perimeter of rusty iron railings, enclosing an open space of some twenty yards by thirty yards, kept the surrounding bush at bay. On all sides the little burial ground was surrounded by walls of rapacious greenery and the twisted trunks of a thousand trees. In the centre of the cemetery stood a large temple tree, and its roots stretched out like the tentacles of an octopus towards the tombstones set around it. The setting sun, peeping through its mask of stormy cloud, sped a last soft lingering look into the still sanctuary.

There in very different earth from that from which they had sprung were laid to rest the bones of youthful Englishmen:

"William Henshaw Pender of Manchester," I read, "who died at Salisbury Factory, Degema, in 1910 aged 25"; "J. Shepherd died aged 29 in the year 1896"; "Captain Bartwell, Her Britannic Majesty's District Commissioner, who died on the Consulate Hulk in 1900 ..." and six and twenty more.

Lying in the midst of these young men there was one woman, Dorothy Amaury Talbot, of whom her stone only bore record that having been born in 1871 she had died in 1916. Looking round at the small group of gravestones I wondered what had been the hopes and joys and fears of these countrymen of mine, and what the tales they might have told.

This visit may perhaps have had a disquieting effect upon me, because the next entry in the journal which I kept at that time reveals signs of brooding and discontent.

"Forgetting all the advantages of my present life," I wrote, "I recall only what I am missing by leading it. Allergic to drab overcast skies, the rain of yesterday and the greyness of today have engendered a dimly reflected feeling of oppression within me. Today I am in my 'why-this-self-inflicted-exile?' mood. It is a questioning mood, a mood in which my thoughts tend to flit aimlessly round the questions 'What am I doing?' and 'Is it worthwhile?' – like moths round a lamp, always fluttering and never coming to rest. It is a self-pitying mood, which brings added realisation of the significance of such expressions as 'far-flung' and 'outpost', expressions which are so light-heartedly and jocularly bandied around when one is at home and the Bush seems far away. It is a mood which holds insidious seeds of doubt: is it all a great mistake? Should I have stayed at home and ... well, found a more normal and ordinary sort of job? Am I missing life?"

My trouble was that I was lonely. My entry for that day came to an end on a plaintive and somewhat poetical note:

"Here I sit on my verandah in the pool of light cast by my lamp, perched on its stand like a miniature lighthouse. I am encompassed by the black velvet curtains of night, night so yearningly tender in its soft voluptuousness, so infinitely beguiling with its myriads of stars. But it evokes only an emptiness within me for 'the night is made for loving ...' and I am on my own."

One lovely evening I crossed by canoe from Degema to the town of Abonnema opposite. Overhead hung a canopy of blue. In the east the azure of the sky had begun to dim; but in the west the sky had the brilliance of a vast fiery furnace. Vivid clouds were rioting through their short-lived life as gorgeously apparelled courtiers in the aurelian palace of the setting sun, to which a path of golden cobbles stretched across the water. Gradually the junketing grew less; the golden bowls were broken; the ruby wine was spilled and slowly ran away. One by one the revellers fell back exhausted, sinking into cushions of rich purple, puce and mauve; and slowly and inexorably the fiery flames were quenched.

In the evening light the river frontage of Abonnema was transformed from its usual scene of squalor to one of beauty and romance. From the canoe in which I was being ferried I could see the stalls jostling each other in the congested market place stretching along the water's edge. I could see some of the wares: lengths of brightly coloured cloth, and pots and pans glinting in the golden glow. A line of gently bobbing canoes moored to the crowded waterfront reminded me of a litter of baby pigs being suckled by a prostrate sow. The matting awnings on the big canoes, which normally looked so drab and dirty, were at that magic hour suffused with the colour of ripe corn. A two-storeyed house was silhouetted against the skyline, also the twin towers of the building, which accommodated the C.M.S. bookshop and the postal agency, the spire of the large Anglican church, and the roof of the Bishop Crowther Memorial School. I could glimpse the three storage tanks at the Bulk Oil Plant, which looked like large round toffee tins with the paper wrapping removed. The purple-red paint of the United Africa Company's go-downs lent colour to the scene. One or two oil-palms, whose straight trunks and feathery fronds reminded me of up-ended washing-up mops, stood out against the sky. On the end of the U.A.C. jetty stood a small crane looking like a sentry on guard.

Abonnema was separated from Degema (which was still referred to as "the Consulate") by about 500 yards of water. Coming from Oguta and the north the Sombrero river swept past Degema and Abonnema on its journey to the sea. The waterway, which I was crossing in the canoe, was but one of the many links joining the Sombrero with the New Calabar and Bonny rivers. Ocean-going vessels regularly plied up the Sombrero as far as Abonnema to take on palm oil.

On the return trip there was nothing to be seen of Degema except tall trees standing high above the fringe of mangrove swamp, the yellow-painted bungalow of the Manager of a French firm nestling behind a trim hedge, close to the water's edge, and the roof of the Magistrate's house in the distance. On the western bank of the Sombrero the mangrove trees, not clearly seen because of the radiance of the sun which was sinking down towards them, looked much like an English wood coming down to the water's edge, and the glint of the light-coloured trunks reminded me of silver birches. All was very quiet and peaceful, as though the setting sun had cast an enchantment over man and Nature alike. The paddler paddled in silence. A man sitting in front of me, and wearing a pink vest beneath his crochet-stitched shirt, also made no sound. A canoe passed us carrying five men, three children and a bicycle. A launch phutted its way upstream. A swift skimmed low over the water. We approached close to the fringe of mangroves, whose many roots curving outwards into the mud looked like the ribs of lobster pots. The paddler had a last hard pull against the ebbing tide to reach the concrete landing steps and the footpath which led across the golf course.

Chapter 4

"Let us forge a new Nigerian personality"

By this time I had been in Eastern Nigeria about seven months, and Chubb decided that I had received sufficient in the way of preliminary training in the art of District administration and that it was time for me to start work in earnest. The large Division of Ahoada was in need of an Assistant District Officer, and thither I was posted.

I left Degema on the launch *Puffin*. With me I had my loads, Philip, Bonniface and one chicken. At Port Harcourt my Boys and loads were transferred to the Ahoada Native Administration lorry, while I collected my car and followed later. Ahoada was situated north of the mangrove swamp area on the western bank of the Sombrero river. On arrival at the river I found the Native Administration lorry parked on the near side, and saw all my worldly possessions balanced on the heads of a crocodile of prisoners who were slowly picking their way across a frail footbridge. Vehicles had to cross the river by a pontoon ferry, which was prevented from being swept downstream by one thin cable.

I moved straight into the A.D.O.'s house. There were only three houses all together: the District Officer's, mine and a Rest-House. My abode was in fact more like a cricket pavilion than a house. It was long and low and open to the four winds of heaven, and I was able to drive my Morris Minor inside and park it in the sitting room. Only the bedroom, washroom and store had four walls. These did not reach the roof and were topped with broken glass to discourage predatory visitors. The building had a concrete floor, and the mud walls were cement-faced and white-washed. The roof was corrugated iron covered with matting; and a matting-roofed corridor led to the shack behind the house which served as a kitchen. The establishment was better furnished than I had expected it would be, having as it did a bed, two tables, two bookshelves, a few upright chairs and a cupboard. There was nothing in the garden except one guava tree, one grapefruit tree and grass.

The government station was quite pleasantly ranged round a miniature golf course, on which no one ever played a game. The only Europeans living in Ahoada at that time were King, the District Officer, and his wife, a Public Works Department engineer (who had been temporarily posted to build a bridge) and his wife and myself; and none of us were golfers. In addition to the District and Native Administration offices there was a Post and Telegraph office, a Police Station, a dispensary and a prison. At some distance from the government station there was a small village, which came to life every eighth day when a market was held. A grisly juju object stood in the centre of the village, a large post adorned with an impressive collection of skulls and with a heap of bones at its base. Signs of missionary endeavour were to be seen in the shape of a small C.M.S. bookshop and Church and a Roman Catholic Church. Seventh Day Adventists and Jehovah's Witnesses also had places of worship.

By virtue of being Assistant District Officer I was Officer in charge of the local prison, and as a result of my time in Degema I was already reasonably familiar with the duties which this entailed. One morning Philip should have woken me at 6.30 a.m. but failed to do so. It was not his morning salutation and shake of my mosquito net which aroused me but the sound of a distant whistle. I looked at my watch. It was 6.48 a.m. It was too late to shave. I rapidly donned some clothes; crammed my unbrushed hair beneath a cap; heard another whistle sound; called for my bicycle; and reached the prison gate just as the last warders were straggling in doing up their belts as they entered. I inspected the line of nine warders and one wardress. There was little to choose between their respective turn-outs, and they all appeared to have risen as hastily as I had. My progress up and down the single rank of warders was watched with much interest by the inmates of the prison, who were squatting on the ground munching their morning meal. Their interest was aroused further when I gave a few simple drill orders, to which the warders found difficulty in responding. Having been dismissed the prison staff shambled off to take charge of their respective gangs. I adjourned to the office where I first congratulated one warder on recapturing a prisoner, and then reprimanded another for having lost one.

The District Officer being away on tour I received a request in the office one Saturday morning to preside at a Public Meeting to be held that evening, at which a Mr. Mbadiwe was going to speak. From Mr. Achike, the District Clerk, I learned that Mr. Mbadiwe possessed several degrees, had spent many years in the U.S.A., and was President of an organisation called "The African Academy of Arts and

40

Research''. At 5.30 p.m. Mr. Achike and Mr. Wodi, the treasury clerk, came round to my house and escorted me to the Native Court where the meeting was to be held. After some waiting I was requested by Wodi to take the Chair, which I was very ready to occupy in preference to the crowded bench on which I had been seated until then. Wodi then called upon Mr. Achike and another gentleman to support me, and in the course of a short and fulsome introductory speech saw fit to liken the three of us to the Trinity.

Mr. Wodi having had his say, without wasting time I called upon Mr. Mbadiwe to speak. Mr. Mbadiwe stood up, and I was the better able to admire the well-cut, double-breasted, palm-beach suit he was wearing. He spoke without a break for the ensuing two hours. He began by explaining the nature of ''The African Academy of Arts and Research''. As I listened I first gained the impression that it was some sort of temple not made with hands, but as time went on I gathered that it was in fact a hostel for African students in New York City. We heard about Mbadiwe's visit to the White House where he had had a half-hour meeting with Mrs. Roosevelt, and about an African Show he had organised in the Carnegie Hall. In the course of his talk Mbadiwe spoke a lot of sense, and there was little I could take exception to. He urged a greater exchange of ideas among Nigerians, and stressed the importance of having aspirations. He advocated the necessity of facing up to present difficulties when aiming for a ''Greater Tomorrow''. He pointed out that one of the main difficulties which the country had to overcome was tribalism. ''Let us forget we are Yorubas, Ibos, Hausas or Effiks, and let us forge a new Nigerian personality.'' He drew attention to the poverty of the country and stated that self-help must be the order of the day.

When Mr. Mbadiwe sat down, I rose and thanked him very much for his excellent talk. An Aladdin lamp, which had been placed on the table in front of me, made me uncomfortably hot and prevented me from seeing those to whom I was speaking. The meeting ended with the selling of button-hole badges. The gentleman supporting me on my left called for donations. He lent across to tell me that someone or other had given two shillings. I wondered whether I could get away with half-a-crown, but reluctantly decided that I must make it five shillings. It was fortunate I paid my tithe when I did, for the next three donations were each allegedly ten shillings! Names and the amounts contributed were called out. A gentleman in the front row stirred himself into action, lumbered to his feet and declared that he would give ten shillings and sixpence. Then a third announced that he would give twelve shillings. I disengaged myself from the fund-raising business first by inviting Mbadiwe to dine with me and then by explaining that I had to go and give necessary instructions to my cook.

41

I had only been in Ahoada a few days when I had for the first time a warring villages' situation to deal with. One night as I was seated and reading my most recent copy of *The Spectator* the Sergeant in charge of our local Police detachment appeared out of the shadows. He reported that he had received information that two villages were fighting because of a land dispute and that several persons had sustained matchet wounds. I told him to send two constables there and then to investigate, and the next morning I followed taking with me another constable and a corporal.

At Mgbuogisi I received an account of the affray from a certain Benson, who claimed to be the village Head. He said that five men of his village had gone out the previous day to cut palm fruit on Mgbuogisi land and that they had been attacked by some twenty men of the neighbouring village of Ohiano. To support his tale he produced three "wounded" men; but when I looked them over I could not find a scratch on any of them. Leaving the constable and one of the two who had arrived during the night to take down statements, I motored a little further along the road to Ohiano. When I finally ran the Headman to earth he persisted in disclaiming all knowledge of any trouble. I did not waste time with the obdurate old man, and we quickly rounded up about twenty suspects.

Leaving the Corporal and the other constable who had come down the previous night to march them up the road to Mgbuogisi I returned there in my car. The two constables were seated in the local school taking statements, while the greater part of the village, who were very interested in the proceedings, pressed around them. I drove the villagers out of the building, but like crabs on the seashore they kept edging back inside when they thought they were not being observed. A man wearing blue trousers, black dinner jacket, white shirt and black bow tie ambled towards me. I asked him who he was, and he replied that he was the Headmaster; and in case that were not sufficient justification for his presence he added that he was just returning from the worship of God.

At this point the twenty men from Ohiano straggled into the school compound. They had one allegedly wounded man with them who had been transported on the carrier of a bicycle. He crouched on the ground with a woebegone look on his face, but when I examined him I was unable to find any trace of a wound.

I organised an identification parade of the Ohiano men as a result of which five of them were detained for questioning. I then returned to Ahoada secretly somewhat disappointed not to have had as much as a glimpse of any gore.

The problems with which one was faced as an Assistant District Officer were frequently both unexpected and involved. At the end of one arduous day in the office, when I was on the point of leaving, the Police Sergeant appeared on the scene escorting a drove of somewhat ill-at-ease persons. I learned that they were involved in a case of neglecting to bury the corpse of a woman who had recently died of smallpox. The body instead of being decently interred had been tossed into the bush, and the said bush belonged to a very righteously indignant gentleman called Matthew. He took particular exception to this act because the dead woman had not belonged to his part of the village.

My problem was to determine upon whom the responsibility for the burial of the deceased rested. She had no father, no brother, no husband – only a lover called Okoro. I inclined to the view that he should have laid his sleeping partner to her last long rest. The Sergeant, however, did not agree. What, bury one's concubine? No indeed, Sir! I gathered that it was in any event probable that Okoro would himself soon be joining his lady love, because he had succumbed to the same disease.

The dead woman's sister, Nwachike, seemed to have been the only one to rise to the occasion – but the question in her case was whether she had risen far enough. From the record of the Native Court hearing of the case I saw that some of the Bench had exonerated her because she was the one who had hired the services of a "stranger" to remove and bury the body. There was in fact no doubt but that the services of the stranger had been bought by Nwachike for the sum of £2. 4s. 1d., one fathom of Indian cloth, two empty gin bottles, one goat and two fowls. Other Court Members, however, were of the opinion that the woman Nwachike had been an accomplice in the perpetration of a dark nefarious deed. By night, I read in one of the statements, Nwachike and the stranger slipped furtively out of the village, the woman leading and the stranger bearing the corpse. Arrived at Matthew's patch of bush Nwachike was heard to say, "Heave it in here". The stranger duly heaved; collected his bottles, goat and fowls etc.; and departed whence he had come with the taint of death upon his hands.

The stranger was a sallow individual. The Sergeant was all for charging him; but while sympathising with his eagerness to do so I pointed out that we would first have to be satisfied that he had undertaken to take, carry and *bury* the body. The stranger looked on impassively while his future for the next few months was being decided. I came to the conclusion that he had been engaged merely to remove the body, and I ruled that no action lay against him.

In his place I was left with a somewhat pitiful potential villain of the piece, a small man who answered to the name of Ben. The point at issue with regard to him was whether or not he was the Head of the dead woman's House. Matthew, pointing an accusing finger at him, declared that he was and was therefore responsible for seeing that his kinswoman was properly buried. As the village in question was divided into only two Houses, Ben took the natural course in the circumstances of

43

insisting that the deceased had in fact been a member of Matthew's House. Impassioned speech by both of them together followed. A means of discovering of which House the dead woman had been a member was to find out to whom her father had paid tax. This was unavailing because I was told that he had died before taxation was introduced. There had, however, been a brother, by then also dead. To whom had he paid tax? Both Ben and Matthew declared it was to the other.

The outcome of this visitation was, I fear, somewhat inconclusive. I decided to leave Okoro undisturbed on his sickbed, to regard Nwachike as having played an honourable part in trying to get her sister's body properly disposed of, to forego preferring a charge against the sallow stranger, and to refrain from pursuing the matter further until it was discovered to whom – if anyone – the deceased's deceased brother had been wont to pay his tax.

It was exciting to go on my first tour in this new Division. I set forth in the Native Administration lorry with Bonniface travelling in the back together with a few fowls and my loads: a small tin trunk, tin bath, bedding roll, camp bed, camp chair, chop box and two empty kerosene tins (to be used as ovens). The latter contained a variety of odd items such as spare Tilley lamp mantles, tins of baked beans and a roll of lavatory paper.

After a lumbering ride of three-quarters of an hour's duration we reached Ikodu on the east bank of the Orashi river. It was market day, and the sellers and their wares spilled over the small market place down the bank to the river's edge. The village was thronged with people, and it was slow work making headway through the press. I had to be careful where I put my feet for fear of treading on articles displayed for sale, or on the squatting or recumbent bodies of the vendors male and female, or on the countless dogs, goats and hens all of which seemed to be experiencing the promptings of a restless wanderlust. Bonniface could not resist the temptation of buying another fowl, which he casually carried upside down while it voiced strong protestations at this unhappy turn of events.

We left Ikodu by canoe for Joinkrama. I travelled in one canoe, seated in my camp chair amidships, with my loads behind me. Bonniface and a consignment of drugs for Okarki dispensary followed in another. It was a bright, sunny morning, and the paddlers sang as they pulled. I did some reading, and unfortunately looked up from my book just too late to see a manatee before it submerged beneath the water. After an hour or so we reached Joinkrama on the west bank of the river, and I paid the paddlers two shillings each for their pains.

Soon after our arrival I made my way to the Native Court, which was quite the most primitive structure of its kind which I had ever seen. It had a roof but no walls, and inside there was room for half a dozen rows of benches only. This was partly due to the presence of three mountainous ant-hills, which erupted like enormous warts from the earthen floor. I had only three reviews to do. The first case concerned a man charged with committing an act likely to cause a breach of the peace in that he took and broke another man's calabash of palm wine. The accused explained that the calabash had accidentally got broken. However, as calabashes do not normally break into pieces if dropped from a height of only two or three feet I considered his explanation to be unacceptable and confirmed the fine awarded by the Native Court. The second case concerned debt, and I confirmed a judgement requiring the defendant to return six bags of palm kernels or their monetary equivalent to the plaintiff. In the third case the Plaintiff was dissatisfied by the amount of dowry refund awarded to him as a result of his wife going off with another man. I discovered that he had made contradictory statements on two material points, and so, having no sympathy for him, I confirmed the Native Court judgment.

In the evening accompanied by a bevy of local dignitaries I walked through Joinkrama on a tour of inspection. The village straggled along the top of the river bank. At that time of the year it was some twenty feet above the water, but during the rainy season the river rose considerably and frequently overflowed its banks. Shadows were cast across the single winding street by the sun which was soon to sink behind the hinterland of high bush. The east bank of the river was bathed in the full glow of its warm light. There was the smell of meals being cooked within the sun-baked mud houses. Blue smoke gently permeated through the matting roofs. Here and there the crackle of fires could be heard. While the women cooked, the men sat in the doorways, from time to time exchanging greetings with passers-by. Groups of youths clustered together playing draughts and ludo. As I returned to the American Baptist Mission where I was putting up during my stay in Joinkrama all that remained of the earlier brightness and beauty of the setting sun was a fast fading flush on the face of the cloud-free sky.

Two American ladies looked after a small hospital and a number of chapels in the neighbourhood. The hospital buildings were made of mud and matting, but primitive though they were the theatre was equipped with overhead arc lamps and a very up-to-date operating table. The ladies seemed in no way daunted at living in that very out of the way spot, and contentedly contemplated the prospect of spending three years there before going on leave. During my second evening with them a woman in labour was brought to the hospital. She was apparently in a critical condition and the Americans decided that the only chance of saving her was to take her to Port Harcourt. They gave instructions that they would leave at dawn the following day. At 4.30 a.m. we had some breakfast, and an hour or so later we

45

began our canoe journey. The canoe was quite a small one, being only about thirty feet long. The sick woman lay on a mattress in the middle, and beside her was placed a boy suffering from some spinal affliction who was also being taken to Port Harcourt. I was appalled by the number of people and loads crammed on board. In addition to the two patients, the two Americans, their cook who operated the outboard engine (a unique means of propulsion in those parts) and myself, there were six other passengers. There was no more than one inch of freeboard; and when the canoe swayed we shipped water. As time went on and the seemingly inevitable did not happen, I ceased bothering about what I would do when we capsized and instead began to enjoy the early morning outing. Going against the current it took an hour to reach Ikodu. Having seen the Americans and their patients start off in their station waggon on the long road journey to Port Harcourt the cook and I returned to Joinkrama.

Later that morning Bonniface and my loads left by canoe for a place further down the river called Okarki. I decided I would travel overland; and my interpreter and I set off on the fifteen-mile journey on the two best bicycles which Joinkrama was able to produce. There had been rain during the night, and in many places the bush path was unridable. Three or four times we had to carry our cycles across creeks spanned by the trunks of felled palm tress, and one creek we had to cross by canoe. For the most part the path followed the course of the river, and in some places where the floodwaters had eaten away the bank it ran along the very brink of the cliff. The path had been neglected, and we had to cycle quite long distances through almost solid walls of grass, twelve to fifteen feet high. *En route* we passed a party of hunters cutting up an elephant which they had shot the previous day.

Rather the worse for wear I took my seat in Okarki Native Court at 11.45 a.m. Three hours later I had a half-hour break during which I ate a picnic snack. At 6.00 p.m. I left the Court having heard all but one of the cases on review. To my surprise I learned that the Rest-House in which I was to spend the next two nights was on the other side of the river. I received a bigger and yet more unwelcome surprise when I saw the place. It was no more than a mat-roofed mud shack with an earth floor, having no door or windows and devoid of all furniture. A small separate building, the size of a kennel, with a hole in the ground, was the lavatory. I foresaw myself after breakfast the following morning poised over this hole in a literal agony of suspense. The "Rest"-House was bounded on three sides by bush and on one by the river. That night mosquitos came in their millions. Creeping things wandered over the floor, and four frogs entered looking for prey. At 10.00 p.m., on the instructions of the Court Clerk, a Court Messenger arrived to guard me from wild beasts during the night – the Rest-House being the only habitation on the east bank of the river.

The day after my return from tour, August 21st, was my twenty-fifth birthday, and I spent it on my own in Ahoada. I recalled previous birthdays, particularly my twenty-first in 1945, when I was on leave in Poona. It was about then that the atomic bombs were dropped; the Japanese war came to a sudden end, and my efforts to make my way to the Burma jungle were no longer necessary. It was then on reaching the age of twenty-one that I realised I would have to come to some decision as to what I wanted to do on doffing my khaki drill. My thoughts had returned to the Colonial Service, a calling for which I had felt an attraction in my teens. I filled in forms. I attended interviews in Delhi and London. I did a year's training course at Cambridge, followed by several months studying Ibo at the School of Oriental and African Studies in London. And there I was four years older and again wearing my khaki drill (but shorn of its badges of rank). Formerly it had been India and Malaya. Then it was Eastern Nigeria. Where would the future lead me, I wondered. It was an exciting speculation.

I saw the two American missionaries on their way back to Joinkrama from Port Harcourt. I gave them a belated breakfast; and at their request presented them before they left with an admonitory letter to "all whom it might concern" that the Government took an interest in the well being of the twin children recently born to one Sunday and his wife, Lydia, of Ogbologo village. I was told that if the father were able to flaunt such a piece of paper it would assist in ensuring that neither of the children was murdered. We also drafted at the breakfast table a specimen Birth Certificate to be used in future by the Mission.

After seeing my friends off I returned to the office at 12.00 and from then until 2.30 p.m. I was visited by a continuous succession of people. One man wanted to be employed as a road labourer. Asked what work he had done previously he replied: nothing. A carpenter brought in an apprentice with a request that he be excused from paying tax. A woman divorced by her husband "on the grounds of dislike" came to seek assistance to retrieve her personal possessions from her former husband's house. Two men wanted permission to visit remand prisoners. Another man came on behalf of a relative to complain that having divorced his wife he had not been refunded the dowry he had paid. The Police Sergeant brought in the man whom I had arrested at Joinkrama on a charge of rape, to enquire what action I wanted taken. Three men came from Obuogisi, one of the villages which had been warring the previous weekend. They were about to plunge into details of their long-standing land dispute, but I cut them short and said that I would listen to what they had to say in due course when I heard the land case. Two men arrived to report that

47

the corpse of a woman who had died of leprosy had been left unburied at the foot of a palm tree. The Headman in charge of the Ahoada sleeping sickness team wished to know where next to begin work. A contractor who had undertaken to make certain furniture for a Native Administration school for £42 came with a request that this figure be raised by fifty per cent! A young man asked me for a "book" (i.e. a note) authorising him to sell drugs. Another bearing his muzzle-loading "Dane" gun with him applied for a licence to shoot elephant. A young woman complained that a Head Court Messenger before agreeing to serve a summons on her behalf had demanded the sum of seventeen shillings and a bottle of gin. Such were some of the purposes which brought people to my office. A few further callers came to see me in my house after I had lunched.

My District Officer, King, was keen on "community development". Self-help had recently become one of government's leading aims in the field, and King was determined that the people of Ahoada Division should set a shining example in this sphere. It was decided that efforts should be directed initially towards building a motor road between two villages known as Ozuzu and Umuaturu, some ten miles apart and separated by a number of rivers. I was sent off on tour to launch this venture. The pontoon ferry at Ahoada took an hour to transport my car across the 100 yards' width of the Sombrero to the east bank. I then had a forty-mile drive, for most of the way along narrow tracks hemmed in by towering walls of dense bush.

On arrival at a village called Ise I parked the car and summoned the men to assemble. After a few minutes I found myself confronting a motley collection of dotards and children with scarcely a young man to be seen amongst them. When I enquired as to who were the Chiefs of the village I was far from impressed by the appearance of the three disreputable-looking old men who were pointed out to me. I explained to my audience that the purpose of my visit was to arouse enthusiasm for the work of making a road from Ozuzu to Umuaturu. I pointed out to the Isu-ites the benefits they would derive from the existence of such a road, cut off as they were from the outside world. I told them that if they and the people of other villages in the neighbourhood undertook the construction of the road and embankments the Government would provide the materials and necessary supervision for the construction of the two bridges which were required. My listeners signified their readiness to turn out *en masse* the following morning to begin construction of the road under my directions.

Having preached the gospel of self-exertion to the people of Isu I repeated the performance in a number of other villages. The response was encouraging and when I returned that evening to the Rest-House where I was staying I was faced with the prospect of large numbers turning out to work on the next two days. This was excellent; but I was uncomfortably aware that I had not made as much as a foot of road in my life before. What directions was I going to give on the morrow to the legions of able-bodied young men who would appear equipped only with half-crown Birmingham-made matchets and some head pans? I studied the chapter on road-making in my manual of Field Engineering. While this gave valuable information as to the measurement of gradients with clinometer or abney level it supplied no advice on how to build a road through swamp a foot deep in water when no rock or stone was available within miles.

The next morning the villagers came to life when I appeared in their midst. With much blowing of horns and beating of drums they trooped down to the river, emitting whoops and catcalls as they went. I had to come to a quick decision as to what I wanted them to do. I pointed to the bush and told them to cut it down, and with weird howls of what I supposed was glee they immediately began to attack the undergrowth.

I sited a series of sticks along the route which I proposed the road should take. Chopped up tree trunks and branches were piled on top of each other in the swamp; and women and children helped by carrying earth in baskets and headpans and dumping it on top. Unfortunately some three or four hours later ardour was dampened by a heavy fall of rain. The horns and drums ceased to sound. Wading knee-deep through the ooze beside the spreadeagled trunks of the trees they had felled with their frail hand matchets the road-builders silently and disconsolately made their way home. The next day, however, they turned out again, and more progress was made. I urged them to keep at it; and promised to return again soon to see how they were getting on and to bring them some axes.

Back in Ahoada I had a wide variety of different matters with which to deal. We were in the process of acquiring some land in order to extend the Government Station. This involved paying compensation for cash-crop trees and negotiating an acceptable rent. A dozen or so sons of the soil congregated in my office and unanimously expressed dissatisfaction with the rates of compensation fixed for various varieties of trees, and equally vigorously they repudiated the proposed annual rental of ten shillings per acre. I failed to resolve this matter there and then; and as the numbers of cash-crop trees on the land in question were in dispute I instructed an Agricultural Assistant to undertake a fresh and comprehensive count.

The usual succession of people visited me in my office: Court Messengers, Sanitary Inspectors, Road Labourers, Leprosy Inspectors, tax clerks, farmers, palm-fruit cutters, contractors, hopeful men, disappointed men, indignant men, old men and women, young men and girls, deserted wives and husbands claiming refund of dowry. One thing they all wanted and that was a "book" written by the

A.D.O. What was written in the "book" mattered little; and provided they were able to leave clutching a piece of paper on which I had written a few words they felt that their visit had not been in vain.

The Sergeant, looking very like a School Prefect, brought before me a small boy aged about ten or eleven. He admitted having stolen a roll of cloth from a market stall. I let him go, at the same time recommending the owner to give him a hiding.

The Sergeant informed me of the untoward death of a village Headman who had fired a cannon to celebrate his success in a land case. It was a very ancient cannon and had exploded when the charge was fired. From the police report I learned that his left leg had been retrieved from forty feet away, and that his windpipe had been found wrapped around his jaw.

Allegations of rape were made fairly frequently, but the circumstances and the nature of the parties involved varied considerably. The Sergeant brought two to my notice. In the first the woman had unwisely allowed herself to be persuaded to accompany the villain along a lonely road. He had forcibly had his pleasure of her once, and then, having continued their walk some way further, had prepared to repeat the performance. At this second attempt, however, the woman had succeeded in escaping his clutches. The second case concerned a blind old man of about seventy. He admitted that he had endeavoured to "have connection" with his house-maid, believed to be aged about eight. After a valiant attempt in one so old he had given up, confessing as he did that he had found that the object of his desire was too immature.

I paid a visit to the Warders' lines to pour oil upon troubled waters. The wife of one of the warders had in a fit of pique bitten a chunk out of the right ear of the wife of one of her husband's colleagues. Although it was three days since the incident had occurred the victim with head bandaged lay moaning on her bed. While the assailant, with arms resolutely crossed over her well-endowed bosom, stood strong and silent, I tried unsuccessfully to make peace between them. The biter refused to voice any regret for her action; and Mrs. Nwaeri, the one bitten, merely went on moaning. Mr. Nwaeri accompanied me back to my house and on the way told me how the women had first come to blows and had then "gripped" each other. Before anyone had had a chance to separate them, Mrs. Odoro had bitten off the lobe of his wife's ear which she had then "spitted" out of her mouth. Mr. Nwaeri had diligently searched for the missing fragment, and on finding it had taken both it and his wife along to the Dispensary, where the Dispenser had carefully stitched the severed morsel back onto the ear.

Accommodation in the prison was inadequate, and in one of the cells it was necessary to house both convicted murderers and debtors. On one side six murderers lay on their bed-boards chained two and two together. On the other side were four debtor prisoners. The debtors considered themselves a cut above their cell mates; and the murderers for their part did not appear to waste much love on the debtors. Each side accused the other of having been responsible for defacing the walls of the cell. Despite the unpleasant fate hanging over them I found the murderers a more cheerful and likeable lot than the debtors, and when I left the cell after my chat with them they cordially wished me goodbye.

In the course of my rounds of the prison one of the inmates, a colossal prisoner of six foot six called Sunday, told me very earnestly that he had good reasons for knowing that certain enemies were plotting to poison him. He assured me that they had given £8 to the warder on gate duty as an inducement for him to accept some bad medicine. This he was to give to a certain prisoner working in the kitchen. He was also to give him three of the eight pounds as a consideration for putting the poison in his, Sunday's, chop. Sunday, towering above me, explained rather pathetically that he was an only child and he wanted to know what his family would do in the event of his death. Confessing my inability to answer that question, I turned to the Chief Warder, who was with me, and enquired on how many occasions prisoners had died of poisoning in the prison. He replied that as far as he knew this fate had never befallen anyone. Sunday refused to be reassured, however, and said that in that case he feared he would be the first.

The Police Sergeant one morning brought three men into my office, two of whom were juju men. They were accused by the third man of having assaulted and robbed him of £6. 7s. 0d. The two juju men were unpleasant-looking fellows but, as they were normally dressed and not wearing their cult clothes, they were not particularly awesome. One was a well-built man with a shaven head, and he kept his arms folded across his broad chest like a butcher. The other was a gaunt individual with one glazed eye. On my making some enquiries the complainant admitted that it was not £6. 7s. 0d. which had been taken from him but only seven shillings. In view of his self- confessed false statement I felt that, much as I would have liked to have had the two juju men in the prison for a spell, I could really do no more than caution all of them. Thereafter I surprised the two juju men by asking whether they had yet paid their tax for the year. Their hauteur somewhat ruffled they admitted that they had not. I intimated that thanks to the money they were able to extract from their credulous compatriots they should be able to set an example in prompt payment of tax. The shaven-headed one made no comment; but his companion informed me that he himself was a tax collector. With the persuasive power of his calling to support him I imagined that he experienced little difficulty in getting those on his tax roll to pay up.

The next person the Sergeant produced was a small and rather frightened young man, who he said had confessed to murder. I read the statement which was placed before me. In this the young man said that he had been returning to his village after cutting palm fruit in the bush when a man stopped him and enquired why he had cut the fruit. The young man took umbrage at being questioned and sliced his interrogator's right arm with the matchet he was carrying. He followed this with a slash at his left thigh, and before he knew where he was he had dismembered the stricken body. In the spirit of one preparing a treasure hunt he buried limbs in different places and then returned to his village. Apparently it was fear of juju that had subsequently induced him to come forward and confess his crime.

I read his statement over to him, and having satisfied myself that he fully understood its contents and that he had made it of his own free will I countersigned it. That meant one more to swell the gang of basket-making prisoners awaiting trial for murder.

At this time a very troublesome man convicted of serious wounding was admitted to the prison. The Chief Warder reported to me that he was exceedingly strong and belligerent and that he suspected he was mad. I went to visit the terror, and found a naked body lying on a blanket on the floor of the cell. I told the body to stand up. When it did so I saw that the chains linking the steel bracelets around each ankle and wrist had been snapped, and the Chief Warder told me that the first thing the prisoner had done on being finally locked into the cell had been to break up his bed-boards into small fragments. The man was of medium height and well built. He was very prognathous and had furtive shifting eyes. I told him that I had heard he had been making a nuisance of himself, and asked what was upsetting him. To my surprise he said he wanted to be allowed to go outside and wash, and he complained that he had not been issued with any soap. He also alleged that the Chief Warder had knocked out his two front teeth. I examined his mouth, and it was quite evident that he had been without the two teeth in question for a long time. Having observed him for some moments I came to the conclusion that he was wilful rather than mad. I left him with a promise that he should have a bucket of water to wash with, but added that he would receive no soap until I had had proof of his good behaviour. It was not until then that I enquired what the name of this troublemaker was, and of all improbable things I learnt that he was called Innocent!

I went off on tour again, this time to Omoku where there was a large number of outstanding cases to be reviewed. Omoku Native Court was the largest in Ahoada Division. It was a corrugated-iron roofed building about 100 feet long, and on my arrival I found it already full of people. I took my seat behind a table on a dais at one end, and as usual I was flanked by Court Members and Elders of the town. In the body of the Court men sat on one side of the centre aisle and women on the other. More men and youths stood two or three deep round the outside of the building and looked in over the low walls. After I had greeted the Court and Council members, the parties in the first case were called; the relevant record of the Native Court proceedings was placed before me, and the work of the day began. Some of the cases I was able to deal with in a few minutes, but others kept me occupied for as much as an hour each. I dealt with the criminal actions first, and did not waste much time over one in which a young man having been found guilty of contempt of court for failing to remove his cap before entering was fined £3. I reduced this to five shillings, and there was a rumble of approval from those present.

In one of the civil cases the plaintiff claimed £10 damages for having been falsely accused of witchcraft. On looking at him I could not help but think that there might have been some truth in the allegation. He was a tall, tottering old man with a gaunt face and yellowish skin stretched over his bony limbs. His eyes were penetrating. He wore a length of cloth over his right shoulder, while his left shoulder was bare. He leaned heavily on a long staff and carried a lotus-leaf-shaped fan made of leather. The defendant was a woman. The circumstances of the case were disappointingly tame. The defendant's son had been caught by the plaintiff stealing oranges from a tree in his compound and had been given a beating. On returning home the mother, having found her son crying, became annoyed and spoke her mind to the plaintiff in the course of which she called him "a wizard". I came to the conclusion that the plaintiff's reputation had in no way suffered as a result of this remark made in the midst of a slanging match, and I reversed the Native Court's judgment which had awarded him £5 damages. One statement made by the plaintiff did not, I thought, have a convincing ring about it. In the Native Court record he was quoted as having said that the only reason why he did not like small boys to climb his tree and take his oranges was his fear that they might fall and break their necks!

Light relief was forthcoming in the next case. In this three men were accused of having stolen palm kernels. The complainant had two witnesses, one of whom was both deaf and dumb. We had a splendid game trying to discover how many bags of kernels he had seen loaded into the canoe of the accused. I could not feel that the afflicted man's evidence was very satisfactory. At the same time as he tried to indicate answers on his fingers he also made repeated, rapid and seemingly inexplicable movements with his hands, and periodically emitted violent inarticulate grunts, pointing the while an admonishing finger at one of the accused.

One case was a judgment debtor case in which the defendant, a man from a different part of the country, admitted borrowing £6. 2s. 0d. from the plaintiff and agreeing to repay him £22. He said he used to work for the plaintiff and had borrowed the money in order to marry. The Native Court had ordered him to pay the £22 in full. I explained that interest of 300–400 per cent was excessive and reduced the amount to be refunded by the defendant to £6. 12s. 0d.

In one of the final cases I dealt with at Omoku I recognised as plaintiff a middle-aged man whom I had frequently seen outside the Court wearing a Boy-Scout hat. He had always given me punctilious Scout salutes whenever our paths had crossed. This gentleman was claiming the return of one cow which he said had been given to the defendant as part of the dowry when he had married his daughter. The daughter having since divorced him he wanted the cow back again. From the Native Court proceedings it was difficult to keep track of this cow's comings and goings. It was constantly changing hands, more frequently in fact than even the defendant's daughter! Many of the statements made regarding this cow were puzzling, for example, "Question by Court: Was the dowry you received paid to you on behalf of the cow or it was a different dowry altogether or not? Answer: It was not for the cow at all." In the end I felt I could do no better than confirm the judgment of the Native Court, which ignored the cow (and the calf which it had reputedly borne) and merely awarded the plaintiff the sum of twenty-six shillings.

From Omoku I moved further north to Okwuzi. *En route* we had to abandon the Native Administration lorry because the road was flooded. Nwanuma, my Interpreter, and I crossed the water by canoe and continued the remainder of the journey by bicycle. Escorted by Philip a gang of labourers carried my loads the nine miles to the tumble-down Okwuzi Rest-House. During my stay at Okwuzi I prospected for a site for a new Rest-House, and found a suitable one close to a Leper Camp.

The next day began badly because as I was shaving I was pestered with the importunings of various local men who wanted jobs. After breakfast I walked across to the small Native Court and as usual proceeded to deal with the accumulation of outstanding reviews and appeals. In the course of one of the cases an interesting point arose as to whether according to native law and custom a woman under menstruation was permitted to swear on a certain juju. I confessed myself ignorant on this point and appealed to the Elders present for guidance. A splendid figure, swathed in a black, gold-embroidered Japanese kimono, slowly hoisted himself out of the deck-chair style seat in which he had been reclining and then delivered himself of the dictum that a woman under menstruation was not allowed to take an oath on that particular juju.

Child dispute cases were fairly common, and I had one such to deal with at Okwuzi. The plaintiff, a tall dour man, claimed ownership of a small girl called Ojiji from the defendant who was older and had a frizzle of white hairs around his head. The mother of the child in dispute stood between the two parties. She was a singularly unattractive-looking person, having one blind eye which remained heavily fixed on me throughout the proceedings. Beneath the yellow duster she was wearing on her head a wad or two of matted hair protruded. Her blouse was nonchalantly hitched up to allow the child she carried on her hip to reach her sagging breast. On reading through the record of the Native Court hearing I discovered that within the space of a few years this woman had been married to the plaintiff three times and to the defendant twice. I did not envy the unfortunate Ojiji either of her two would-be fathers and did not give much consideration to their rival claims for ownership. For the child's sake it was clearly desirable that she should remain with her mother. The mother was at that time living with the plaintiff, who assured me that he fully intended to remain married to her. The mother confirmed that she intended to remain with the plaintiff; and in view of this I gave judgment that he was the rightful owner of Ojiji. There followed an unedifying tussle in Court in which the small girl, bewildered and crying, was snatched away from the grasp of the old man with the white hairs who protested indignantly – much to the amusement it seemed of those present.

Having disposed of the cases I held the customary informal "Citizens' Advice Bureau" session. A file of people formed up in front of my table, and one by one they made their respective requests, enquiries or complaints. My interest was aroused when a pretty, well-dressed girl in her teens came forward. She told me that as a child she had been given in marriage to a man old enough to be her father, that now that she was grown up she had found a man for herself whom she wanted to marry. I was pleased to further the ends of true love, and my Citizens' Advice Bureau became a Marriage Bureau. I sent Beatrice, for such was her name, accompanied by a Court Messenger to fetch her father, her husband, Rufus – the one she loved – and his mother. In due course they were all assembled in front of me. Rufus, I was glad to see, looked a likeable young man, and I thought that he and Beatrice made an excellent pair. Beatrice's husband shewed no reluctance to divorce her provided he received his dowry back. Only her father was querulous for he feared that he would lose financially over the transaction. I tried to reassure him, and I felt that as a result of our meeting I had succeeded in paving the way for the young couple. I told them that I hoped they would in due course do as I suggested and be married in Church or by the District Officer.

When I was back in Ahoada after completing my tour I paid an informal visit to the Prison and made a round of the cells. I was pleased to find a somewhat more peaceable and law-abiding Innocent. The Chief Warder told me that he had become a good basket-maker. Innocent took the opportunity of my visit to fire a volley of staccato words at me. His complaint was that his belly was not full, and to prove his point he hoisted up his shirt to shew me the portion of his anatomy in question.

I learned that the visiting Magistrate had during my absence dealt with the case of the warder's wife, who had bitten a chunk out of the ear of a neighbour, and had imposed a fine of £7.

Two human legs sticking out of a box on the carrier of a bicycle being wheeled through the station caught my eye. The rest of the body was covered with coarse matting, around which swarms of flies buzzed noisily. I drew the attention of the Police Sergeant to the unusual load; and he later informed me that the body had been brought to Ahoada in connection with a report of a death by drowning.

Soon I was off on tour again, this time to Umuaturu to see what progress the villagers had made with the construction of the road to Ozuzu. It took forty minutes on the pontoon ferry to cross the Sombrero river at Ahoada. We took the main road to Owerri. The earth surface was appallingly corrugated and driving over it was sheer agony. When passing through Owerri I called at the government hospital, displayed a poisoned toe and was given a large shot of penicillin. It was about a further sixty miles to Umuaturu and I did not arrive there until 1.45 p.m. I ate some sandwiches and then entered the Court. At 4.30 p.m. I received a message that the lorry bringing my loads had not arrived at Ozuzu seven miles away, from where they had to be carried by porters to Umuaturu. About an hour later, however, a Court Messenger reported they were on their way. I remained in the low-ceilinged Court until 6.15 p.m. by which time it was so dark that I was no longer able to read the judgment books. By then it had been raining for an hour. I drove to the Rest-House, which was in darkness and deserted. There being nothing else to do I dozed in my car, lulled by the beating of raindrops on the roof. From time to time I was aroused by the voices of porters who arrived in ones and twos and deposited my belongings. At 7.45 p.m., Philip having lit a Tilley lamp, I emerged from the car. I had a splitting headache. Everything and everyone was soaking wet. It was still raining heavily, though the thunder and lightning had decreased. I bandaged the thumb of a porter who had come to grief, and then visited the shack which served as a kitchen. Wretched Bonniface was at sixes and sevens and had only the light of his fire by which to work. To my annoyance he informed me that he had no bread. I told him to heat a tin of spaghetti and brew a mug of coffee for me.

There being no furniture of any description in the Rest-House and my one canvas camp chair being sodden I returned to the car, where I waited for my spaghetti to appear, and in the meantime Philip fixed up my camp bed and mosquito net. In due course I swallowed a lukewarm snack, took two aspirins with my coffee and retired for the night amidst a litter of petrol cans, tins of oil, chop boxes, office boxes, etc. The noise of the cascading rain on the matting roof reminded me of the seething sound of boiling jam. However, neither that, nor the intermittent lightning flashes, nor the pain in my head prevented me from quickly falling asleep.

The rain had stopped by the following morning, and after breakfast I sallied forth to inspect the Umuaturu – Ozuzu road. I was disappointed but not unduly surprised to find that very little progress had been made on this project since I had launched it a month earlier. I spent the day suitably haranguing the inhabitants of various villages in the vicinity.

The next Rest-House in which I stayed a few days later was another very unprepossessing one. When I arrived in the evening I found a derelict building awaiting me with crumbling mud walls and a matting roof perforated in many places. Once again there was not a single item of furniture. The kitchen and boys' quarters were in an even more advanced state of decay than the main building. Bonniface used the garage to cook in, and in the absence of a place for themselves he and Philip spread their sleeping mats in the second of the two Rest-House rooms. This room contained my food supplies, kitchen equipment and crockery. Some things were scattered over the floor while others were still in the boxes. I told Philip to get everything sorted out and arranged, at which he enquired how he was to arrange anything with nothing on which to arrange it. I saw his point and left discreetly without making any more bright suggestions.

Philip always looked glum, but I thought that on this occasion he was looking more gloomy than usual. This might have been due to the lack of accommodation and the prospect of getting wet during the night when the rain began to spray through the roof of tattered palm-leaf mats; or it might have been because I had taken him to task earlier that evening about the speedy way in which my sugar had been disappearing. If I were to believe him I had consumed sixteen pounds of sugar in as many days!

On my way back to the Rest-House the following evening, my attention was caught by a crowd of happy laughing people. I got out of my car, and arrived on the scene in time to see a cow drawing her last breath. A squalid compound in a jungle clearing was the final resting place of this beast which in happier days had roamed over the wide, open grasslands of the Northern Region. There she lay on her side on the brown earth, her hooves lashed together with rope. Beneath her half-severed neck a large white enamel basin had been placed in a hollow in the ground. Men stood attentively by her flank and legs ready to suppress the slightest movement. Another bent over her head, with a thumb gripping tightly in one nostril and forefinger in the other. When so many connections seemed to have been severed it was odd still to see some signs of life in the recumbent body. From time to time a shudder shook the stricken beast. Rapidly the life-blood was being pumped away. A man with his hand inside the gaping neck depressed the pipe from which it spurted towards the enamel basin. The flow of blood grew less, and the basin was almost full. Willing hands reached within the gory cavity to scoop and squeeze and win the very dregs, while the women and children standing round shrilled excitedly and one thin dog licked furtively at a red stain on the ground.

Chapter 5

"Snuff up his arse"

About this time I paid a visit to Enugu, the headquarters of the Eastern Region. After an enjoyable weekend I left on Monday morning on the return journey to Ahoada about 250 miles away. At the top of Milican Hill I paused for a moment to look down on the aluminium roofs of Enugu flashing with a chromium-plating glitter in the sun. For twenty miles or so we bowled merrily along the tarred Onitsha road. Oil bean trees lined the route, and elephant grass grew high on either side of the road. At times we passed men wearing only the briefest of loin cloths, who stared wonderingly as we sped by; at others we passed groups of Hausa men wearing the long flowing robes of the Moslem North. Branching south off the Onitsha road, we took the laterite-surfaced road to Awgu, Okigwi and Owerri. Streaky like a long rasher of bacon the road stretched on mile after mile, the magenta red of the laterite giving place here and there to the yellow and white of sand. There were views of grass-clad hills and terraced slopes and sometimes a glimpse of bush-covered plain in the distance. After Okigwi we came to the end of the open countryside and once again found ourselves encompassed by bush and oil palms. Some twenty miles north of Owerri the laterite petered out, and from then on the surface of the road was either earth or sand.

On leaving Owerri we ran into an electric storm. It grew prematurely dark, and I had to switch my headlights on. The rain teemed down, and visibility through the windscreen was very limited. The narrow road was quickly awash, and for many miles I drove through water three or four inches deep. I could scarcely hear the thunder above the noise of the rain, the engine and the churning of the wheels through the slush. Lightning struck downwards repeatedly at the tree-clad countryside, each time cracking the grey-blue bowl of the sky. These flashes momentarily threw the road, the puddles and the trees on either side into sharp relief. A sizzling searing shaft of lightning accompanied by an instantaneous crash of thunder made me involuntarily press harder on the accelerator, and I swerved too fast for comfort into the next trough of water. At one point my companions and I had to leave the shelter of the car to break off the branches of a tree which had fallen across the road. Further on we came on another similar obstacle, through which someone before us had already cleared a way.

I reached home wet and tired, and having had my supper I planned to have an early night. At 9.30 p.m., leaving the Tilley lamp in the sitting room, I went into my bedroom. I sat down and in the gloom removed one shoe and sock. I placed my bare foot on the mat beside my bed. It was not until then that I became suddenly and painfully aware of a multitude of strange bodies on the floor. I grabbed my torch, and by its light saw to my horror that the entire room was alive with ants. I leapt up, hopped wildly around not knowing where to put my unshod foot and called frantically for Philip. By the time he arrived I had donned a pair of mosquito boots, which afforded reasonable protection.

For two and a half hours Philip, Bonniface, Christian (my small-boy) and I waged war on the invading army of ants. Philip and Christian kept on energetically sweeping the floor. Bonniface kindled a small fire in one corner of the room on which he burnt the only india rubber I possessed and thereafter various leaves which gave off a pungent smell. I supervised operations and sprinkled Jeyes fluid on concentration areas. When the campaign began I was wearing only shorts, but later on I put some long trousers on over them and also donned a mackintosh. However, in spite of these precautions ants took their toll all over my body.

The ants were entering my bedroom by a single route, which it was fortunately possible to seal with a liberal application of Jeyes fluid. However, before I had discovered their presence they had already overrun the room. Floor, walls, ceiling, furniture and my mosquito net were all swarming with small black specks, specks which were all on the move weaving to and fro between each other. We burnt, we swept, we beat and we stamped; but although one heap of dead bodies after another was flung out of the window we did not seem to make any impression on the invading hordes. I went outside and was appalled by the hosts of ants I found surrounding the house. The grass in the front garden looked as though it had been covered with a black carpet. I remained outside for only a moment because I was immediately being bitten in a score of places.

It was as well that I kept my eye on the troop movements outside for thereby I noticed a column about to enter the sitting-room. Bonniface scattered embers all along the side of the house, which had the desired effect of keeping the marauders at bay.

At midnight I pronounced the coast to be reasonably clear, and the boys left. Hardly had I removed my mackintosh, however, before I heard a cry go up that ants were approaching their own quarters. On closer inspection we found that they were heading for the kitchen. We did not attempt to interfere with the progress of their march, but simply evacuated all food supplies.

I fell asleep in a reek of Jeyes fluid, burnt rubber and the charred remnants of miscellaneous pieces of greenery. On leaving for the office after breakfast the following morning I observed at the end of the drive a line of ants heading out of my compound in the direction of the Rest-House. I wished them a hearty good riddance.

Mail was delivered twice a week to Ahoada from Port Harcourt provided the road was passable. Local letters usually afforded some amusement. "To the Helper of the Helpless, the Honourable District Officer" began one petition. The next one I opened, which the writer wished to have forwarded to the Resident, was addressed to "His Imperial Highness the Senior Resident". Concluding lines were sometimes quaintly phrased. "I shall be waiting for your sweetable reply, Sir," ended Elajan Osokoro, whereas another petitioner preferred to finish with the words "I stop here appending my autograph on the album". For many the District Officer was a patriarchal figure and many of the letters we received were couched in terms similar to the following: "Trusting that your worship as a Father in this Division will give your kindest considerations as far as justice is concerned. Thanking your worship for time spent in reading. Awaiting your Fatherly reply ...." Letters were frequently written by professional letter writers, who were wont to wax both emotional and lyrical, as the following examples reveal: "Your worship may know the step to deal upon this case because through your wings we the cheated ones shelter. I close with tears of my stolen yams" and "I ardently appeal to your worship to view this my jeremiad with the utmost sympathy". Writers of letters took a pride in their handiwork, and tended to indulge in so much verbosity that the message they sought to convey frequently became obscured. A letter from the Secretary of an Ex-servicemen's Association included these sentences: "Yet as an Ex-Military high-ranked officer you are, and Ex-Servicemen we are, we feel that meeting you in this manner should be ceremonised with some military activities, gestures and articulations. But, taking into consideration our present life as Civilians, we just acquiesce in this simple manner of meeting". Some people were constantly writing to the District Officer. One such was Sunday Dibea. In one of his screeds he commented "I really believe that a black man's tricks can easily be discovered by a yellow race, since we achieve our Civilisation from you". In a letter from the Ogba Community League I was surprised to find myself termed "A

61

'Churchill' the public admires". The people of Ogba were apparently conversant with conservative characteristics because in another letter complaining about a Chief I read, "He considers himself higher than every one in the village, he being one of the tory-lords of Ogba Clan". A woman wishing to explain the reason for her absence from Court wrote, "Sir, you know a woman will not empty her bladder in the public. So I was away urinating when my case was called".

One evening I visited the Prison kitchen garden. After I had been inspecting the beds a few moments the figure of the Chief Warder appeared through the narrow entrance. Beneath his voluminous khaki cape I saw a scarlet shirt and a brightly coloured loin cloth. Between the asparagus beds the Chief Warder came smartly to attention.

"Everything correct, Sir. No complaints, Sir."

"Good evening, Mr. Eziashi. I am just taking a look at the garden. It does not seem to be in such good condition as when I saw it last. Are prisoners still working here?"

"Certainly, Sir. See where I have planted more seeds. Actually I was coming to plant some things this evening."

"These tomatoes look pretty dreadful."

"Very bad, Sir." The Chief Warder with a grimace of dissatisfaction on his face stooped and stirred a long creeping growth lying on the ground. "No tomatoes at all, Sir."

"What's this called, Mr. Eziashi?"

"That is okra, Sir. It gives man power."

We made our way round the garden, looking at cabbages, lettuces and carrots. On leaving the enclosure we passed the Prison. Warder Onuora, one of the best warders we had, was standing by the entrance. By the look on his face I knew he wished to speak to me about something. While I halted some yards ahead, Onuora had a few words with Eziashi. Then with an apologetic smile on his face Eziashi approached me.

"I am sorry, Sir. This is not the right time to see you, but Onuora wishes to take this opportunity of speaking to O.C. Prison."

"Well, what is it, Onuora?"

"I want to ask O.C. Prison to get me transferred to a prison anywhere else, Sir."

"Why do you want that?"

There followed a few more words between Onuora and the Chief Warder. The latter then spoke.

"Warder Onuora has many enemies here, Sir, and he fears that they are planning to harm him. Actually, Sir, he is afraid they will poison him. Black men fear poisoning too much."

"So, you think there are people who want to poison you, Onuora?"

"Yes, Sir. I have found two pins about this size, Sir, covered with black stuff stuck into my house, Sir. One in the ceiling and one in the floor of my bedroom. Even the Chief Warder could witness to it, Sir."

Eziashi laughed apologetically. "As for myself, Sir, I have no fear for poisoning."

"Well, Onuora, in spite of these pins you have not come to any harm; and it would have been worse if they had been stuck into you instead of your house."

Onuora seemed slightly reassured.

"Actually, Sir, I have no much fear for poisoning; but I think my enemies may seek to make trouble for me by putting incriminating articles in my house."

"Warder Onuora recently saw one scientific man who advised him that his enemies might try to incriminate him, Sir."

"What sort of incriminating articles?"

"Such things as counterfeiting materials perhaps, Sir."

"What you should do, Onuora, is to report to the Police that you have reason to suspect that certain persons may attempt to place incriminating articles in your house, and they can then be on the lookout."

There followed another aside between Onuora and Eziashi. The latter replied, speaking in a very confidential manner.

"It seems that Warder Onuora and the new Police Sergeant were formerly stationed in the same place some four or five years ago, Sir. At that time there was some palaver between them as Onuora discovered the Sergeant making arrangements to have sexual intercourse with his wife; and Onuora fears that the Sergeant will have no love for him now if incriminating articles are found in his house."

"Is it only fear of your enemies which makes you want a transfer?"

"Yes, Sir."

"If you remained we might catch the people trying to incriminate you. We would put them inside the prison, where you would be able to look after them. Would you like that, Onuora?"

"I would like, Sir."

"Well, what I suggest is that you let it be known that the O.C. Prison is anxious to catch anyone who attempts to spoil your fair name. That may make them think twice. You can let me know later if you have any more trouble."

"Yes, Sir."

"That is good, Sir. I don't want to lose my best warder, Sir."

"I quite agree, Mr. Eziashi."

"It is only fear of my enemies that pressed me to ask O.C. Prison for a transfer. I am very happy to work with Chief, who is my good brother, and with the O.C. Prison. It would please me very much to stay in Ahoada."

"Well, we will do nothing now, Onuora. Let me know if you have any more trouble in future. All right?"

"Very good, Sir."

Onuora saluted smartly, and then his mouth with its two protruding front upper teeth split into a beaming, jagged smile.

In the course of my travels around Ahoada Division I sometimes came upon interesting sights. Motoring from Umuaturu to Egwi I saw a young woman, wearing vast brass bangles, slowly walking along the road. I stopped the car in order to have a closer look. The girl took fright and disappeared as fast as these impedimenta would allow her into a field of cassava. After some minutes of cajoling my interpreter, Nwanuma, succeeded in persuading her to emerge from the greenery and display her charms.

The bangles consisted of long coils of brass which extended from the ankle to the knee, becoming wider at the top. They looked rather like two immense inverted candle snuffers. I estimated that each bangle weighed between seven and ten pounds. To prevent them chafing the girl had wrapped pieces of cloth around both her ankles on which the bases of the bangles, coiled like great springs, rested.

I was told that girls in that neighbourhood, whose parents could afford to buy such bangles, wore them during the months spent in the Fattening Room prior to marriage. Normally one did not see them wearing these bangles because they did not frequently emerge from the confines of the Fattening Room. The less exercise they took the fatter they became and therefore the more desirable in the eyes of potential husbands. This girl told me that she expected to wear her bangles constantly for five months. At the end of that time she looked forward to going to her husband-to-be whom she intended marrying in Church.

On another occasion when I was driving, a young woman with her head painted a bright yellow caught my attention. I stopped, and Nwanuma called her over. She obligingly came and stood beside the car. From my seat inside I had difficulty in seeing her head, but her bosom was agreeably framed in the window. Her body was tattooed with a floral design, which took root so to speak in her navel whence there sprouted tendrils which weaved between and around her two firm breasts. Her nipples were tilted slightly upwards like two small flowers looking towards the sun.

On getting out of the car I was able to study her head and hair style. Except for certain tufts of hair the whole of her head and neck were painted a cadmium yellow. This effect had been achieved by the application of a special kind of earth applied moist and left to harden. Her hair was gathered up into a high "cock's comb" which projected from the top of her head rather like a fireman's helmet. In her hair, her ears and at either side of her nose were placed small silver-coloured ornaments of a floral design. She had bangles on her wrists and a cloth round her loins.

On other occasions I saw other women with yellow heads but without the "cock's comb" hairstyle. I also saw one or two very small naked girls with yellow heads. I was unable to discover the significance of this form of ornamentation. All that people could or would tell one was that every year women and girls participated in a special dance to which they went with yellow heads, and that their heads remained in that state throughout the month of November.

One day I came upon a cavalcade of some fifty widows. I would never have known that they were widows had not their singularly dreadful appearance so aroused my interest that I stopped the car. The female forms stood by the side of the road uncertain whether to advance or stay. They were only identifiable as such by their dejected, dangling dugs. The only article worn by them was a small square of cloth over the fork which left the backside bare. All hair had been shaved from their heads, and their tonsured skulls had a coating of red earth baked hard by the sun. Their limbs and bodies had been rubbed with the same red earth. Some of the female forms were wizened and cadaverous while others had great distended bellies as full and round as large meat dish covers. They carried grasses in their hands, holding them as if they were candles or tapers. It was through Nwanuma I learnt that they were widows mourning for their late lamented husbands.

Passing through Rumuji village I saw a native dance band practising. Two men sat on the ground on either side of a cumbersome instrument resembling an outsize xylophone. The instrument comprised two six-foot lengths of banana palm trunk laid alongside each other on the ground. Pegged close together across these two trunks were logs of wood stripped of its bark, each about two inches thick and three inches wide and varying in length from eighteen to thirty inches. The two players, who had hammer sticks in both hands, sat facing each other and belaboured the "keys" for all they were worth. In addition there were two drummers. One was beating what appeared to be a solid log of wood. The other sat astride two drums, the tightly drawn skins at the ends of which he sometimes caressed and sometimes thumped with his two hands.

Later on I saw the local men dancing to the rhythm beaten out by this band. The dance was what was known as a "masquerade" dance. On a stand in a stringed-off enclosure in the middle of the circle of dancers there was an elaborate, brightly painted carving of a twin-engined aeroplane with a wing span of at least three feet. From time to time one of the men would remove this from its stand and would dance with it balanced upon his head. Close to the circle of dancers at the foot of a large tree there was a small juju shrine, identifiable as such by reason of a few pots and bottles stuck in the ground and one or two manillas, bones and some feathers scattered around them.

In a clearing outside another village elsewhere in the Division I was puzzled by a number of wooden "stalagmites" a foot or two in length sticking up out of the grass. I gathered that these objects were concerned with some especially erotic dance performed by young women which took place at a certain time each year and which could only be witnessed by the initiated. It seemed that having worked themselves into a frenzy of excitement the women brought their dance to an end by throwing themselves onto these smooth polished phallic devices.

Dancing was particularly indulged in when the moon was full. On bright moonlit nights one would hear the drums pounding away from dusk to dawn. Almost stupified by the pulsating rhythm dancers circled endlessly round and round oblivious to everything around them. One night in Ahoada I could not get to sleep because of the sound of singing and drumming on the edge of the village at the other side of the open space we called a golf course. I got out of bed and walked across to see the fun. The band consisted of one man, who was beating two drums of different sizes, and another, who was distributing blows between six flagons embedded in the ground and filled with water to different levels. There was a choir of women who clapped their hands and ceaselessly chanted the same refrain. By the light of the moon I was able to discern a circle of some forty women, who maintained a constant and convulsive oscillation of their bottoms as they slowly progressed round and round the music makers.

During my eight years as an Administrative Officer in Eastern Nigeria I was constantly faced with the task of organising and holding elections of one kind or another. However, on a certain day in November 1949, happily unaware of the onerous Returning Officer duties which the future held in store for me, I rather looked forward to conducting my first election. The scene was Egbeda village; the purpose was to elect a village representative to the Group Council; and the method was secret oral ballot. I was accompanied by my orderly, Walson by name, Nwanuma, Ukpabi, the road Overseer, and a Court Messenger.

Three or four hundred men were gathered in Egbeda market place. To give them time to organise themselves I dawdled for a few moments by my car. This proved to be a waste of time because Nwanuma entirely failed to induce them to arrange themselves in any sort of order. I elbowed my way through a mass of jostling bodies until I reached a small table at which I seated myself. The crowd, laughing and talking excitedly, surged around me. Walson, Nwanuma, Ukpabi and the Court Messenger did what they could to force the press of bodies back, and having won a few square feet of breathing space they did their best to keep it. Nwanuma mounted the table and through him I endeavoured to explain to the men of Egbeda the purpose of holding an election. I stressed that it was Government's intention that villages should be represented on Group Councils by freely elected persons and not as hitherto by the nominees of the village Elders. Then I described how the voting would be carried out: I would remove myself and table to the compound of a school alongside the market; one by one they would come to me at the table and say the name of the man they wished to represent them; I would record their choice; they would then go to the other end of the compound and remain there until everyone had voted.

It sounded such a simple procedure, but in the event it proved impossible of fulfilment. As a first complication, no sooner had I taken my seat in the centre of the school compound than all the schoolchildren numbering several hundreds formed a crescent around me at a distance which allowed them the maximum proximity compatible with safety from the sudden sallies of Nwanuma who strove valiantly to keep them at bay, but whose efforts appeared to succeed only in provoking considerable hilarity.

It was not only the schoolchildren we had difficulty in keeping at a distance. The entire adult male population of the village came streaming through the hedge into the school compound; and despite the combined efforts of Nwanuma, Ukpabi, Walson and the Messenger it was impossible to regulate them to one at a time. I left my seat to reason with them above the hubbub. I reseated myself, and they again broke their ranks. Walson, Ukpabi and the Messenger found some sticks. Armed with these and assisted by two or three public-spirited men they vainly tried to control the villagers. In an attempt to preserve the principle of secrecy I moved to another spot behind a Church in the same compound, where I hoped the lie of the land might make it feasible to restrain the over-eager electorate.

It proved to be a vain hope. Within a matter of moments I was surrounded by clamouring men. With the whole village about to converge around me, I was in despair to find somewhere whither I could retire to escape the mob, and where it might be possible to regulate the voters one by one. One of the "public spirits", at that time immaculate in white shirt and white sun-helmet, cleared a path through the crowd by laying out to right and left with a long pole and conducted me to the school storeroom. The moment it was unlocked I nipped inside followed in quick succession by Nwanuma, Walson, the Court Messenger and the "public spirit". We immediately barricaded the entrance. The store, which was at one end of the school building, had a second door opening into the long schoolroom. The children ubiquitous as ever, were back inside the building, and were interested spectators of my movements.

I seated myself on a stool in the middle of the storeroom. Walson and his assistants, who now also included one willing teacher, let in the first man and beat off those behind who attempted to force admittance in his wake. He whispered the name of his choice to me – an unnecessary precaution in view of the din going on outside. He was then propelled by Nwanuma through the door into the long school-room; and Ukpabi then helped him on his way out of the building. Meanwhile the next man had been admitted. I recorded his vote, and he followed the first man out of the building. And so it continued hour by hour: the Messenger and Walson at the door belabouring incessantly the press of bodies seeking to fight their way over the threshold; the willing teacher hurling pot after pot of water onto those outside in an attempt to dampen their ardour; the "public spirit" expostulating with, rebuking and entreating his fellow villagers; and I noting the votes on a sheet of foolscap, which became increasingly crumpled as time went on.

At an early stage the door and door frame gave way under the strain, but fortunately the walls held firm. Periodically bodies would succeed in slipping through the doorway beneath the blows of those on guard. At such times I left my stool for a brief space to render physical assistance to my hard-pressed lieutenants. My contribution, small though it was, was sufficiently well delivered to cause the soles of both my shoes to come adrift.

When they finally gained admittance to the store, as a result of their exertions the men were pouring with sweat, panting and spent with fatigue. The clothes of many hung in tatters, while others appeared wearing only shorts rolled up around their thighs. Many, I was certain, had no idea for what reason they were struggling to get inside, for once in the store some would have staggered straight past me and out through the other door had I not stopped them and asked them for whom they wished to vote. As often as not their faces remained blank, and I had to give a brief resumé of the purpose of my visit.

After a while we began to spot people coming through a second time. Once inside the store and they were recognised as having already voted, they received a series of thumps in quick succession, and were then chased screaming with feigned terror down the schoolroom building to the great delight of those undergoing tuition therein. The punishment inflicted on these persons did not, however, deter countless others from attempting to register a second vote. After giving Egbeda three hours of my time, and there still appearing to be as many persons remaining to vote as there were when I began, I decided to call it a day. My small party made an honourable retreat, having fought a good fight against overwhelming odds. The "public spirit" forlornly protested at our departure as we climbed into the car. The villagers, however, appeared to be in as cheerful a holiday spirit as when we had arrived; and we left to a rousing cheer.

It was a relief to return home that evening and to drink many cups of tea as the sun sank below the line of high bush onto which my house faced. At 6.00 p.m. two prisoners carrying a bucket of water entered my compound through a gap in the hedge. Quietly stepping over the grass they began to water the line of zinnias in the bed along the front of the house. Having no watering can with a rose to spray the water, one man held a small hand broom while the other took a mess tin full of water from the bucket and poured it over the broom, which had the effect of spreading the water about. When they reached where I was sitting they wished me a good evening. Having finished their task they retired through the hedge and walked slowly back across the golf course to the Prison, which was to remain their home for many months to come. One of the prisoners I knew – a young man serving a two-year sentence for counterfeiting. There was something moving about this sight of two bad men being good.

In the absence of "mod. con." we were very dependent upon the services of prisoners. The water gang visited my house every day and filled up the forty-four gallon petrol drum which stood outside the kitchen. Some of this water found its way via kettle and filter down my throat, while some of it after being heated in a kerosene tin on the decrepit wood-burning stove in the kitchen went to fill my bath. Philip was usually summoned to "pass bath" at about 6.30 p.m. A few minutes later I would be sluicing various parts of my anatomy in turn, it being impossible to immerse more than a very limited portion of myself in my tin tub at any one time. The limited capacity of my bath had the virtue, however, of making a little water go a long way. By dint of wedging as much of myself as was humanly possible into it I was able to raise the level of the water from three or four inches to a foot or more.

My lavatory was a small separate building behind the house. Beneath the wooden seat there was a kerosene tin (empty four-gallon kerosene tins fulfilled many useful purposes; flattened they were used for roofing houses) and beside it a box of sand. Regularly every morning just before 8.00 a.m. the latrine gang came to my compound. The warder and prisoners engaged in friendly conversation with my boys. Sometimes there was a knock on the little wooden hatch while I was still installed, and I had to call out a warning to wait. On my leaving the knock was repeated, the wooden hatch was opened and the kerosene tin discreetly removed.

Sometimes after tea I played tennis with King. Following our exertions it was delightful to sit on the verandah of his house and down a succession of cold drinks. While we imbibed the sun sank below the level of the high trees on the far side of the golf course. Then we saw the sky grow bright with a rosy radiance like a theatre curtain when the footlights start to glow. For a few minutes we watched the final flare-up of the passing day intensify like a Roman Candle which throws up a brighter brilliance just before it dies. Then very swiftly the colours toned and the shadows deepened. Behind us a crescent moon was already riding high; and before us the evening star shone brightly, a harbinger of the host which would shortly follow in her train.

Back in my own house on looking into the garden through the open doors of my sitting room a little later I could see only an inky void. The rhythmic blending noise of myriads of insects suggested a peaceful Nature gently snoring as she sought repose.

One evening while I was on tour in a distant part of the Division I was handed a note from King just as I was finishing in Court. It said, "Return immediately. Trouble in Port Harcourt". I walked over to the Rest-House and reluctantly told Philip to dismantle my camp bed and pack up. While bicycles were being procured for Nwanuma and myself I had a quick meal.

We had to cycle twelve miles to reach the place where my car was parked. The ride was uneventful, and a quarter moon gave us a little light. The bridge over one river being in disrepair we were ferried across in a canoe. Every time we cycled through a village every dog within miles came to life and rent the silence with barks and howls. In places where the track was sandy our wheels could not get a proper purchase and we were liable suddenly to find ourselves slithering wildly to and fro. Having transferred to my car we drove the remaining twenty-two miles to Ahoada. Seen in the light of the head lamps the corrugations in the surface of the road stood out darkly like ripples on the sea. We reached Ahoada soon after 11.00 p.m. King gave me a few facts and told me that I must leave forthwith for Isoba, a place fifteen miles from Port Harcourt, where I was to establish a headquarters. This sounded simple enough but I had little idea as to the purpose my headquarters was intended to serve; furthermore I had neither boys nor loads with me.

I collected a few things from my house and King lent me a camp-bed. Shortly before midnight I drove my car onto the pontoon ferry. Twenty minutes later, having reached the east bank of the Sombrero, I prepared to drive off. As I did so a long expected mishap occurred – one of the ramps slipped. I braked immediately; and the car came to rest with its two rear wheels still on the pontoon, one front wheel on the second ramp and the other in the river. It took an age to transfer my little Morris Minor safely to *terra firma*. While the rescue work was going on I heard a noise like the sound of a motorcycle in the distance never getting any nearer. When I enquired what it was one of the ferrymen told me that it was a crocodile snoring. I rather wished I had not asked, and looked thoughtfully at the water in which I was standing up to my waist.

Because of the delay I did not reach Isoba, which was forty-five miles away, until 3.45 a.m. My arrival awoke the Inspector of Schools who was staying in the Rest-House. Considering the hour he was remarkably friendly, and while we chatted his steward, who had miraculously materialised from nowhere, set up my camp bed.

At 7.00 a.m. the Inspector of Schools left, so our acquaintance was a brief one. Having nothing with me I was unable to breakfast. Taking no thought for the body therefore I set about establishing my headquarters. This I achieved by shifting a desk from the bedroom onto the spacious front verandah. Uncertain what to do next I was delighted by the appearance of Ukpabi, the road overseer, on his motorcycle. He had some splendid rumours to pass on to me: the streets of Port Harcourt were littered with bodies; the European residential area had been raided in the early hours of the morning; the Superintendent of Police had been mauled and killed by an angry mob; sympathisers were marching from Aba to join the rioters .... I sent Ukpabi off to reconnoitre the lie of the land, while I considered what action to take if an unpleasant situation were to arise in the immediate neighbourhood. In the event my planning was to no purpose. Ukpabi returned at midday and reported that he had visited Port Harcourt and had found the shops open and everything back to normal. I locked the one shotgun and four cartridges, which had been surrendered to me, in the bathroom, and then drove a couple of miles to the nearby Leper Settlement to inform the four Europeans there of developments.

Later in the day I received a note from the Resident saying that he required my assistance in his office, and for the next day or two I was kept busy decoding and encoding telegrams.

On leaving Port Harcourt I went to Umuaturu to see the progress made by the villagers on the construction of the road to Ozuzu. Much work had been done on the embankments since my last visit, and I thought it would be possible before long to begin construction of the two bridges. It was a hot noonday, and having sat down in a shady patch on the new road to eat my sandwiches I was loth to get moving again. It was too hot to make much of a meal, and I contented myself with only a mouthful or two.

I did the cycle ride back to Umuaturu at a steady and somewhat stately speed. The sun shone down. The track, which on my previous visit had been wet and slushy, was dry and dusty. When going through a village all the children came

71

swarming after me, and broke into an excited chorus of "Onye ocha! Onye ocha!" (White man! White man!) which persisted long after I had passed.

The old mud Rest-House at Umuaturu having been demolished I spent the night in a small mud hut used by visiting Roman Catholic Fathers. It was a very small building situated inside the compound of the Mission school. A narrow verandah allowed Philip just sufficient space in which to erect my camp-bed and mosquito net, and the two box-sized rooms accommodated my food supplies, tin bath and wash basin. I had my evening meal in the open at a table placed on the sandy threshold of the hut beneath the spreading branches of an oil bean tree.

I passed an uncomfortable night because a stomach upset kept me constantly on the run. I had no time to reach the kennel-like structure which served as a lavatory even had I wished to make use of it; and by the morning the vicinity of the hut was strewn with evidence of the many calls I had had to answer.

One afternoon while on tour in another part of the Division after finishing my lunch at 3.15 p.m. I set off in my car from the Rest-House accompanied by Nwanuma and Walson. We drove to Umudioga, where we enquired as to the whereabouts of a village called Akpabu; and to my horror we were told that it was thirteen miles away. Bicycles were produced and a helpful individual, Isiah, was kind enough to shew us the way. In spite of the hot afternoon Isiah wore a woollen pullover over his shirt throughout the ride to Akpabu. We cycled in single file along a bush path, which for the greater part of the distance threaded its way through high bush, and which for many miles was so narrow that my legs were constantly brushed by the undergrowth on either side. Sometimes I had to duck down in order to avoid low dangling foliage, and sometimes I had to brake suddenly when the path veered unexpectedly in order to avoid a fallen tree trunk. In places we passed bunches of palm fruit left unattended beside the path but safeguarded by juju in the shape of an oil-bean pod or a piece of palm frond. We were cycling westwards, and at times I was dazzled by the contrast between the bright sunlight and the dark green shadows.

I welcomed the brightness of the sun after the drab, overcast days of the past months. The sunshine breached the tall, circumscribing walls of greenery, and here and there introduced a variety of colour into the awful uniformity of the bush. As a result of the interplay of light and shade the rank undergrowth and fleshy vegetation became alive and interesting. On pausing in a patch of high bush and seeing the path and the greenery on either side spattered with golden drops of sunlight I marvelled, when looking upwards at the denseness of the foliage overhead, that a single ray of sun was able to penetrate to the forest floor. When the sun shone the whole complexion of life brightened: the chromium plating on new Raleigh bicycles flashed more proudly; the kerosene tins containing palm-oil, carried on the backs of older machines, looked less jaded; the head-ties, blouses and fathomlength skirts of the women became gayer; the white sun helmets of village Elders looked more pristine; the polished mud walls of houses turned redder; and the matting roofs instead of appearing crestfallen and bedraggled looked crisp and brown like the crusts of well-baked loaves.

We arrived at Akpabu before 5.00 p.m. and found that the village was not prepared for our arrival. There was much calling and beating of drums before the villagers assembled in the market place. With an eye on the setting sun I explained as quickly as possible the reason for holding an election. The proceedings passed off swiftly and satisfactorily – very differently from the performance at Egbeda a few weeks earlier. We did the return cycle ride at a preposterously rapid rate, and succeeded in arriving back in Umudioga before dark.

In an open place near the C.M.S. school some 400 members of the Umudioga Women's Association dressed in their best were seated patiently awaiting our arrival. I sat down behind a small table, on which an alarm clock with an emphatic tick kept me constantly conscious of the passage of time. I began by telling the ladies how splendid they were and how the life and well-being of the village largely depended upon them, and then congratulated them on the interest they had shewn in improving their conditions by their own efforts. We then discussed the three projects, about which they were particularly keen: a well, a maternity home, and some market stalls. They were evidently pleased with what I said, because they surged around me as I was about to get into my car and several of their leaders almost literally unbosomed themselves of a vast quantity of eggs. I was amazed at the size of the huge pile which was heaped onto a calabash and carefully placed between Nwanuma's legs on the floor of the Morris Minor. In addition a couple of buckets of oranges were poured onto the back seat.

Murmuring with surprise and appreciation when I switched on the headlights, the crowd hastily withdrew from in front of the car. Moving slowly in order to preserve our fragile load we left the village to cries of, "Are you going?", "Go well", and "Thank you".

On returning to the Rest House we counted the eggs and found there was a total of 182! These I shared out between Nwanuma, Walson, Philip, Bonniface and others.

There followed many more election meetings, which often entailed journeys to villages I had not previously visited. In the course of one week Nwanuma, Walson and I motored 400 miles and cycled more than 100. Immediately upon our arrival at some seemingly deserted village it suddenly came to life. Children shrieked with joy at seeing a white man. Men called out excitedly that the A.D.O. had come. Drums were beaten and horns were blown; and in due course the village gathered round. After explaining the purpose and procedure of the election, there followed the tedious business of recording the votes. As the men of the village bent down beside me to mutter a name in my ear, I received wafts of many strange new smells and a close-up view of craw-craw, elephantiasis, yaws, tropical ulcers and other diseases and afflictions. At the end of polling the villagers closed around me to hear the results. Having announced them a polite clap was given for the winner, but as soon as I moved towards the car babel broke out and the kith and kin of the successful candidate loosed forth wild howls of jubilation.

After a week of this activity ending with an election held after dark on Friday in a remote village, which involved a return cycle ride of seven miles through thick forest on a moonless night with only one lamp between five of us, it was something of a contrast on Saturday afternoon to attend the birthday party of the six-year-old daughter of friends in Port Harcourt. A dozen little European boys and girls dressed as fairies and elves sat on the grass in the shade of a frangipani tree and played Hunt-the-Slipper and Blindman's Buff. Taking my ease in that friendly setting, it was hard to believe that the events of the past week – the cycle rides along narrow bush paths, the tumult of excited villagers, the whispered names, the bad breath – had been real.

The following Monday I was back in my office at Ahoada faced with a stack of files which had accumulated during my absence on tour the previous week. I was prevented from dealing with these, however, because of the inevitable crowd of persons wishing to see me. None of these was satisfied unless they obtained some sort of note written by me. What I wrote in it appeared to be more or less imma- terial. The important thing was to secure an "akwokwo" ("book", i.e. paper) written and signed by "Nwa Bekee" (literally "Son of Baker", i.e. white man). These scraps of paper scribbled on by an impatient A.D.O. seemed to evoke the same sort of blind faith in the recipients as that which they had in the juju powers of certain objects or in the effectiveness of a five shilling injection as the panacea for all physical ills.

King told me one day that instead of a "book" he had given one of his callers a Rennie's tablet. This visitor complained that somebody had invoked juju on him and refused to revoke it. King, putting his hand into his pocket, happened to find a Rennie's tablet there, and this gave him an idea. Placing the tablet on his desk, he said: "This is White Man's powerful juju, which I will give to you. Take it back with you to your village, and call the people into the market place. Tell them you have a juju more powerful than all other jujus. Put it in your mouth and chew it. Say that you spit on the juju invoked against you. Then spit, and all will see that your spittle comes out white." The complainant, clutching the powerful tablet, left well content.

On one occasion only I had recourse to a similar ruse. A man visited me to make a complaint about the theft of some of his properties. Despite his assurance that he was telling the truth I doubted his story. A lump of lead on my desk, which served as a paperweight, caught my eye. Picking it up I asked whether he was willing to swear to the truth of what he had said on my juju. He was not prepared to do so.

Sometimes the utter lack of comprehension of those who came to see me made it difficult for me to retain my patience, particularly when there was a mass of work waiting to be attended to. For example a young man wearing Scout uniform entered my office one day. He handed me a letter, in one sentence in which he stated a wish to join the Navy and in the next remarked that he understood there were many vacancies in the Army. Puzzled by this apparent inconsistency I asked him which it was he wished to join, the Army or the Navy. He seemed mystified by my question, but finally replied: "The Navy, Sir." I asked him whether he knew what the Navy was, and he said: "The Navy is the Army, Sir." "What does the Navy do?" I continued. A pause, then "Watchmen, clerical works, and office works." "What sort of work do you hope to do if you join the Navy?" "I hope to serve as a clerk," he replied promptly. My hopes that this was a young man fired with a spirit of adventure were dashed. He was just one more "Standard VI pass" looking for an office chair.

The amorous activities of the persons amongst whom I worked were a constant source of amazement to me. In my office one day I had a one-eyed man and an aged and singularly unattractive woman – someone else's wife – who had committed adultery together. They were followed by a young girl of eleven or twelve with a broken leg who was carried in by her brother. I was told that she sustained this injury when preventing some fellow from having "forcible connection" with her. Next came an unfortunate man with paralysed legs as thin as drum sticks. He shuffled in on his hands and squatted before my table. His request was that he be allowed to go to Degema hospital instead of Port Harcourt for a blood test, which had been ordered to establish the paternity of a child whose ownership was in dispute. I looked at the figure crouching on the floor and refused to believe that he could be the father .... An unusual case between a young man and an old woman came to my notice in the course of hearing some reviews. The latter was charged with "unlawfully assaulting the complainant by holding and drawing the complainant's penis and rendering some injuries to it". In his statement the young man said, "the accused bent down and held my penis and drew it very strongly." After this rough handling he went and shewed his injured person to the Court Clerk and the Sanitary Inspector, who on inspection found it to be badly swollen. The Native Court took a very serious view of the matter and expressed the opinion that "but for the help of God, the accused actually wanted to finish up the life of the complainant by holding his penis and drawing it, and this always caused sudden deaths to men ..." The old woman had been fined £3, but on going into the matter I found that she was not guilty as she had been attacked first by the young man. I expressed mild surprise that the complainant had not been better able to look after his private parts.

When siting a well in Abua a bevy of women approached my car, and a half-naked spokeswoman came out with a request that they be supplied with drugs to increase their fertility as they were unable to produce as large a number of offspring as they would like. Through Nwanuma I expressed sympathy and told them that unfortunately I could not help them. Afterwards Nwanuma told me that in another part of the Division the imbibing of "Quink" ink was considered to be very efficacious for this purpose.

In December the Harmattan wind blew for a few days, and the air was full of particles of sand carried southwards from the Sahara. During this all too brief period the nights were relatively cool. After sunset the dew fell heavily, and in the morning the countryside was veiled in mist. Looking into the garden when I got out of bed I saw the grass, the hedge, trees and bushes all covered with countless dew-spangled spiders' webs, the silver threadwork of which reminded me of the winter artistry of Jack Frost at home. It was not until about 10.00 a.m. that the last shreds of the morning mist dissipated in the sunlight.

The year ended with some excitement, which was occasioned by a decision to make a deviation in the P.W.D. Trunk road B which ran north from Ahoada via Omoku and Okwuzi to Oguta in the neighbouring Division of Owerri. The proposed deviation was only a few miles in length, and its purpose was to avoid a low-lying piece of ground which became flooded every wet season and rendered the road impassable for four to five months each year. Construction of this deviation, however, meant that the village of Obrikom would be by-passed, and the people of Obrikom, in particular the women, were very incensed that the main road would no longer pass through their village.

I visited Obrikom in order to try to allay the fears of the villagers that they would suffer as a result of the road deviation. A stormy reception awaited me, and no one present shewed any sign of being amenable to reason. The women protested angrily that the road had always passed through Obrikom since they were piccins; why therefore should it not continue to do so? I replied patiently but unavailingly; the people of Obrikom refused to see any advantage in the deviation. As it seemed profitless to remain any longer, I rose to go. I succeeded in elbowing my way out of the congested mud building in which we had held our meeting, but once outside my way was blocked by gesticulating women, and a dozen horny hands held onto my bicycle. By leaving that in their possession I eluded further obstruction and walked out of Obrikom with most of the villagers at my heels. Later on I was overtaken by Nwanuma who had somehow or other succeeded in retrieving both our bikes.

Further proof of the earnestness of the women's displeasure was given by the unexpected appearance the following day at Okwuzi of eighty of them, who had marched in a body from Obrikom nine miles away. They repeated their protestations in the Native Court, and later in the day straggled home in twos and threes, all shouting loudly as they passed the Rest-House where I was staying.

Women were given to demonstrating; and the next occasion when this happened was when King and his wife were staying in Omoku. Their lunch was interrupted by 200 angry woman who marched up to the Rest-House to protest against the closure of a market insalubriously situated in the middle of the town. King was able to halt them halfway up the drive, and having spoken with them they were dispersed by the District Interpreter and King's Orderly wielding bamboos. The latter somewhat incensed by a bite he sustained dealt very severely with a young man who rashly proclaimed (in Ibo) that the D.O. had "snuff up his arse".

I saw New Year 1950 in at Degema. While I was there Newington received a report of a regrettable incident which occurred at a village just inside Ahoada Division. Six policemen from Degema who were carrying out an investigation were chased out of the village by a mob armed with matchets. "Inside the Ahoada boundary, so it's your palaver, old man," I was told. On January 1st I crossed by canoe to the road end at a place known as Degema Hulk. From there I drove to Ahoada, taking two of the Degema constables involved in the incident with me. Except for a short, ineffectual chase after a man wearing a garment which looked very like a pair of prison "knickers", and who I thought was probably the prisoner who had escaped a few days previously, our journey was without incident.

After discussion with King I set off in my car for the refractory village of Rumudoga, followed by a Corporal and three constables in a lorry. My intention was to arrest such persons as the Degema policemen might be able to identify as having been amongst those who had assaulted them. On arrival at the village I called for the Chief, who was slow in coming forward. We received a message that for some obscure reason he was having to change from a pair of black leather shoes into some white canvas ones. While he was doing this, some 200 young men gathered round. One of the Degema policemen slipped up to me and said that he

77

had recognised two amongst the throng. I told him to point them out to the Corporal and to arrest them. We had the pair of them in custody for only a moment or two before the crowd forcibly liberated them, and then some individuals began to throw clods of earth and pieces of wood at our small party. We withdrew, and it was only with difficulty that I succeeded in preventing the police from leaping into the lorry and ignominiously heading for home. We came to a halt thirty or forty yards from the assembled villagers. In due course things quietened down, and I called the Chief forward and told him exactly what I thought of him and his village. I instructed him to report to the District Officer in Ahoada at 8.00 a.m. the following morning; then in an effort to twist the situation to our advantage I informed him that I had intended investigating the land dispute between his people and infiltrators from Degema Division, but that in view of the reception I had received I was not prepared to stay a moment longer.

The Chief failed to come to Ahoada, but that was immaterial because King and I, accompanied by a European Police Officer and twenty-five rank and file from Port Harcourt, visited Rumudoga instead. We found the Chief, this time already wearing his white canvas shoes, and told him to beat his drum to summon the village together. Only three men responded, one of whom was recognised as having been hostile the previous day, and some handcuffs were slipped over his unresisting wrists. More were rounded up later and were escorted back to Ahoada. After an active day King and I returned home, and left the police contingent to enjoy for the next week or so whatever Rumudoga might have to offer.

Chapter 6

"My heart is in two places"

A day or two later the angry ladies of Obrikom and the recalcitrant young men of Rumudoga seemed very far away; the Rest-Houses, the dusty road, the cassava plots, the sprawling bush, the District Office, the Prison and my own quaint pavilion-like house all seemed remote. While in Ahoada another working day had begun and office messengers were busy sealing and taking letters to the post office to catch the morning's outgoing mail, and King was struggling to reduce the files in his "in" tray, and prisoners in their various gangs were drawing water, emptying latrine buckets, gathering firewood and cutting grass, the Assistant District Officer lay comfortably abed in Port Harcourt Nursing Home. A small hernia sustained some time since my arrival in Ahoada accounted for my presence there.

The trolley came for me at noon, and a moment or two later I transferred myself to the operating table in the theatre. "Hold out your arm," said the surgeon, "I am going to give you something which will make you sleep." In fact it did no such thing, but instead made me feel pleasantly tight. Two sisters propped me up while I was given a further injection in the spine. Numbness soon began to creep up my legs, and after a moment or two I could no longer waggle my toes. The surgeon, who, although he appeared to have nothing on but a white overall, was perspiring freely, hitched up my quaint hospital garment and placed a piece of lint across my eyes. Using my chest as a repository for his various implements he proceeded with his small repair job. The sisters chatted with me while the needful was being done, and then began talking to each other about providing spinach for the patients' lunch. I felt that that was neither the time nor the place for a discussion on such a very uninteresting vegetable, and appealed to the surgeon who replied that for his part he believed in informality in the operating theatre.

79

"Elastoplast or bandage?" enquired the surgeon in the same tone of voice as one would use when offering a choice between white or black coffee. "Elastoplast," I replied for no particular reason. As I was being trundled out of the theatre I heard the surgeon telling one of the nurses to clean up the blood. Back in my bed I lost my earlier blithe spirits as the stimulating effect of the injection in my left arm wore off.

While I was in the Nursing Home Bonniface stayed with a "brother" who had a shop in Port Harcourt. He came to see me every morning at 8.30, sometimes wearing a pale blue vest and sometimes his khaki uniform jacket; and while I was confined to bed his assistance in holding a mirror while I shaved was most useful. I asked him whether he was enjoying his holiday in Port Harcourt. He big eyes roved around, and he worked his banana lips but made no reply. I asked him again, and after a short pause he said: "My heart is in two places. I like it here in Port Harcourt, but then I remember Master lying in hospital ...."

Soon the time came to say goodbye to the spring mattress, the iced water in thermos jugs, the neatly laid meal trays, the running hot and cold water, the bedside lamps and the electric fans, and to return to my own frugally appointed home.

After leaving the Nursing Home I stayed for a few days in the Rest-House at Isoba overlooking the New Calabar river. At 8.00 a.m. one Sunday Philip filled my wash basin with hot water. I stirred at the sound, and turning my back on the light from the uncurtained windows I tried without success to recapture sleep. For a few minutes I lay inert and contemplated the outside world through the protective walls of my mosquito net, feeling rather like a joint of cold meat beneath its fly-proof cover. Deciding to miss no more of the morning's freshness, I rose and, stepping over the low windowsill onto the grass outside, looked down on the limpid river below me and across at the dense vegetation on the far bank still wreathed in morning mist. As the sun rose higher in the sky this slowly vanished away, and the phalanxes of screw-pines on the other side of the river came into clearer view. The dew beading the grass around the Rest-House disappeared and the compound was dappled with the shadows thrown by the many flame-of-the-forest trees flanking the drive. A single harmattan lily was in flower at the base of a venerable old tree which stood on the edge of the river bank. Lizards basked on its sun-baked buttress roots, from time to time awaking from their drowsy state to indulge in some vigorous copulation. The compound was the resort for many birds. Swifts at their endless game of tag darted between the trees, swooping low over the cut grass. From time to time I saw the blue flash of a kingfisher; and black and white fish eagles perched on branches of trees overlooking the river. Canoes travelling with the current sped gracefully in mid-stream, while those making headway against it kept as close as possible to the bank. Sometimes I heard the sound of singing coming from the river, sometimes only the plashing of paddles.

I was once again busy hearing reviews and appeals at some of the fifteen Native Courts we had dotted around the Division. I always enjoyed this aspect of my duties as an A.D.O. because of the insight it afforded me into the thinking and behaviour of those amongst whom I lived and worked.

In one criminal case the charge recorded in the Native Court judgment book was as follows: "unlawfully invoking and placing juju to kill complainant and his people in the complainant's house". In the course of her statement the accused said: "Ogbowu then produced the juju and I swore that if I had been used by a man called Gad the juju should kill me and that if not the juju should not kill me." Invocation of juju, and swearing on juju featured constantly in both criminal and civil actions. In the Court record of another case I read, "As the accused and I are Christians, I brought forward my brother and I held him at the hand and he swore the juju that if I called the woman again in order to use her the juju should kill me". Being a Christian he himself could not swear, but it was in order for his brother to do so on his behalf. In an action for the return of a goat the plaintiff stated, "I met the defendant to give me juju as was previously ordered by the Court, and he refused on the grounds that he would give me a certain poison known as 'Agaba' to take internally after swearing on it." This was the first time I had come across a reference to what in fact amounted to trial by ordeal. The Native Court I was glad to see had not countenanced this suggestion, and they recorded in their findings that, "Agaba is a very strong poison when taken internally on oath, and therefore the Court does not allow this nature of oath in order to safeguard the dear lives of litigants".

In another case the complainant stated, "I was looking for my goat, when I felt a smell of a goat being put on fire", whereupon he cleverly traced the smell and was able to identify the roasted goat as his own missing one! In the recorded proceedings of a civil action I read that, "Oke was suffering from elephantiasis of the scrotum and died. There was no body of the relatives of the deceased who came for the interment. I and my husband hired people who cut off the scrotum and buried the corpse." An insight into marital relations was afforded by the statement of a complainant which went as follows: "As my custom is I usually sleep with my wife before I leave to sleep ordinarily. I then placed my hand over the accused's body and drew her near me in order to intromise my penis into her uterus, then all of a sudden she bit me at the cheek, and I drew backwards and while querying her why she should bite me, the accused got up and landed this piece of stick at my forehead ..." at which point the aggrieved husband tendered as exhibit a hefty log of wood.

On investigation I discovered that the reason for the woman's unaccommodating attitude was her husband's failure to pay her the customary thirteen shilling initial sleeping fee.

As I have already mentioned we were continually receiving at the District Office letters on a wide range of topics, many of which were very quaintly expressed. I received one addressed to me personally and marked confidential from one of my warders. In this the writer drew my attention to the feats of valour he had performed in capturing a prisoner who had recently escaped. He concluded his self-laudatory paeon with the words, "I have not much to talk; Master knows the best for his poor servant. Your's Loving Son, J.N. Odu." I also received a simple little note addressed to the Right Honourable A.D.O. It was short and to the point:

> "Sir,
>   I have the honour most respectfully to submit
> you this my poor application if there shall be any
> job of carrying excrement or latrine at your end –
> or anywhere at all I am ready to persevere.
>   Hoping this my poor wishes will not fail me.
>   May the Lord be with till end.
>   I am your's awaiting the reply please.
>   I have the honour to be, Sir,
>   Your most obedient servant,
>
>   Benson Adoji"

Another began "My very dear Mr. Arrowsmith, I have the pleasure to write you this letter just to break the dull monotony of silence which lies between us as a big gulf." It ended very effusively with the words: "Good morning, Good afternoon, Good evening – I am, Sir, Your friend (teacher and photographer) Joseph O. Eli".

Prisoners who were inconsiderate enough to escape were liable on recapture to be awarded a flogging. This was not carried out until a medical officer had examined the person concerned and certified his fitness to receive the punishment. One morning I had to supervise the flogging of two prisoners both of whom had been sentenced to twelve strokes. In turn they lay down on their stomachs on some wooden bed boards which had been placed on the ground in the prison yard. Their wrists and ankles were firmly held by fellow prisoners who appeared to be eager to assist. A damp cloth was laid across the buttocks of the otherwise naked recipient; and the beating was administered vigorously and efficiently by the Chief Warder.

One of the prisoners bore his painful punishment in manful silence, but the other made lamentation loud and long.

One evening I received an urgent note from Mr. Ukpabi, the Road Overseer, asking me to go "one time" (i.e. at once) to Isoba because the Treasurer there would not pay the road labourers their month's wages and he feared there would be trouble. The following morning as soon as I got up I was handed another missive. This was a lengthy one from the Treasurer who also begged me to go with all haste to Isoba because the road labourers were about to "matchet" him. It seemed advisable to pay the place a visit, so I drove there after breakfasting. I found about 100 labourers encamped around the Treasury Office; and the Treasurer only left the relative safety of his nearby quarter when he was confident that I had arrived. Without much difficulty the issue was resolved. The labourers received both their pay and also a blast from me for not carrying out their duties sufficiently conscientiously.

Certain occupational hazards appeared to be attached to the Treasurer Isoba's job. The previous holder of this post, an alert young man in his early twenties, had the misfortune to be the victim of some juju spell as a result of which he became as paralysed as a log of wood and was carried off to his home village to die.

As I entered Isoba on my way to settle the road labourers' palaver I noticed beside the road a dog and a bitch joined end to end, and was somewhat surprised that no one had taken the trouble to release them from their awkward predicament. I was even more surprised, when returning to Isoba the following evening, to see the same dog and bitch still not disengaged. Hearing the car one tried to go in one direction and the other in the other, and as a result they stayed more or less where they were in the middle of the road. As I braked I gently bumped into them, thereby doing them a greater service than anyone in the village had done, because the mild shock of impact had the happy effect of releasing them from their protracted union.

Erema had the reputation of being a progressive village. This was because it boasted a Community School, which was a purely locally supported enterprise. The villagers, not so very many in number, raised £700 a year for teachers' salaries and upkeep. When I visited Erema I saw a huddle of very dirty and scantily clad old men squatting in the shade of a tree just in front of the entrance to the school. They were gossiping and drinking in turn from a fly-ridden calabash containing some foul-smelling tombu (palm wine). Aligned beside the calabash there were half a dozen or so little sticks, which looked somewhat like bones. They varied in size, but none was more than a foot long; and each of them had at one end a thick lump of unidentifiable matter resembling a meatball. I learnt that the disreputable old men were the Elders of the village and that these unsavoury looking objects were their "ofors", i.e. their magical symbols of office.

Each Clan Council kept a record of its meetings in a Minutes' Book, which used to be examined by the D.O. or A.D.O. when on tour. An unusual entry caught my eye when looking through the Minutes' Book of the Ogba Clan Council. In recommending that a well keeper be appointed to look after the wells in Omoku town the Council stated that amongst other things it would be the duty of this official "to check women from standing astride over the wells and drawing water, thus contaminating the water with menstruation". The entry concluded somewhat abruptly with the statement: "This is a nuisance".

Menstruation featured fairly prominently in native law and custom. Women were considered to be unclean while menstruating, and were barred from taking part in certain juju rituals. In one of the cases I reviewed I came across an unusual expression to describe this condition. An ex-husband posed the following cryptic question to the plaintiff, his former wife: "Were you under flowers when you ran away from me, or had the flowers gone from you before you ran away from me?". The Court Clerk explained to me that a woman was considered to be as it were "flowering" when undergoing menstruation.

On visiting one of our Maternity Homes I was told that a child had been born a couple of hours before my arrival. I looked around the place, and in the delivery room I saw placenta lying uncovered in a large kidney basin. On enquiring why it was there, the midwife told me that the father would shortly be coming to collect it and that he would bury it either inside or on the threshold of his compound and would plant a palm tree, a pear tree or possibly an iroko tree over it.

It rained heavily on Empire Day 1950 in Ahoada, and the customary march-past of schoolchildren had to be cancelled. King gave instructions that they should assemble instead in the hall of the Government School, where he would read the Governor's Message to them. The school band played the National Anthem when King and I arrived. The message, which did not take long to deliver, exhorted the schoolchildren to prepare themselves to be good citizens of their country which was approaching man's estate, etc., etc. It was clearly above the heads of those to whom it was addressed. The eyes, normally so bright, in the rows of shiny black heads in front of us were fixed blankly on King, while the Interpreter rendered as best he could in the Ekpeye tongue such words and phrases as "integrity", "citizenship", "man's estate", "equal partnership" and "British Commonwealth of Nations". When we rose and turned to leave the hall I saw chalked in the corner of the blackboard in front of which we had been sitting the single word "urine". Why it was there I could not imagine.

King and I were invited to attend a Masquerade dance in the village of Upatabo. When we arrived at about 4.00 p.m. we found the village *en fête* and the dancing already in progress. We were ushered within the ring of spectators to seats behind a table, covered with a flowery cloth, placed near the entrance to a wooden building from which the dancers emerged having donned their finery within. The open space in the centre of the village was thronged with onlookers, who left the dancers only meagre space in which to perform their antics. Opposite us at the other side of the dancing area there sat a row of old Chiefs, who were clothed in the traditional nightshirt style of garment stretching almost to their ankles. Several of them wore spotless white sun helmets, and the majority held smart ebony walking sticks with ivory handles. They were supplied with liquid refreshment from an earthenware pot carried by a young boy. From this their drinking horns were constantly refilled. I noticed that one of the old worthies could hardly keep his eyes open, and swayed on his chair first to one side and then to the other.

The scene was one of indescribable movement, babel and colour. Spectators, "controllers" and dancers alike remained in a perpetual state of flux. Never before had I seen a crowd of people so imbued with life. The whole place seethed with movement, as does an ants' nest when disturbed. The spectators jostled each other, surged forward, were driven back or themselves broke into dance; the "controllers" pushed the crowd back and lashed out with sticks to keep a space cleared for the dancers; oblivious to all else the dancers rhythmically oscillated the cheeks of their bottoms, and a man in a masquerade pounded up and down in their midst. All the time there was a ceaseless stamping of feet mingled with the hoarse cries of men, the excited shrieks of women, shrill blasts on whistles, the rattle of the seed-pod anklets of the masquerade dancers, the hollow notes of a horn, the clash of pangas, the slapping of leather fans, the clapping of hands, and singing and laughter. And dominating everything – weaving as it were a single fabric out of this riot of sound – there was the ceaseless irresistible rhythm of the drums.

The medley of costume and colour was overwhelming in its variety. The women wore vivid headsquares and boldly patterned cloth around their waists. The dress of the men ranged from palm-beach suiting and co-respondent shoes to nothing but a loin cloth. Young men wearing collars and ties rubbed shoulders with others wearing strings of leopards' teeth around their bare necks. Sun helmets and trilbies mingled with elaborately embroidered native caps sporting golden tassels. Bare feet, feet in sandals and feet in patent leather all helped to raise the dust. Men in trousers, men in shorts, men with a "lapper" of Manchester cloth around their loins capered together in wild abandon. Many of the men, irrespective of the kind of garb they had on, had made themselves gay by knotting brightly coloured scarves around their waists – as they were wont to do when wrestling. A large number had one or more eagle feathers stuck at varying angles in their crinkly coiffures. Some had bands of fur around their arms above the elbows. The bright hues of the garments and the constant movement of the crowd made a veritable kaleidoscope of colour.

Those who were dancing carried an amazing assortment of things in their hands: electric torches, fans, umbrellas, kerosene tins, pangas, Dane-guns, handkerchiefs and walking sticks.

A trio of half-naked women each clutching a flashy-looking torch danced their way up to us and remained for some minutes wriggling their bodies in the conventional manner. They were followed by a quaint female couple who entertained us on the other side of our table. They both looked a great age; their heads had been half-tonsured, and their dugs flapped against their hillock-like navels. They were not prepossessing specimens of their sex, but for sheer lewdness they took a lot of beating. They wriggled and writhed in a most suggestive way. One of them wore a girdle of large conch-like shells around her middle which jangled together as her backside rose and fell. As this girdle jerked up and down the other women lightly stroked the wrinkled body it encircled with a feathery instrument like a fly whisk.

My attention was caught by one of the male dancers who wore only a loin cloth and a thing which looked half-cap, half-wig. A frill of strings hanging close together around it gave the wearer the appearance of having an Eton crop; and this becoming effect was in no way marred by the small skull which was attached to the front of this headgear. Entering into the spirit of the occasion King seized this thing, donned it and himself joined in the dancing much to the approval of those present. Having finished his exhibition dance, King planted the object on my head. It slipped forward, and as I jiggled to and fro the skull bumped against my spectacles in what I feel certain must have been a most unbecoming manner.

Over one end of the open space an awning of sorts had been erected on a few bamboo poles stuck into the ground. Beneath this the band sat, and I am sure they appreciated such scant shade as the awning offered because it was an exceedingly hot and sunny afternoon. The music was provided by members of the band pounding hollowed logs of wood, which emitted notes capable of carrying a long distance.

The star of the show was a venerable old man who looked like an Old Testament prophet, and who sat with the Chiefs and not with the Band. He wore a toga-like garment and his head was decorated with three long eagle feathers. Before him there was a carved wooden drum about three feet high. A skin was drawn tightly across its top, and on this the old man periodically beat with one or other of the drum sticks which he held in either hand. The drum was an impressive instrument, in appearance as solid as a Norman font. On its front was carved the head of a man; and the whole of it was dotted with white spots. I was told that it was a very important drum, which could only be beaten by a man renowned in valour who had proved his worth by killing either leopards or men. As the venerable figure crouched over the symbol of his authority, or sidled around it, from time to time he landed a blow on it in an apparently offhand manner, much as a lesser mortal is wont to lash out at a persistently irritating fly. Accompanying his sporadic poundings and standing close beside the drum there was a younger and less striking individual who blew sustained and mournful notes on a long horn.

As for the masquerade dancers they presented a weird and grotesque appearance. There was a certain similarity in their costume and masquerade paraphernalia. They were all enveloped from head to ankles in thick, brightly coloured cloths, leaving only their feet bare. The cloths over their heads had the smallest of slits for seeing through. In their hands, which were also enveloped in heavy wrappings, they carried pangas which they periodically clashed together. They wore anklets of seed pods which rattled noisily as they danced. Projecting at varying angles from their gaudy raiment were long feathers. However, it was the elaborate wooden contraption which each bore upon his head that was the most striking feature of the dancers' appearance. These were as much as five or six feet long, and were painted in the brightest shades of blue, yellow and red. Some of these carved devices were so imaginative that I was unable to recognise what they were intended to represent. One such was, I learned, a hippopotamus but it bore no resemblance to the pachyderm in question, which was said to inhabit the rivers in that part of the country. I was, however, able to identify correctly an aeroplane, a dog and a porcupine.

The masquerade dancers emerged one after the other from the "Changing Room", one returning before the next appeared. As fast as his heavy and unwieldy impedimenta would allow him he made a preliminary canter up and down the open space. Thereafter, no doubt to give himself an opportunity to regain his breath, the dancer wandered somewhat aimlessly around. A few minutes later, clashing his pangas together, he broke into the wild abandon of a sort of Highland fling to the cheers of those watching and to the imminent danger of all within range of his massive careening headgear. The first time a dancer after a headlong dash came to an abrupt halt on the other side of our table and brandished a panga over the puce tablecloth in my direction, I was at a loss to know what was expected of me. Mr. Nwanuma, who was sitting beside me, explained that to return his salute I had to cross the blade of his matchet with something of my own or failing anything then with my arm. This I did, and the monster retreated apparently satisfied.

After watching the proceedings for an hour or so King and I allowed ourselves to be persuaded by one of the Elders of the village to adjourn to his house for liquid refreshment. Our host, who must have been very hot inside his voluminous robe of wine-coloured velvet which he was wearing over a pair of grey flannel trousers, was clearly in need of a drink. Gin, whisky, brandy, beer and a bottle of Phospherine Tonic wine were produced. We sat for some time, our glasses being constantly refilled, listening to the sounds of the dance continuing in the distance. Later, as the shadows were lengthening, tables were placed together in the compound outside our host's house, and many of the Government staff from Ahoada took their seats around them. A considerable collection of bottles was ranged in the middle to the evident appreciation of those about to be regaled. Notwithstanding the general babel someone offered a blessing, and then the distribution of liquor took place. This service was undertaken by the Dispenser, who was no doubt considered to be the one best qualified to apportion the precious fluids. I watched him with great care measuring tots of gin and whisky, pouring them into the same tumbler and topping up with beer.

We left the festivities some three hours after our arrival, by which time a full moon was already high in the evening sky.

Chapter 7

Cameroon Mountain

In March 1950 I was granted some local leave, which I decided to spend with a colleague who had been transferred from Rivers Province to Buea in the British Cameroons. I left Port Harcourt in a De Havilland "Dove", and found myself for the first time looking down on the flat, bush-covered landscape of Ahoada and Ogoni Divisions from the air. In places I could see the dark green patches of bush long left undisturbed. Lighter patches indicated bush of lesser standing; and areas shewing signs of brown earth in place of the omnipresent green revealed where cultivation was taking place. We landed at Calabar and remained there for twenty minutes while the plane was refuelled. Soon after taking off again we were flying over the sea. Cloud obscured our view, but I was pleased to be able to catch a glimpse of the 9,000 ft. peak on the Spanish island of Fernando Poo rising above a collar of cottonwool. As we neared our destination we skirted the foothills of Mt. Cameroon, following the coastline beneath us. When over Victoria the plane turned inland, and we passed only a few hundred feet above a thickly forested mountain ridge. A few minutes later I saw banana plantations beneath me; and a little less than two hours after leaving Port Harcourt we landed at Tiko.

The airfield at Tiko was only identifiable as such by the presence of a single dejected airsock. The grass strip was surrounded on all sides by banana palms. A narrow gauge plantation railway line ran behind the solitary airport hut; and while I was waiting for a car to collect me, a Lilliputian engine went by drawing half a dozen empty trucks.

The drive of twenty miles or so to Buea took nearly an hour. The road climbed steadily all the way, and in places the gradients were steep and the corners sharp. Before long we were able to look down on the banana plantations which stretched away towards the creeks of the Cameroon river. As we drove along we passed many

89

lorries laden with bananas going to Tiko where a "banana-boat" was being loaded.

For the most part the road, when not skirting a steep hillside, was flanked by high walls of elephant grass. Villages were few and far between. The houses, which were of the same shape as those in the Rivers Province, had walls of planks instead of mud. The local inhabitants looked much the same as those from where I had come. It was a new sight, however, for me to see women supporting great baskets on their backs by means of bands around their foreheads. There were the inevitable sheep, goats, fowls and ducks straying on the road, and in addition many errant porkers which retreated grunting indignantly as we all but ran them down.

Buea, formerly the German dry-season capital of the Cameroons, was situated 3,000 ft up the lower slopes of Cameroon Mountain. A small Schloss, once the residence of the German Governor, dominated a number of white-painted bungalows scattered on the hillside below it. The Schloss with its minstrels' gallery and stags' heads on the wall had the air of a baronial hall; and added glamour was lent to the place by a ghostly visitant, who reputedly played the piano in the drawing-room at irregular and mysterious hours.

Staying in Buea I found it hard to believe that I was on the west coast of Africa and only four degrees north of the equator. The huge mass of Cameroon Mountain, girdled with a belt of forest to a height of 6,500 ft., towered behind the small Government station. In front there was a glorious view extending for many miles southwards in the direction of Duala and the French Cameroons. Buea was like one large garden with flower beds everywhere, encircled with some of the many smooth grey stones which littered the hillside. The soil was a rich black colour, and English flowers and vegetables grew in profusion. Roses abounded on all sides; and it was a joy to see again lupins and violets, dahlias and carnations. Scattered around the station stood many fine trees: mahogany and tall, slender silk-cotton trees, eucalyptus, bushy-topped mangoes, casuerinas and graceful jacerandas. Sheltering behind sturdy bamboo hedges were the bungalows of Buea's fortunate residents, all raised a few feet above the ground on concrete supports. Each had a chimney because the chilly evenings on the mountain made a fireplace necessary.

Buea had three European-managed farms, which supplied fresh milk and butter. I visited Upper Farm, and saw a couple of ponies grazing in a field, calves in pens, pigs in styes, cows being milked and butter being churned; and I smelled again the familiar smell of dung and straw. Behind the farm and below the forest belt cattle munched at the lush grass, the bells round their necks tinkling as they moved from tuft to tuft. Up there I picked wild raspberries and steeped myself in the tranquillity of the mountain scene. Birds chirruped, and a few insects droned. At long intervals a car or lorry passed along the single road through the station below me. In the stillness I could hear clearly the distant cry of a child, the hammering of workmen, and a bell in the American Baptist Mission at Great Soppo striking the half-hour.

In a storm Buea was anything but serene. The wind lashed round the mountain from the north-east. Huge banks of cloud raced by just overhead. The roar of thunder reverberated and lightning stabbed blindingly. The earth itself seemed to shake; and then one was reminded of the fact that Mt. Cameroon was volcanic and liable to eruption. Down on the plains the wind flattened 40-50,000 banana trees and acres of elephant grass were laid low.

At 9.00 a.m. one day I set out to climb the mountain, accompanied by a guide called Simon and four porters. Simon had an extra finger on his left hand, which dangled from his little finger like a chippolata sausage. The porters distributed amongst themselves my blankets, spare clothing, food, water, cooking utensils, stove and hurricane lamp. Ngongi, who carried the box containing my food supplies and bottles of water, bore his load the whole way balanced on his head! The others lashed their loads into wicker frames, which they carried on their backs.

It was fine and warm when we started, and I wore only shorts and a pair of old canvas shoes. Soon after passing through Upper Farm we entered the forest. There the going was cooler, because great trees interlaced with networks of thick foliage hid us from the sun. Here and there we passed a few small clearings where cocoyams were growing. The floor of the forest was covered with a deep mulch of rotting vegetation and studded with rocks and boulders. At times the narrow trail skirted the edge of clefts in the hillside; at others it led us across gaily running streams. Rampant everywhere both on the ground and as parasites on other vegetation were ferns, ranging in size from small ones similar to those one might find in an English garden to tree ferns standing twenty to thirty feet high. Except for an occasional raucous bird call it was silent in the forest, and we saw no wild life.

At 6,000 ft. in a small clearing we came on Hut 1, the first of three erected by the Germans before the Great War for the benefit of climbers. In fact it was a well-built bungalow rather than a hut, and roses were in full bloom on the small terrace in front of it. I sat on the verandah while I drank some coffee, and I saw with disgust that the walls had been disfigured with the names of earlier climbers.

We emerged abruptly from the forest at 6,800 ft., and then came a gruelling climb up a grassy boulder-strewn slope, which as time went on seemed to approach ever nearer to the perpendicular. I marvelled at the dexterous manner in which Ngongi made the ascent with the wooden box still balanced on his head. The sun continued to shine brightly, but clouds beneath us hid Buea from view. At about 9,000 ft. we topped this steep slope. Before us there was a gently rising shelf corrugated into hillocks covered with rocks and tufts of grass, which extended to a second steep mountain face. Not long later Simon and I arrived at Hut 2, our journey having taken three and a half hours.

Hut 2 was a very different structure from Hut 1. More than anything else it resembled a shoddy public latrine. It was a windowless shed, built of corrugated iron, and divided into three partitions. I had one room; Simon and the porters had another; and the third, which was very small, seemed to serve no useful purpose. There was a sloping shelf in my partition made of boards and covered with a thin layer of straw which served as a bed. A decrepit camp-table was the only article of furniture.

The hut was situated in a fold between two hillocks. The land around it was bare except for one or two stunted lichen-covered trees and a hardy plant looking rather like heather which had taken root here and there. During the afternoon I remained outside, except during a short squall of rain. I moved from cranny to cranny among the rocks in my endeavour to find a place which was in the sun and out of the wind, which was blowing keenly. I had no alternative but to idle away the time because the porter bearing the load containing my book and writing and sketching materials did not arrive until three hours after ourselves. At 5.00 p.m. I began preparing my evening meal, which consisted of a tin of vegetable soup, fried sausages and bread and butter, washed down with copious draughts of Nescafé. After eating I went outside to watch the sunset hues fade from the sky. The top of the wall of mountain behind me glowed pink. Buea and the plains were hidden beneath a silver-fox cape of cloud. Ahead of me night was already spreading wide her darkling wings; and the stunted trees, silhouetted against the paling western sky, looked like fantastic wizened gnomes staggering up the mountainside.

I passed a very uncomfortable night, but realised that it must have been worse for the porters. Within their partition they lay on the ground huddled around a fire, which gave off plenty of pungent smoke but little heat, each wrapped in a single tattered blanket. For my part I had three good blankets and a couple of sweaters, but nevertheless I was frozen.

Shortly before 6.00 a.m. the following day I was roused by a bang on the corrugated-iron wall. I dressed promptly; and at 6.15 a.m. set out with Simon and Ngongi for the top.

We made this early start in the hope of reaching the summit before the clouds had had time to pile up and obscure the view. At the time we set forth the sun was just rising above a bank of cloud. Looking down I could dimly see Buea and the plains, still shrouded in the grey-blue of early morning twilight. Ahead of us the first rays of the sun caught the tip of the mountain; and as the sun rose higher so more and more of the mountainside was bathed in its warming glow.

Having scaled the second steep slope it was possible to see ahead of us the final lap of the climb leading to the actual summit. On our way we saw a couple of deer which went bounding away when Simon and Ngongi halloo-ed. The landscape had become even bleaker. There were no longer any trees, shrubs or plants, but only boulders, stones and spongy mounds of moss. Further on we were stumbling in loose ash, our feet slipping with each step we took.

I was thankful to reach Hut 3 which was situated in a hollow within 100 ft. or so of the summit. I shared my tin of spam and loaf of bread with Simon and Ngongi, who crouched over a small fire which they attempted to coax into life in the middle of the hut. I was amazed at the length of time they left their hands and feet actually in the flames. A thermometer inside the hut registered 43 °F. – at times it fell below freezing I had been told, so we were comparatively fortunate. Nevertheless outside a biting wind was blowing, and I felt cold right through to my bones. Having eaten and written my name in the Climbers' Record Book, accompanied by Simon and Ngongi, I scrambled up to "Bottle" peak, so called I suppose because of the eleven bottles, full of scraps of paper bearing the names of earlier climbers, which were stuck into a small cairn of stones.

We did not spend long on top of Cameroon Mountain. We were hidden in swirling cloud and could see nothing at all. I was not able even to see into the crater, the rim of which we skirted.

We were soon back at Hut 2, and after a rest – as I saw no reason to spend a second uncomfortable night on the mountain – we returned to Buea, reaching home by 4.30 p.m.

A few days later I took off from Tiko's little airstrip. We passed over Victoria's botanical gardens, skirted round the south-western buttress of Cameroon Mountain and then set a course for Calabar and Eastern Nigeria.

Chapter 8

"You, young man"

In the summer of 1950 I went on my first home leave. On my return to the Rivers Province at the end of the year Chubb gave me the job of District Officer, Port Harcourt. There followed the busiest eighteen months of my life. I had very little leisure and no available time for keeping a record of my doings.

Life in Port Harcourt was very different from life in Ogoni, Degema and Ahoada. I had no touring to do, no Native Court cases to deal with, no village community development projects to encourage, and no mud and thatch Rest-Houses in which to stay. I lived in a large house in a large compound, and Philip and Bonniface enjoyed the luxury of well-appointed boys' quarters and a static life. I went each day to the District Office, my time being spent either at my desk, or at meetings or in going around the town. Although my urban work bore little re-semblance to the work I had previously done as an A.D.O. in the bush I neverthe-less enjoyed it and found it intensely interesting.

My *ex officio* appointments were many and varied, ranging from President of the Town Council (for a time) to Chairman of the Catering Rest-House Management Committee. I was Registrar of Marriages, Secretary of the Liquor Licensing Board, Chairman of the Tax Appeal Committee, Secretary of the Port Operations Commit-tee, Chairman of the Port Harcourt Town Planning Authority, Chairman of the Port Harcourt Branch of the Nigerian Ex-Servicemen's Welfare Association, Assistant Food Commissioner, and Chairman of the Local Broadcasting Committee.

Problems of one sort or another arose in constant succession: the overdue com-pilation of estimates for the coming financial year; the refusal of a Railway official to vacate a Rest-House quarter; a Nigerian Ex-Servicemen's Welfare Association drive to raise funds which resulted in a loss; an office messenger sentenced to eighteen months for embezzlement; a Town Council resolution to demolish some

Government quarters; and the refusal of squatters on Crown land to apply for occupation licences.

One hot evening I found myself seated in a studio in our small local broadcasting station. Two members of the Advisory Committee and the Broadcasting Officer were with me. Also in the room were a score of women packed close around a microphone poised on its slender stalk. "One, two, three, four!" said the Broadcasting Officer, at which the ladies broke raggedly into song accompanied by the clapping of their hands. We should have been seated in another room listening to the artistes, but a broken-down loudspeaker necessitated this closer proximity. The babel continued for some minutes until the Broadcasting Officer cut it short. I turned to the two committee members, seeking an indication from them as to the merit of the performance. They were in no doubt.

"Splendid timing," one said.

"Beautiful tone," said the other.

"Approved," I noted on my agenda.

The audition continued and a bevy of young men replaced the women around the microphone.

"One, two, three, four!" said the Broadcasting Officer. A cacophony of sound broke out as the young men began lustily beating pieces of wood together. This lasted a few minutes.

"Stop, stop!" bellowed the Broadcasting Officer. "Can you give us something different?"

The young men muttered among themselves; and when they launched into the second item in their repertoire I could perceive little difference in the din, except perhaps that it seemed even more deafening than before. When silence was restored I turned once again to my two companions to take my cue from them.

"Not good enough," they both said.

"Require more practice," I noted down.

In the case of a young man who crooned American songs unaccompanied and a trio, who achieved a poor imitation of the "Inkspots", my two African colleagues looked to me for guidance. At the end of the audition I announced the decisions of the Committee to the motley collection of men and women waiting outside.

Prior to the hearing of appeals by the Tax Appeals Committee announcements were made on the Port Harcourt Radio-diffusion Service and by the Town Crier. The appeals were dealt with in my office. I sat at one end of a table along one side of which were seated the members of the Committee. At the other end sat the Senior Tax Clerk, who acted as major domo of the proceedings. He had an impressive collection of files spread in front of him, and he ushered the appellants in turn into our presence. The Committee members were each provided with a list giving details of those who had appealed; and they shared a very battered Ready Reckoner which was kept open at the fourpence-halfpenny page, because tax on incomes up to £500 was at the rate of only fourpence-halfpenny in the pound.

We could hear very clearly from outside the excited voices of those who had assembled in the hope of having their tax demands reduced by a shilling or two. A host of men were thronging the unfortunate District Clerk's office and were jammed together on the flight of stairs leading up to it. When someone was admitted, those outside endeavoured to keep the door ajar in order to glimpse the proceedings and to hear what was said.

The appellant was asked his name and occupation, and the same procedure was followed in the majority of cases. For most categories there was a standard sum of tax to be paid, for example £1. 10s. 0d. by Native Doctors, and eighteen shillings and sixpence by fish traders. Most of those we interviewed came under the general classification of "petty trader". Depending on the nature of their answers to the questions put to them and on the manner in which their appearance struck the members of the Appeals Committee they were required to pay either £1. 0s. 3d., £1. 5s. 2d. or £2. 5s. 0d.

Those who were plot holders had to state the number of rooms rented out by them, and whether they were back or front. Members then carried out arithmetical calculations, looking over each others' shoulders to see if their results agreed. Mr. X would say a figure. I would then suggest a higher one. Mr. Y and Mr. Z, having had the proposed figures repeated for their benefit, would then agree with that of Mr. X or on a compromise between the two. Sometimes Mr. X recommended no reduction, in which case I suggested an increase, whereafter the procedure remained the same.

One after the other young men and old men, all wearing their most worn-out clothes, entered the office and left a few minutes later either with an alteration made on their demand note or with the figure shewn on it confirmed. Intent on our task the morning slipped rapidly away. At 1.30 p.m. one of the members began to feel the pangs of hunger.

"You, young man," he said to me. "You strong and no need chop. But I be old man and my belly cry for chop."

He begged the rest of us rather pathetically to break off for a meal, but we all preferred to carry on and finish the business. Through the sultry hours of the afternoon we continued to sit. Gradually the noise of those waiting outside grew less, as their numbers dwindled. With only half my mind on the profits of petty traders and the front and back rooms of grasping landlords, I became increasingly conscious of the torpor of siesta-time settling upon the town. The noise of the traffic along station road grew quieter. Even the wasps clinging to their dangling nests overhead made fewer sorties; but the fine dust of dried termite excreta continued its gentle unremitting descent from the wooden ceiling above.

The first couple I married were Nigerian. After the requisite notices had been posted for the required length of time and the necessary affidavits had been sworn we agreed on a day for the ceremony, and I asked them to come to the District Office at 9.00 a.m. On reaching the office at 8.00 a.m., wearing tie, long trousers and jacket in place of my usual open-necked shirt and shorts, I took a quick look at the Marriage Ordinance. By doing so I discovered that persons might only be married between the hours of ten in the forenoon and four in the afternoon. Bride in a pink dress and Bridegroom in a dark suit had therefore to wait patiently for an hour. At 10.00 a.m. they were ushered into my office and were followed by half a dozen smartly clad witnesses. The proceedings lasted barely five minutes. I read the required portions of the Ordinance, concluding with the somewhat terse warning that a second marriage by either party while the other remained alive and not legally divorced would constitute bigamy. There followed the signing of the marriage register; and I then congratulated Gertrude and Vincent on having become man and wife.

Every morning a venerable old man wearing a shapeless khaki uniform entered my office carrying a dog-eared ledger in one hand and a battered sun-helmet, symbol of his authority, in the other. He was known as "Time Keeper". He placed the ledger reverently on my desk, open at the latest entry. I glanced through the distribution of the Township labour gangs, and had difficulty in making out both the Time Keeper's spidery calligraphy and his unorthodox spelling.

"What on earth is this?" I asked on the occasion of his first appearance, pointing to the words "Gulief Corse". After a little questioning I discovered that this was the way in which he spelt "Golf Course".

I noted that nineteen labourers were working on Diobu "Futbal" field. One morning I took the Time Keeper with me in my car, and we visited his various gangs. At the Futbal field we found nine men sitting in the shade of a tree, eight standing and talking and two absent without leave. As we approached the "labourers" regarded us with tolerant indifference, secure in the knowledge that they would all be two shillings and twopence the richer by 3.00 p.m., when their period of duty ended. Elsewhere we saw labourers allegedly cutting grass on roadside verges, working in the township's single park and digging graves in the cemetery. The impression I obtained from this outing was that no matter how efficiently the Time Keeper might keep time it was evident that his labourers preferred to waste it.

Amongst the various visits paid from time to time by people from overseas to Port Harcourt I was privileged to receive one by Mr. Monkhouse, the assistant editor of the *Manchester Guardian*. I made arrangements for him to give a talk in the town's only public hall, the erstwhile Roxy Cinema. Before the meeting I gave Mr. Monkhouse and his British Council escort tea in my house. The latter laughingly mentioned in the course of conversation that at one place visited by Mr. Monkhouse during his lecture tour no seats had been provided for those attending. I hope I looked suitably amused, but I could not help but remember that the Roxy was usually more or less devoid of furniture and that I had given no express orders for seating accommodation to be provided. However, all was well, for on arrival I found that some chairs and benches, albeit few in number, had been ranged in front of the platform. My own chair caused me a moment of acute worry. While Mr. Monkhouse was speaking, suddenly and without warning the back came adrift, and the Chairman all but found himself un-chaired.

The Roxy was in a busy part of the town, and throughout Mr. Monkhouse's talk I was painfully aware of the cries of children playing in the street immediately outside, the blare of motor horns and the metallic hammering of an energetic iron worker somewhere in the vicinity.

At the end of the talk I invited questions. An aggressive member of the local press promptly said he wished to make a suggestion, and proceeded to do so without more ado. He was evidently of the opinion that the British press was guilty of deliberate distortion of facts, because his suggestion was that on his return to England Mr. Monkhouse should summon the editors of all leading newspapers to a conclave at which he should charge them to tell the truth about Nigeria in their columns.

The majority of the questions asked were critical and hostile. The most absurd was one put apparently in all seriousness by a young man, who wished to know what steps British newspapers were taking to dispel the idea prevalent amongst English people that all Africans had tails!

A more friendly occasion was the send-off party given by the Town Council for their departing British Town Clerk. The festivities began with a group photograph taken on the tennis court outside the African Club. After this was over we straggled inside, and seated ourselves at a number of small tables, onto which clean cloths had been drawing-pinned. The others in my group were a Town Councillor, an ex-postmaster friend and a Lebanese trader. There were a dozen or so Europeans among the fifty or sixty present. With one exception, the editor of a scurrilous local newspaper, everyone seemed happy and friendly. This individual sat silent and aloof, no doubt regarding the proceedings with disapproval as an opportunity enabling black and white to meet on cordial terms. Seeing him clad in his ill-fitting, double-breasted jacket and disregarded both by Europeans and his fellow country-men alike, I had it in me to pity his misguided and self-inflicted estrangement.

In due course someone was called upon to take the Chair, and two others were called upon to support him. Amidst clapping these dignitaries then occupied the seats reserved for them. The Chairman, a well-known local ecclesiastical figure, was extremely unctuous. While admitting that until that evening he had not had the pleasure of meeting Mr. Coatswith (the Town Clerk) he proceeded to discharge a string of superlatives testifying to his noble character. He then went to great pains to express appreciation of the great honour accorded to him by being asked to preside at such a noteworthy gathering. When he finally finished a buxom young woman stepped forward and read an address in appreciation of Coatswith's services, which she then presented to him. He then expressed suitable thanks; and bottles and glasses were distributed. My Lebanese companion immediately removed the tops of several beer bottles with his teeth, and wasted no time in getting down to the serious part of the evening's activities. Toast followed toast, each affording the proposer a splendid opportunity to express his views on matters in general and on the affairs of Port Harcourt in particular. Eventually I was called upon to propose the toast of the invitees. Having no wish to discourse at length, I explained that, knowing as I did that the virtuous qualities of those present spoke for themselves, I was at a loss to know what there was left for me to say. Happy in this knowledge I asked them therefore to rise and drink to "Ourselves, the invitees".

Before the proceedings were able to come to an end we had to sit through the Chairman's protracted "Closing Remarks", which were followed by a rendering of "For he's a jolly good fellow".

During my stay in Port Harcourt a new High Court building was constructed; and I recall one particular occasion on which I had to appear in this Court to give evidence regarding a confession which had been sworn before me many months earlier.

Two fans revolved gently overhead; and on the benches some score of Africans slumbered or ruminated peacefully. Three bangs heralded the entrance of His Honour the Judge. The bodies stirred and rose unsteadily to their feet. The Judge bowed. Those in Court bowed. The Judge seated himself on his rostrum, and below him the Clerk of the Court rustled through his papers. One or two black-gowned barristers adjusted their wigs, and behind them the public settled down again on the benches. The accused, Lucy Amadi, was called. A few moments later she entered the Court escorted by two Constables, and took her place in the dock. Lucy, charged with murder, was a young peasant woman in her middle twenties. Her feet were bare, and she was simply clad in a cotton blouse and a fathom of cloth wrapped round her waist. Her hair was stylishly gathered together in small tufts, which stuck out from her head like pins out of a pincushion.

Hearing of the case of the Queen versus Lucy Amadi was resumed, and I was called to give evidence. Standing in the witness box I noticed that I was the only white person in the Court. I stated that in May of the previous year the accused had of her own free will made a statement of confession before me. I was followed by a Mr. Okeke, who looked both hot in his tweed sports coat and ill at ease in his unfamiliarly prominent position. He confirmed that it was he who had interpreted Lucy Amadi's statement of confession to her. The Doctor who had carried out the post-mortem on the victim was then called; and he unemotionally informed the Court that death had occurred as a result of the infliction of eight wounds by means of a sharp weapon.

The fans revolved dispassionately. The barristers exchanged remarks amongst themselves; and the younger generation collected around the entrances to the Court and peered in.

The accused was called by her defending counsel to give evidence, and she answered the questions put to her without hesitation. She had been married to her husband for seven years. Recently her father-in-law had died, and her husband had inherited one of his wives. One evening after she had finished cutting cassava in preparation for supper, Lucy went to her husband's house and happened to carry with her the knife she had used for preparing the cassava. Finding her husband sitting on a bed with his inherited wife, she left; but on her way back she was overtaken by the other woman, who proceeded to beat her. Lucy tried to defend herself, and in the struggle which ensued the knife she was carrying lodged itself in the deceased.

Counsel asked for exhibit "A" to be produced, and the Clerk searched fruitlessly for it amongst the conglomeration of stuff on his table. A constable was then despatched to look for it, and returned a few moments later bearing a handy-looking little dagger. On being questioned by her defending counsel the accused confirmed that the exhibit was the knife which had lodged itself in the deceased.

The defending counsel sat down, and the prosecuting Crown Counsel lumbered to his feet. He fired a succession of questions at the accused which had the effect of revealing the circumstances surrounding the death in a rather different light. He concluded by declaring in strident tones that the accused was a wildly jealous woman who had gone to her husband's house deliberately to kill his inherited wife taking with her for the purpose a dagger, a weapon quite unsuitable for the cutting

100

of cassava but admirable for the infliction of a mortal wound. With this weapon she had stabbed the deceased no fewer than eight times.

The fans revolved imperturbably above the white wigged heads of Judge and Counsel, above the pincushion head of Lucy, and above the heads of Clerk, interpreter, police and public.

Defending Counsel on his feet again, having passed a cheery aside with his prosecuting opponent, stated that it was not the intention of the Defence to deny the infliction of the wounds, but to contend that they were inflicted in self-defence at a time when the accused was in danger if not of her life at any rate of grievous bodily harm. The deceased was a larger woman than the accused; she was armed with a stick; and at the relevant time the accused was in a weak state of health having only recently recovered from the effects of a miscarriage.

The accused, back in the dock, stood up waiting for the Judge to pronounce his judgement. She, who had been kept waiting for this moment for the past ten months, was not left in suspense much longer, His Lordship accepted the defence of self-defence; and accordingly reduced the charge from one of murder to one of manslaughter. But while force may be used against force, the amount so used must be no more than is reasonably necessary. The infliction of eight wounds, any one of which might have been sufficient to prove fatal, was excessive.

"Sentenced to eight years' imprisonment," said the Judge.

Nobody stirred. Nobody sighed, cried, laughed or sang; and Lucy Amadi was led out of the Court looking outwardly as calm as when she had been led in.

I remained District Officer, Port Harcourt, for a full tour of eighteen months. By the end of that time I had acquired a fairly intimate knowledge of the town and its environs. The single road into Port Harcourt passed through the shanty town suburb of Diobu. The town's main road ran parallel with the railway line, and was flanked on the side opposite the track by a number of buildings called "factories". These were owned by various British, French, Swiss and Greek Companies. They were a combination of go-down and shop; and in some cases had staff flats on the upper floors. There was only one building amongst them which resembled a shop in the normal sense of the word. This was the "Kingsway Stores" owned by the United Africa Company.

Behind the main road and centred around a kidney-shaped circular road system was the Government Residential Area. This was where the senior Government officers, both British and African, and the managers of the Commercial Companies lived in modest bungalows and houses set in fairly spacious tree-clad gardens. To the east of the Residential Area was the pride of Port Harcourt, the golf course, which extended to the very fringe of the mangrove swamp, which almost completely encircled the town. Apart from Government offices and houses the Residential Area contained the spacious Residency building, the Port Harcourt (European) Club, the Braithwaite Nursing Home (formerly known as the European Hospital) and the diminutive All Saints' Church.

A green belt separated the Residential Area from the town proper. On the far side of this and along Harbour Road prosperous African merchants and contractors had begun to build themselves elaborate dwellings three or four storeys high in an area known as Millionaires' Row. In this vicinity the two open-air cinemas were located.

The African town was laid out on an unimaginative grid system. The main street was known as Aggrey road, and it was there that the majority of the Syrian and Lebanese community and the more well-to-do, middle-class Africans had their homes, shops, offices, and consulting rooms. Many of the buildings flanking this street were of two storeys; but elsewhere in the town the majority, whether dwellings or shops, were single-storey structures.

The port was situated at some distance from both the Residential Area and the town. The quay was on the east side of the New Calabar river, the width of which was barely sufficient to allow enough room for the ocean-going cargo boats of the Elder Dempster, John Holt's and Palm Lines to turn around in. On the west bank of the river there was nothing but swamp and mangroves.

When the time came for me to leave Port Harcourt I took with me a variety of memories: Town Council bye-elections, a fire in Aggrey road, a Red Cross fundraising garden party at the Residency, a Yoruba function in the football stadium in honour of a local Yoruba Doctor awarded the O.B.E. in the New Year Honours, a mammoth parade of schoolchildren on Empire Day, a strike of Port workers, an explosion in the Power Station and the memorial service for King George VI held in St. Cyprian's Church.

Chapter 9

"What for they go waste our time?"

While on leave in England during the summer of 1953 I was married in a small country church, more than 1,000 years old. After a very brief honeymoon we had to return to Nigeria. Parents and relations came to London Airport on a lovely sunny day to speed Angela and me on our way. Having received the summons to embark we said our goodbyes, and like a disorderly crocodile of schoolchildren we walked with our fellow passengers across the tarmac to the waiting plane. We waved to the small group of kith and kin clustered amongst the coloured umbrellas on the terrace outside the Airport restaurant; and then we climbed up the steps, and disappeared within the belly of the Argonaut. Peering through a window we could still see those with whom a few minutes earlier we had been lunching. They waved, but irresolutely because they could no longer see us. Seated within the plane we shared with them the rending moment of departure.

Suddenly the engines came to life. Like performing lions roaring at the command of their trainer, each of the four in turn reached a shattering crescendo; and then, as though abashed by their noisy exhibition, self-effacingly died away. We taxied to the end of the runway, and a few moments later we were high in the sky and looking down on Greater London. Below us there were long lines of suburban houses stretching and converging towards the Metropolis. There were factories and churches, playing fields and railway lines. Soon we were over more open country. We saw fir trees, gorse bushes and bracken; and we told ourselves that we recognised Oxshott Heath, where we had spent our first day together. A little later we crossed the Sussex coast and were over the English Channel.

On arrival at Port Harcourt I was informed that I was posted to Brass, the most remote of the Rivers Province Divisions. Accompanied by Philip, Bonniface and our personal effects, we set off to our first home together in the middle of the Niger delta. We travelled by launch, and the journey took twenty-four hours. It was evening when we came alongside the tumbledown jetty at Brass. There were no other Europeans in the station, and we were led to our abode by the District Clerk. Labourers unloaded our belongings and carried them up a steep flight of steps to our quarters above the District Office on the first floor of an ancient building. It was dark by the time our last box was deposited in the middle of the completely bare living-room. Philip produced a lighted Tilley lamp and we inspected our dwelling place. We were somewhat taken aback to find that it was virtually devoid of furniture, shelves and cupboards and of course of all "mod. con.". In the "bathroom" there was nothing except a thunderbox; in the kitchen, which was on ground level, there was a grimy wood-burning "Dover" stove. Fortunately we had brought a couple of beds and mattresses with us. We also possessed some camp chairs, a camp table, some bookshelves, a desk, a meat-safe and my old tin bath.

One morning three weeks after our arrival in Brass Angela had an acute pain in her stomach. Having both come to the conclusion that it was probably appendicitis, I hastily summoned my launch crew and we set off on our rather agonising journey through the creeks to Port Harcourt. The engineers screwed every rev. they could out of the old engine, and we reached our destination in the early hours of the following day. Later in the day Angela's appendix was satisfactorily removed.

After some convalescence she returned to Brass; but we were not left in peace for long in our distant backwater. A new Resident required my services in his office, and we moved temporarily to Port Harcourt. After five years in Rivers Province I was keen to go to some other part of the Eastern Region, and at the beginning of January 1954 my wish was granted. I was suddenly posted out of the blue to Abakaliki in Ogoja Province in the northern part of the Region. We were given three days in which to pack up and transfer ourselves to our new station. Philip had to return on his own to Brass to collect the remainder of our belongings from there. He was none too pleased at this succession of moves, and I heard him mutter darkly, "What for they go waste our time?" En route to Abakaliki we spent a night in Enugu, where I was given a briefing by the Civil Secretary. He explained that the reason for the suddenness of my move was the fact that the then D.O. Abakaliki's health had broken down and it was necessary to withdraw him straightaway. He then went on to paint a somewhat grim picture of the state of the Division. I gathered that there had recently been a good deal of turmoil due to the introduction of a new education rate levied on all taxpayers. I was told that I must avoid meeting my predecessor, who would be taken from Abakaliki under medical supervision on the morning following my arrival; and it was also made clear that I was merely required to hold the fort in Abakaliki until the return from leave a few months later of a more senior Administrative Officer.

We arrived in Abakaliki the following evening and spent the night in the small Catering Rest-House, where a room had been reserved for us. The next morning after the departure of my predecessor I walked down to the District Office and introduced myself to the staff.

The two or three months we spent in Abakaliki were eventful. There was constant trouble in connection with education rating involving riotous assemblies, the seizure and murdering of local Councillors, and attacks on police and Government officials. Shortly before my departure I accompanied a contingent of some thirty police under the command of the Provincial Superintendent, an Englishman, on a raid on a village well off the beaten track where it was believed a number of ringleaders were in hiding. On arrival we met stubborn opposition, and found ourselves all but surrounded by hostile and armed villagers. With the help of tear gas and the firing of a round or two we succeeded in extricating ourselves and in bringing a few prisoners back with us.

After I had handed Abakaliki over to my more senior colleague on his return from leave I was put in charge of the adjoining Division, known as Ogoja. We remained there for about a year until the end of our tour. In Ogoja too life was not without incident; but trouble instead of stemming from education rating arose from a long-standing dispute about land between two clans. Wearying of the slow processes of the Law the rival factions resorted to arms. I arrived on the scene to find the warriors on the two sides under cover and about half a mile apart. A tremendous hullaballoo was going on, and it seemed as if they were on the point of launching into action. However, by dint of much parleying with both sides in turn, and by remaining in between them, I was able to restrain them from fighting until the arrival several hours later of police in full riot order who had travelled speedily from the Provincial Depot 100 miles or more away. Their appearance had a very salutary effect, and the oiled and almost naked warriors melted rapidly away.

During our year in Ogoja we were fortunate enough to be able to take some local leave and to visit the Spanish island of Fernando Poo. To do so we had to travel to the old port of Calabar on the Cross river. When we arrived on the wharf to embark, we saw the Island's fresh meat supply being loaded on board. One after the other bullocks and cows were lassoed, hoisted into the air by their horns and lowered into the hold of the *Ciudad de Ceuta*. Formerly a ferry boat between Spanish Morocco and Spain, this old vessel had been sent south to finish its days travelling three times a month to and fro between Calabar and Fernando Poo. We went on board after the cattle; and a little later, as the sun was setting behind the mangroves, we were steaming down the river towards the open sea. The many deck passengers — Nigerians going to the Island to work as labourers in the plantations — drummed and sang and made merry. I did not know whether they did so from pleasure at the thought of the money they were going to make, or in order to keep their spirits up as they sailed away from their native land into the unknown.

The following morning we went ashore at Santa Isabel, the capital. A steep road led from the wharf up the cliff to the main square, where many stately Royal palms towered fifty feet high. At the far side of the square facing the sea stood the Governor's residence, and beside it was the Cathedral with its twin spires. Santa Isabel faced onto a beautiful bay; and the 9,000 foot peak of the Island's highest mountain rose up behind the town. Many of the buildings were pleasing, particularly the new Town Council offices which had a Canary Island stype of architecture. Houses were made attractive by balconies, balustrades, shutters, tiled floors and wrought-iron work; and by law they had to be painted externally at least once every two years. The town seemed to be busy and thriving. A lot of building was in progress, and a new wharf was under construction. The streets were full of cars; and lorries travelling along the circular coast road brought cocoa, coffee and bananas from the plantations for shipment.

Coming from Eastern Nigeria we were struck by the prolificity of white people in Santa Isabel: white men serving in shops, driving lorries and waiting at table; white women going shopping and pushing prams; and white children returning from school with satchels on their backs. No matter what the time of day, provided the sun had not set, every white person we saw outside wore a sun helmet.

The British population on the Island consisted only of the Vice-Consul, his wife and daughter, a Chaplain and the Manager of the Ambas Bay Trading Company, a subsidiary of Unilever. The main function of the Vice-Consul was to safeguard the interests of the indentured Nigerian labourers working on the Island. The indigenous natives were Bubis, of whom there were about 10,000. These people were unwilling to exert themselves; and for its labour force Fernando Poo depended largely upon Nigerians, of whom there were usually about 10,000 on the Island. A treaty provided for the recruitment of labourers in Nigeria, and some were engaged as far afield as Ogoja. They contracted for two years' work in Fernando Poo with the chance of remaining for a further period if they wished. It was with the Nigerian population, consisting largely of Ibos, Effiks, Yorubas and Cameroonians, that the British Chaplain also was concerned. In order to cater for the spiritual needs of his flock he had succeeded by dint of much effort over many years in building an Anglican Church almost within the shadow of the Roman Catholic Cathedral and the Bishop's Palace.

In the public gardens on the Punta we were interested to see a memorial to John Beecroft, an Englishman, who despite that fact had once been Governor of this Spanish territory. The British connection with the Island began in the 1820s, when use was made of it as a base from which to suppress the West Coast slave trade. Beecroft was appointed Governor in 1843; and it was not until 1858 that the Island had its first Spanish Governor. We were reminded of the part played by Fernando Poo in the campaign against the slave trade by the many Fernandinos who lived on the Island. These charming and courteous people were descendants of slaves from Sierra Leone and the Gold Coast, who owed their liberation to the British "Clarence" Tribunal, which was set up on the Island in 1827. The Fernandinos comprised the African aristrocracy of the Island, and were respected by the Spaniards. At the time of our visit a Fernandino owned one of the larger plantations and was President of the Cocoa Section of the Chamber of Commerce.

Only forty miles distant from the coastline of Nigeria, Spanish colonists were watching the constitutional changes taking place on the mainland with some misgiving. They were wondering whether Nigerian political advancement would jeopardise the recruitment of Nigerian labour, on which the economy of the Island depended. Cocoa production was all important; and even with 10,000 Nigerian labourers in the colony the output was much less than it might have been because plantations were unable to obtain more than half their necessary labour strengths.

Santa Isabel seemed to us to be a happy, friendly place, free of political agitation. The Governor made the laws, and the people kept them. There was no need to lock houses or cars because thieving was almost unknown. Europeans and Africans worked hard, often side by side, and relations between the two races were good.

In the evening there was relaxation. The bells rang for vespers, and schoolchildren, black and white, filed inside the Cathedral. People loitered chattering in the Square, or drove or strolled along the Punta enjoying the cool sea breeze and passing gardens in which grew roses and gardenias, hibiscus and cinnamon, guavas and avocado pears. Out at sea ships passed bound from Doula to Marseilles. The clouds dispersed from the sides of the mountain, and the whole of the pyramid-shaped Santa Isabel peak was revealed, looking in the evening light rather like a gigantic sandcastle. On clear days the great hump of Mt. Cameroon twenty miles away on the mainland could also be seen.

We sailed from the Island on such an evening, when the sun was sinking down towards the sea. A few minutes later and it was gone. The golden glow in sky and sea like footlights quickly dimmed; and as the *Ciudad de Ceuta* sailed out of Ambas Bay, on that beautiful island four degrees north of the equator another day drew to its close.

During my year in Ogoja, Nigerian Federal elections were held for the first time and I was responsible for arrangements in my Division. The successful candidate was a very pleasant young man called Matthew Mbu. Within the space of a few weeks his status changed from that of a small trader in palm oil and palm kernels to that of a Minister of the Federal Government. When we went on leave a few months later we accepted an invitation he very kindly made us to stay with him during the day or two we spent in Lagos before embarking. He met us in his official car on our arrival at the railway station, and drove us to his ministerial house in the smart residential area of Ikoyi. We had a separate suite to ourselves and his domestic staff were as attentive and helpful as our own would have been. Matthew showed us the sights of the capital and entertained us most hospitably; and at the end of our stay he took us to Apapa where the Elder Dempster mail boat on which we were to travel to England was berthed.

Chapter 10

"Arrowsmith — Eket"

After a wonderful leave we returned to Nigeria by sea. I had assumed that I would be resuming duty in Ogoja, and I received an unpleasant shock when, following our arrival at Freetown, I read in a cable giving the postings of Nigerian Government Officers: "Arrowsmith — Eket". We were both very disappointed to learn that we would not be going back to Ogoja because we had many friends there, whom we had been looking forward to seeing again. As for Eket, I had only a vague idea where it was, and knew nothing about it except that it was "leopard-murder" country.

On arrival at Lagos we made use of the new Atlantic Terminal, which had been opened while we were on leave. It was a great improvement on the old Customs' shed, and made us feel that we were travellers of some significance. Outside the Terminal building there was the usual medley of gesticulating porters, taxi drivers and rag, tag and bobtail. We saw our bags loaded onto a 1920 Public Works Department Albion lorry, and four hours later they were delivered at the friend's house where we were staying.

Lagos was as bustling as ever. Building was going on on all sides. Kingsway Stores, the City's main emporium, appeared to be even larger than it was before; and many more petrol filling stations had sprouted here and there in the town and on the outskirts. We were shown the recently completed House of Representatives building, and were filled with wonderment at the effect of its air conditioning.

We had tea one afternoon with our friend, Matthew Mbu. It was strange to be sitting once again in his house in Ikoyi, where we had stayed five months previously. So much had happened during those months, and Nigeria had seemed so far away — and there we were back where we had started. It was a particularly interesting tea party because we were joined by Dr. Azikiwe, at that time Premier of the Eastern Region, who was staying with his political colleague Matthew. He was strikingly dressed in a flowing white robe, a pair of sandals, a royal blue fez-shaped hat, and a pair of thick-lensed glasses. He removed his headgear after shaking hands. On hearing that I was destined for Eket, Zik showed some interest.

"Ah, Eket," he said "That is where we are shortly going to have our first trial at holding universal adult suffrage local Government elections."

These words sent a shudder through me.

"I am very pleased to meet the D.O. who will be carrying out this job."

He looked at me searchingly, and I detected no glint of pity in his eyes.

Our conversation turned to more general matters; and I was surprised when Zik said that for the first time Nigerian intelligentsia had hoped for a Conservative victory in the British General Election, which had recently taken place. The Labour party was considered to be divided and therefore unsafe; and apparently great confidence was felt in Sir Anthony Eden.

After a two days' stay we departed from Lagos by car. On leaving the town we passed a fine new hotel under construction beside the lagoon, and situated within a mere fifty yards of the City's rubbish dump. Beside the new Railway Station I stopped the car in order to investigate a rattle in the boot. A youth in a blue singlet loafed up and asked: "Where are you going to, Master?" "To Eket," I replied, as I re-entered the car.

Our first stop was Ibadan. I had rung up from Lagos and had made a reservation at the Catering Rest-House for the night. However, on arriving at the Rest-House by way of a forest reserve I found that we were not expected. Fortunately we eventually succeeded in obtaining a room — and just in time because the rain began to descend in torrents. Our room was cheerless in the extreme. It was bare of floor mats and curtains; the mattresses were hard; and the bedclothes felt damp.

The following morning before resuming our journey we drove to the site of the new University. At the junction of the road leading to the campus and the main road there was an overturned and abandoned taxi. The general effect of the University buildings, which were very much on top of each other, was one of fancy concrete work and pastel shades of Snowcem. Everything looked new and impermanent; and I wondered what the result of a few years' weathering would be upon the prettily coloured buildings. We were told that the cost of maintaining them amounted to £90,000 a year! It seemd a pity that so little use had been made of stone. Where it had been used, as to some extent in the Trenchard Hall and in the Anglican Chapel, it shewed up to great advantage.

On our way back to Ibadan we saw in the distance the giant blocks of the new University College Hospital which was under construction.

The next halt on our journey eastwards was at Ife, where we visited the small well-designed Museum situated beside the Oni's compound. We admired the beautiful workmanship of the famous bronze heads believed to be 600–900 years old; and were interested to see that the features were not those of people indigenous to Southern Nigeria. On some of the heads hair, moustaches and beards were indicated by a number of small holes. Also in the Museum there was a small terracotta head from Nok in Plateau Province, which was thought to be 2,000 years old. We were shewn around by a young man, who afterwards led us into a room where he was engaged in modelling heads. He said that he was the only person in Ife interested in doing this.

We continued our journey, passing through Akure and reaching Benin in the evening. The next morning we left early for Asaba, situated on the west bank of the river Niger. An ancient ferry boat arrived soon after we did. Rather than having to back off the ferry at Onitsha, it was considered preferable to back onto it at Asaba. This was something of a feat; and we observed one mammy wagon, with the words "GOD BE WITH US" writ large above the driver's cab, almost drive off the ramps. After much manoeuvring four lorries and seven cars were packed onto the ferry. Crossing the mighty river took nearly half an hour.

That afternoon we arrived at the house of our friends in Enugu, and discovered to our horror that they had not received the telegram I had sent from Lagos two days earlier giving warning of our appearance. The telegram was not in fact delivered until 5.00 p.m. the following day! While in Enugu I met the Permanent Secretary, Ministry of Internal Affairs. He spoke to me about the forthcoming local Government elections to be held in Eket; and to my regret I learned that the new election procedure would involve a formidable number of county, rural district and local council elections in the Division. Furthermore, I gathered that not content with the heavy election undertaking it had also been decided to choose this juncture for a reorganisation of the existing local Government pattern of Eket County. It was with somewhat gloomy foreboding that I contemplated my new assignment.

In Enugu we were joined by our Boys. It gave me real pleasure to see our Steward, Philip, again. He was wearing the same old khaki shirt, a relic of my Army days, which he had worn off and on over a period of years. Philip introduced our new small-boy to us, a lad by the name of Desmond, whom he had recruited during our leave. Desmond had recently left school, having passed Standard V, and had not done any housework before. Bonniface, our Cook, also turned up. After meeting our ways separated again. Bonniface left for Ogoja to collect those of our loads which still remained there together with some of his own. Desmond remained with the Boys of our friends pending Bonniface's return to Enugu; and Philip plus a bundle of belongings done up in a straw mat travelled south with us in the car. Being a very small man it was just possible to make room for him on the back seat wedged beside our suitcases.

Chapter 11

"Two flying machines steering south passed over Eket"

Eket Division was one of the Divisions in Calabar Province. It was bounded by the Cross river in the east, the sea in the south and Opobo Division in the west. The Headquarters of the Division was at Eket, a small place, situated some eight or nine miles up the Qua Iboe river from its outlet to the sea. From our house we could sometimes hear the breakers on the shallow bar at the mouth of the river. Mr. A. A. Robertson of Glasgow, Agent for the firm of Miller Brothers, crossed this bar in 1871, and is believed to have been the first white man to penetrate up the river. Two years later Miller Brothers withdrew from the Qua Iboe river owing to threats made by bellicose King Ja-Ja of Opobo, who claimed a monopoly of all trade in the district. In 1881 a freelance trader, Mr. George Watts, opened a "factory" at Eket having made an agreement with the Qua Iboe Chiefs. This enraged King Ja-Ja who decided to drive out the intruder and to punish the people. In April of that year about fifty of the King's canoes armed with cannon entered the Qua Iboe river from a side and creek and bombarded several villages. The invaders broke into Mr. Watts' factory and destroyed or carried off much of his stock. They then returned to Opobo taking 100 or more prisoners with them. This act of aggression caused the British Consul in Calabar to intervene; and in due course active hostility between Opobo and Qua Iboe was brought to an end.

Within a few years of British traders becoming re-established at Eket, as a result of an appeal made by the Chiefs of Ibeno for a missionary to come and live among them, Mr. Samuel Bill arrived and settled in Big Town at the mouth of the Qua Iboe river in 1887. Four years later he was joined by his wife, who was the first white woman ever to be seen in that part of the country. The mission they founded, known as the Qua Iboe Mission, was still in existence in 1955 when Angela and I arrived in Eket.

Government followed in the wake of Commerce and the Church. In 1895 a Vice-Consulate was established in Eket. Three years later the Consul was replaced by Mr. A. C. Douglas, the first Political Officer, and the District Office, Eket, was then opened. Douglas was supplied with no staff of his own to begin with, but he succeeded in obtaining from the Consulate at Opobo four Court Messengers, one Marine-boy and an Interpreter. By 1910 the Government staff had increased considerably and consisted of the following: District Commissioner, District Clerk, one Schoolmaster, one pupil teacher, one interpreter, one telegraph operator, one prison warder, one police sergeant, nine police privates, one forest guard, one carpenter, nine beach and canoe boys, one engineer foreman, one quartermaster and one caretaker.

From the earliest days the Government worked for the betterment of the district and its inhabitants. The overland telegraph line from Eket to Oron and thence by underwater cable to Calabar, the construction of which was much opposed by the warlike residents of the country through which it passed, was the first priority. Other developments followed. In his Tour Notes dated 10th May, 1905, Sir Walter Egerton, High Commissioner, wrote: "I have directed that 500 cuttings of *Ficus elastica* be sent down here. It would be well to plant them along the new road to Oron on the opposite side to the telegraph wire." In 1955 many of these rubber trees planted along the side of this road were still to be seen. Thanks to the encouragement given by the Government the cultivation of rubber became an important industry in Eket Division.

As long ago as 1878 efforts were made to bring to an end the killing of twins. Article One of an agreement concluded with the Chiefs of Calabar on 6th September that year read as follows: "Whoever wilfully takes the life of a twin child or children shall be judged liable to the penalty of death. Anyone wilfully concealing any fact that may come to their knowledge of the murder of twins shall be considered accessories after the fact, and shall be liable to such punishment as the Consul shall direct. Twin mothers in future shall have full liberty to visit the town and buy and sell in the markets, the same as any other women of the town, and they shall not be molested in any way . . ."

In spite of the terms of this agreement the dreadful treatment meted out to twin babies continued. Mr. Bedwell, acting Provincial Commissioner, when visiting Eket in 1906 wrote in his Tour Notes as follows: "TWIN PALAVERS. This is an old-standing difficulty here. Mothers of twins will, even if living at the Mission, try to starve twins to death . . . It has been arranged to have a 'Twin Compound' at the Mission, to which all twins and their mothers should be sent at the expense of the town . . . A Matron will be appointed to have charge of the compound in the

Mission. I will give a sum not exceeding £20 to pay the Matron's wages and to contribute towards first expenses. A report must be made in six months' time as to results. Provision should be made in draft estimates 1907 to support this.''

A very poisonous bean, known as the Esere bean, was to be found throughout Eket Division. It was thought to destroy witches and wizards and the like but to be harmless to ordinary mortals. Recourse used therefore to be had to it to establish the innocence of those accused of witchcraft. Five beans were certain to cause death, and even one might do so if water were drunk after eating it. The toxin caused loss of eyesight and speech and inability to control the limbs. Thereafter the affected person became unconscious, and his body was wracked with short sharp spasms until he died. The Eket Annual Report for 1916 contained a reference to trials by ordeal through the swallowing of Esere beans. "The outbreak of trials by Esere bean poisonings occurred in the Ebugha portion of the district . . . An enquiry was held under the Collective Punishment Ordinance and the deaths of 44 persons were proved to have occurred in the course of the trials by ordeal. As a result of the Enquiry fines amounting to £825 were imposed on the towns concerned."

A few years later more drastic action was necessary. In 1919 eighteen persons were publicly executed before an estimated crowd of 4,000 onlookers in Oron market. The Annual Report for that year stated: "The number of victims who succumbed to the Eserine poisoning is much greater than is generally realised. From one of the Warrant Chiefs, who understood that for him there was no reprieve, I learnt a few hours before his last walk that in one town over 100 were destroyed in this manner. I should put the number of victims for the last epidemic at about 500."

Not all Esere bean poisonings were due to trials by ordeal. Owing to the wiping out of some families almost *in toto* by the influenza epidemic at the end of the Great War — it is estimated that 8,000 persons died of 'flu in Eket Division in 1918 — in many cases bereaved and melancholy survivors committed suicide by Eserine poisoning.

The bulk of the population of Eket Divison consisted of Ibibio, believed to be one of the most ancient peoples in West Africa. To the Ibibio rocks and rivers, ponds and trees all had an indwelling spirit. Many villages had their own sacred groves, trees or pools, which were believed to be inhabited by their protecting guardian spirits. All lived in the shadow of juju; and shrines and juju houses were to be found throughout the countryside. A fairly typical one was described by P. Amaury Talbot, at one time District Officer Eket, in his book *Life in Southern Nigeria** as follows:

115

"To the central pillar of the little juju house a strange object was bound. This was a piece of gnarled root or branch, sculptured, it would seem, by the hand of Nature herself . . . Here and there upon the head of the fetish small feathers were stuck, while a cavity beneath the bend of the neck was filled with these. A rough oval, formed from wild rubber or some other adhesive substance, had been smeared upon the pillar itself, a few inches above the strange growth. Upon the space thus prepared, chickens' feathers had been thickly plastered. At the base of the column lay an ancient skull, encased in a network of copper wires, and behind that again was a little pile of trade-gin bottles, the contents of which had been poured out as libations. Near the door stood a great drum of the usual type, carved from a solid block of wood. On both ends of this, little tufts of feathers were to be seen, held in place, like those already mentioned, by some sticky substance. Toward the back of the room a curtain of plaited palm-leaf screened off an inner compartment, in the midst of which a row of fascinatingly mysterious objects were propped — one, a short spear with haft elaborately carved in the form of a human figure; strange sceptre-like staves of much the same shape, but without iron tips and with curiously flattened faces, and a queer red-painted instrument, ending above in two horns like those of an irregular crescent. This latter the priest of the Juju declared to be a whistle or trumpet by which "the call of the spirit" was sounded. Before these also a heap of skulls was laid."

Juju could be either placated or invoked. Invocation with or without the administration of poison could lead to the sickness, paralysis and death of the person against whom it was directed. Placation of a juju was effected by sacrificing to it fowls, sheep, goats or even human beings. Talbot in the same book tells of a renowned juju situated near Jamestown on the west bank of the Cross river. The frequenters of this juju formed themselves into a society. They held their principal rites at the time of the new yams. If any non-member chanced to pass by and witnessed even the smallest part of the ceremonies, he had to bring a sacrifice consisting of sheep, goats, salt and fish, otherwise he would be stricken with sleeping sickness as a punishment. Talbot was told that this Society had been stopped by Government in about 1904 because members were in the habit of sallying out and seizing upon passers-by to offer up to their juju.

Ibibio men were very addicted to membership of secret societies, sometimes known as Ekpo societies. The Calabar Annual Report for 1923 defined an Ekpo Society as not being "a law-giving or law-making society. Rather it was and is a lawless band of brigands who backed their words with the edge of the matchet. Hence its demands and decrees were held in awe and the disregard of them viewed with terror". Members of these Societies, their identities concealed beneath hideous black wooden masks, and clad in skirts of grass, used to participate at times in frenzied dances. For a woman who witnessed any of the proceedings it was death. Members of Societies were ruthless in their dealings. In the Eket Annual Report for 1918 Jeffreys wrote: "There exists a good deal of friction between the Ekpo Society, the tradition-keepers of the tribe, and the younger generation known as the school-boys . . . Feeling runs high at times especially at the full ceremonial dances, when through the matcheting of a school-boy or two by an infuriated dancer the comedy of the play becomes the tragedy of the Court. The society continues a strong, though covert existence, and any relaxation in the vigilance of the Government would enable it to revert openly to all its former terrorism and villainy."

Elaborate and costly ceremonies had to be undergone by young men wishing to become members of Ekpo Societies. In some cases this used to involve a human sacrifice. Talbot described how a Chief who wished his son to become the member of a society either chose a woman from among his slaves or purchased one from another town or tribe — only young and beautiful women were acceptable. She was led to the sacred enclosure, where she was strangled. This form of killing was adopted because "no blood might flow, for this was a warrior's society, and the victim was offered to the war god that he might rejoice in her agony and accept it as the price of his aid to the youth who that day entered the ranks of fighters, so that no drop of the latter's blood need be shed to appease the thirst of the deity."

The most notorious of the Eket secret societies were the Leopard Societies. Members of these societies used to don the actual claws of leopards and slash their victims to death. From the nature of the wounds inflicted it was difficult, if not impossible, to establish with certainty whether the killing had been caused by a genuine leopard or perpetrated by a member of a Leopard Society. There had been an outbreak of these ritualistic murders a few years before my arrival in Eket, which resulted in the hanging of a number of men.

The Ibibio believed that the initiated had the power of changing themselves into various sorts of birds or fish or animals. In the case of Leopard Society members it was thought that they did actually become leopards when they went out on their foraying expeditions. This power of metamorphosis was believed to be used for evil purposes only — one such purpose being to gain admittance, for example in the form of snake, frog or bat, to locked premises at night in order to have sexual intercourse with some unsuspecting female. The Eket Annual Report for 1929 contained a reference to "an outbreak of the 'Uben' Juju, by which persons in possession of it are said to be able to gain access to houses and copulate with any women inside without their being aware of it."

Ibibio women used to undergo a painful form of circumcision, which was usually carried out during their stay in the Fattening Room prior to marriage. A piece of coconut shell was shaved very thin and a hole was made in it. The clitoris was drawn through this hole, and was then cut off with a sharp knife or a splinter of glass. It was necessary that the woman should make no sound while this operation was carried out.

In 1927 a curious phenomenon, which later became known as the "Spirit Movement", developed. It made itself more apparent in adjoining Divisions rather than in Eket itself. During the summer of that year a revivalist movement began, fostered by Mr. Westgarth of the Qua Iboe Mission. This led to gangs of hysterical church adherents terrorising the countryside. The Calabar Provincial Annual Report for 1927 described the situation as follows: "They declared themselves to be inspired by spirits, or, as they put it, actually to be spirits . . . They called on persons to confess their sins, and put those who refused to do so to torture. The victim was bound with ropes tightened with levers and by pouring water on to them. Then he was left to perish. The gangs lived in the churches of the locality and terrorised the whole countryside . . . A strong detachment of police was hastily assembled. Twenty-nine trussed up persons were rescued in time to save their lives. About 200 'spirits' were arrested and put on to making a road. Manual labour caused an almost immediate return to sanity."

With the passage of time enlightenment and development progressed. Following the establishment of the Government school in Eket in 1906 many more schools were opened all over the Division. This was due largely to the efforts of various Christian Missions. Methodists and Roman Catholics were well established early in this century. They were followed by others, including American Lutherans, Salvation Army, Assemblies of God and Apostolics. A Methodist Hospital was built at Oron; and after the last war a well-equipped Hospital was built at Eket by the Lutheran Mission. The Native Administration for its part established dispensaries in a number of centres.

In his Tour Notes dated 2nd September, 1925, the far-sighted Resident of Calabar Province drew attention to the need to develop the oil-palm industry in Eket. He wrote as follows: "I would remind the D.O. that he should constantly impress upon the Chiefs of his district that they must cultivate the palm tree. Their sole wealth is oil, and hitherto they have been the sole producer in the world's market. Now the Malay States are coming into the market and their oil is better than the wild West African article, because it is cultivated. Again the Germans have purchased the plantations in the Cameroons and are planting, exclusively, oil-palm trees. Although therefore the competition is not immediate it is very real, and the Chiefs

118

should be told that times are changing and what held good in their father's father's time will not hold good tomorrow and they must look ahead.'' The people of Eket did not attempt to emulate the British in Malaya and the Germans by establishing plantations. Some progress was, however, made, and production of palm-oil increased from 2,833 tons in 1909 to 4,069 in 1932.

Within a period of sixty years enormous progress had been made; and it is to the credit both of the people of Eket and of those who came from overseas to work amongst them that so much was achieved so quickly. The days of tribal warfare, secret society murders, Esere bean poisonings and the slaying of twins were past. The modern age had come. On 11th December, 1930, according to the Annual Report, "two flying machines steering south passed over Eket." During my stay in the Division some twenty-five years later the helicopters of an oil company flew constantly overhead.

---

* Life in Southern Nigeria, P. Amaury Talbot, Macmillan 1923.

Chapter 12

"On a day being a day not within seven days of the day"

It was pouring with rain when we arrived at Eket, and the one road into the station was flooded. However, we found our way without difficulty to our house. A sandy drive with a line of rubber trees on one side and a small "golf course" on the other led to a double garage and the rear of the District Officer's residence, a largish building raised about five feet above ground level on a number of brick arches. Wooden steps at the front of the house gave access to the sitting-room; and another flight at the back led from the covered way, connecting the kitchen with the house, to the pantry which was behind the sitting-room. There was also a concrete stair-case up to the bathroom of the main bedroom, which was used by Philip when bringing buckets of hot water for our bath. The kitchen and Boys' quarters were on ground level. Under part of the house there was a store. Elsewhere a mass of clobber, which included one jeep and five mowing machines, had accumulated in between the arches. The house had a red corrugated-iron roof. Guttering — an unusual feature of buildings in Eastern Nigeria — ran along the edge of this, and at one corner of the house there were two large iron water-storage tanks. The house was spacious. It had two bedrooms, each with its own bathroom and lavatory, a large sitting-room, a dining-room, a pantry and a store. The rooms were bright and airy. Half or more of the front of the house consisted of windows with wooden panels below them, which could be propped open for additional ventilation. The house was well equipped with "mod. con.". Both bathrooms boasted full-length baths, and one had running cold water in both bath and basin. One lavatory was equipped with a W.C., the other having a thunderbox.

The house was reasonably well supplied with furniture. There were four beds, two with interior-sprung mattresses and two with mattresses stuffed with coconut fibre. There was a fine looking dining-room table, which we soon discovered provided a permanent home for an army of tiny sugar ants. There were some dining-room chairs, a sideboard and, in the sitting-room, a sofa and two or three armchairs. The most attractive piece of furniture was an old chest of drawers with brass angle brackets at the corners and inset brass handles for each of the drawers. We saw a replica of it in the Residency of Calabar; and I liked to imagine that it came to Nigeria along with other Victorian furniture in the days of H.M. British Consul.

In front of the house towered a lofty flag-pole, from which a Union Jack flew on days when the District Officer was in the station. At its base there was a Nordenfelt machine gun bearing the date 1901. About a quarter of a mile away and some fifty feet below the house there flowed the Qua Iboe river.

We arrived in Eket, one of the wettest places in Africa with a rainfall of about 150 inches a year, in the middle of the wet season. It rained continuously for three weeks following our arrival. In order to avoid a fine spray being blown into the house we had to keep the windows all along the front of the house closed. In spite of this moisture seeped in. Shoes and handbags become mildewed overnight; and the covers of our books — particularly dark-blue ones — became mottled and discoloured. In order to keep our clothes as dry as possible Angela placed oil heater lamps in our wardrobes. Though depressing the weather nevertheless had the merit of being cool, the temperature in our house never exceeding 75 °F at that time of year.

Soon after our arrival in Eket I went to a meeting of the Eket County Council. A system of local Government had been in operation for the past three years. The Division formed one County Council area, four Rural District Council and twenty-six Local (i.e. Parish) Council areas. In a Division where local Government obtained the Councils were responsible for managing their own affairs. However, by the new Eastern Region Local Government Law which had only just come into effect the District Officer, in his capacity as Local Government Commissioner, exercised control over the conclusion of contracts and the engagement and termination of certain grades of staff. He also had the right of access to all books and records for purposes of inspection.

The headquarters of Eket County Council was eleven miles from Eket, but because of a bridge which was under construction one had to take a longer route which involved a journey of sixteen miles. It took me seventy minutes in my new MG Magnette to cover this distance. The road was in an appalling state. In one swampy place the surface was barely above the level of the water on either side. There were other places where the road had been churned up into a lake of liquid slush. Elsewhere the road surface was wavy, with water lying in the troughs between the undulations. Driving over it was more like an outing in a motorboat than a ride in a car. All the way the road was pockmarked with deep potholes, and every incline was scarred and eroded by streams which rushed down on either side. One timber bridge was in a very shaky condition. I had a look at the bearers and runners and found them covered with a green slime; and there was a gaping hole in the carriage-way where one of the decking planks had broken.

The Secretary of the County Council introduced me to the meeting, and the Chairman said some words of welcome. I sat down beside him, and counted twenty-eight Councillors sitting at tables put together to form three sides of a square. Some wore trousers or shirts; some were in native dress. The Chairman had on shorts, shirt, pullover and Wellington boots. In addition he sported an Anthony Eden hat and a leather briefcase. Amongst the Councillors I saw one or two sun helmets equipped with pale sea-green waterproof covers, blue plastic mackintoshes and gumboots, and a trilby hat garnished with a peacock feather. Fifteen Councillors had spectacles, but only four wore them. The remainder fiddled with theirs or kept them on the table in front of them as a status symbol. One man wore a pair of sunglasses throughout the proceedings notwithstanding the murkiness of the day.

I felt myself to be in a familiar setting, and my heart warmed towards these representatives of the people trying to grapple with an agenda. In their own way they did very well. The meeting opened with a prayer. Then followed "confirmation of the minutes of the previous meeting". As the minutes had not been circulated in advance the Chairman went through them item by item in order to give members of the Council a chance to satisfy themselves as to their exactness. All went well for the first half dozen items or so; and then we came to a long one dealing with a proposed new road to connect with a new pontoon ferry. From the minutes it was evident that there had been a division of opinion as to the route this road should follow; and a decision in favour of one of the two ways suggested had been carried by a small majority. It was at this juncture that the proceedings became disrupted. A little man in a dark-blue flannel blouse with a zip-fastener up the front jumped to his feet and made it clear that he did not support the decision which had been recorded. Others jumped up agreeing with him. They were followed by others who vigorously defended the decision reached at the previous meeting. All round the tables Councillors were on their feet shouting "Mr. Chairman" and "on a point of order", and at the same time Dark-Blue Blouse was doing his best to move a resolution that the former decision be rescinded. This was not to the liking of the Chairman, who came from the part of the Division in question. The Secretary came to his rescue by begging leave to read from the Council's Standing Orders. Enunciating very carefully he read out the Order dealing with a motion to rescind a former

122

resolution. This stated that such a motion, supported by the signatures of at least one fourth of the Councillors, had to be submitted in writing in advance of the meeting at which it was hoped to make the motion. Dark-Blue Blouse was finally persuaded to sit down and to take action accordingly if he wished. As I had found to be the case elsewhere, the Councillors clearly did not or would not understand that by "confirmation of the minutes" was meant only a confirmation of their correctness as a record, and that this was not intended to be an opportunity to enter into debate over decisions taken at the previous meeting.

After an hour and a half we came to the end of the first item on the agenda! With the Chairman's permission I then intervened and gave members a brief description of the programme for the County, District and Local Council elections. No sooner had I finished my outline than the Council unanimously resolved that the Minister of Internal Affairs should be requested to extend the period for the holding of these elections from December 31st until March 31st of the following year. This was telegraphed to him, but to no avail.

I returned home to study and to submit a report to the Resident, Calabar, on the draft Regulations governing the method of conducting the Eket Local Government elections. It was not an attractive weekend holiday task. The draft Regulations, the work of some Legal Officer in Enugu who would probably never even vote in a local Government election much less face the herculean job of having to organise one, contained reference to Voters' Lists, Nominations, symbols, and sealing of ballot boxes. One particularly unintelligible Regulation began: "On a day being a day not within seven days of the day . . ."

After we had been in Eket a month I became aware that we had settled. Our regret at not returning to Ogoja had not waned; and Eket had not revealed any unexpected charms or attractions. It was simply that we had adapted ourselves to the change. I had not grown any more enamoured of my duties as Electoral Officer in charge of the local Government elections; but I had become attached to the little District Office with its slate roof and to my staff. Similarly our house had become home. There was a daily routine. At 7.00 a.m. Philip knocked on our bedroom door. After contemplating the morning for a few minutes through the mosquito net, I reluctantly emerged and entered the bathroom. On my opening the outside door, Philip climbed the steps bringing some shaving water in our one and only blackened kettle. We always wished each other good morning. Sometimes if cleaning my teeth I could only gurgle it. Sometimes Philip had a chewing stick in the corner of his mouth, which he would remove before greeting me. After shaving, I walked across the grass to the office 200 yards away bearing any files or telegrams which I

123

had had at home. Also I always took my umbrella. If it were not raining when I set out I could be pretty certain it would be before my return.

I left the house the back way, passing Desmond sweeping the pantry and Bonniface, who had nothing to do until breakfast time, lounging outside the kitchen — possibly engaged in combing his crinkly hair. Walking along the sandy path across the golf course I usually met a warder and a gang of prisoners; and warder and prisoners in succession wished me good morning. At about 9.30 a.m. I returned home for breakfast. We had this on the verandah in front of the dining-room, from where we enjoyed a wonderful view across the garden to the river and the forest on the further side. Some mornings I brought some mail back with me, which we read while eating our fruit, cereal and toast and marmalade. After the meal I went back to the office and remained there usually until about 2.30 p.m.

While I dealt with my files and interviewed my callers, Angela supervised Philip and Desmond doing their housework, gave Bonniface instructions regarding the day's meals, issued tins from the store, cooked some delicacies on her oil stove, did some gardening if fine or perhaps some dressmaking if wet, and wrote numerous letters. At lunch we compared notes. I told Angela about my doings in the office: the uncivil letter from a P.W.D. officer; the prisoner who had escaped; and the man the sergeant had brought before me charged with attempting to murder his own son. For her part Angela told me of the difficulties she had experienced in making our gardener, Vincent, understand what she wanted him to do in our small and pathetically unproductive kitchen-garden.

From about 3.00 p.m. to 4.30 p.m. we slept or read in our bedroom while a refreshing breeze, blowing straight into the house, made the curtains billow. After tea we strolled around the station, looked in at the African Staff Club, called at the Post Office, visited the Lutheran Hospital, or maybe drove somewhere to inspect a road, a bridge or school. We bathed at about 7.00 p.m. Sometimes before and sometimes both before and after dinner I had to wade through a stack of files which an office boy had brought across to the house earlier in the day. We always had our evening meal by the light of two pink-shaded candle lamps. After serving dinner Philip retired for the night, leaving Desmond to wash up and then to shut the house up. Angela and I read, wrote, chatted or listened to the wireless (usually Radio Brazzaville) before going to bed. Lying beneath our mosquito net we could see through the uncurtained windows of our room the silver streak of the Qua Iboe river glinting in the moonlight; and we could hear the rhythmic croaking of a host of frogs disporting themselves at the water's edge.

At teatime one afternoon a large figure in a flowing garment appeared at our house. With difficulty I identified this caller as my Senior Warder. He displayed some committal warrants and said with indignation that the visiting Magistrate had that day sent him two very bad men. He explained that he was anxious to get rid of these "habitual criminals" by transferring them to the large prison at Calabar, which was permissible as their sentences amounted to more than two years each. He was somewhat disappointed when I inspected the warrants and observed that as sundry sentences were to run concurrently they had in fact only eighteen months to serve. The Senior Warder smiled coaxingly at me.

"They be very wicked men, Sir," he said. "They no like to stay for bush prison. They want the amenities: electric light, radio and fresh fish when they catch sickness. They never get fresh fish in Eket. If they stay here I fear they go make plenty palaver in the prison."

I remained unmoved by the desire of the two men in question to enjoy the "amenities" of a civilised prison. I told the Senior Warder that I was not prepared to transfer them, and that he would have to ensure that they caused no trouble. He was rather crestfallen by my attitude and obviously thought it would have been wiser to give in to their wishes and to send them off to enjoy the relative luxury of life in H.M. Prison, Calabar.

One day I had to visit Eket County Council Headquarters to enquire into the dismissal of the Treasury cashier. A sheaf of typescript had been sent to me which explained the grounds of complaint against this young man and his rebuttal of them. I had found it interesting reading. In one place the Treasurer had written: "Mr. Inyang's conduct is intolerable in any decent society and for that reason he is no longer useful in the Treasury Department of your Council, if the progress of it is our principal aim". Elsewhere I read: "In fact his daily misconducts are numerous and only a volume of books to the size of a Bible can contain same if such were to have been written. This is no exaggeration but a living truth from the pen of a truthful man in my person . . . I shall be most grateful to you if I am freed of this pest."

Inyang I discovered was also able to express himself eloquently on paper. He wrote of the Treasurer: "He is fond of styling himself and that very proudly as one paid by the Council to become a Dictator"; and again: "Mr. Ubot, a vaunt, obscurant, funk, haughty human being who delights himself in the use of obscene and unchaste language against innocent and decent creatures of God, and who likes to boggle and bungle difficulties . . ."

I had previously given Inyang an opportunity of having his say; and on arrival at the County Council Headquarters I listened attentively to the Secretary's and the Treasurer's accounts of his behaviour, knowing that on returning to Eket I would be faced with the task of sending my comments and recommendations to the Permanent Secretary of the Ministry of Internal Affairs. After our discussion Mr. Isong, the Council Secretary, fortified me with a whisky and orange in his house. He also gave me some rose cuttings which I took home to Angela as a peace offering for not arriving for lunch until 3.30 p.m.

The time arrived for us to go on tour for the first time in our new Division. From 8.00 a.m. to 10.00 a.m. confusion reigned in the house. In between serving and clearing away breakfast Philip was busy gathering together and packing up camp beds, bedding, crockery, lamps, tins of food, water filter and so on and so forth. Desmond stood around looking bewildered. Bonniface, having packed up his kitchen things, lurked in the rear quarters; and Vincent and our tame prisoner did their best to keep discreetly out of sight. At 9.00 a.m. the Eket Rural District Council lorry arrived. Having backed as close to the rear of our house as possible, the crew of six disembarked and squatted in a row along the covered way leading to the kitchen. Sundry station labourers stood around waiting to place our loads on board.

I was in the office when the lorry finally left. A few minutes after its departure Angela saw two labourers return to the house. Apparently Philip had suddenly remembered that he had omitted to pack a milk jug, and he had stopped the lorry and despatched these two men to collect one. Angela was just in time to prevent Desmond from giving them a silver one. We left in our car a couple of hours later, taking Mr. Usip, the District Interpreter, with us.

On our way we came upon a Shell Company drilling lorry at work. We stopped for a few minutes to watch, and I was impressed by the deft manner in which the African operators handled the machinery. The lorry was jacked up off the ground; and at its rear there towered a contraption like a pile-driving frame. Down this frame the drill gradually sank into the ground. Having drilled to the depth of one length of pipe, another length was screwed on and drilling was resumed. It was encouraging to see these men, unsupervised by a European, working so efficiently and energetically.

We reached the Rest-House at Oron to find the lorry about to leave having only just delivered our Boys and belongings. It was raining hard, and I was glad to be able to drive the car straight onto the verandah of the house. The Headman, Mallam Labaren a Hausa, and two labourers, Alfred and Michael, were present. Mallam was a tall man, and in his turban and long white robes he looked an impressive figure; and I was soon to discover that he had a fairly lively sense of his own importance. The Rest-House was a huge building, quite twice as large as it need have been. Its whitewashed walls were clean and the roof of palm-leaf mats was in good condition. In the bathroom there was a huge concrete bath, which looked as though it might have been the brainchild of an Epstein or a Henry Moore. From the

126

verandah there was a good view of the Cross River. The compound contained a tangle of bushes, some scattered oil palms and a flagpole. Alfred and the numerous members of his family occupied an outhouse near the Boys' quarters.

During our stay in Oron I heard reviews in the Native Court and held a meeting of the Township Board. I prospected a site for a proposed cinema, and attended meetings of the Boards of Governors of two Methodist education establishments: the Oron Boys' High School and an Elementary Teacher Training College for girls. Fathers Flanagan and Hannigan invited us to supper one night at the Roman Catholic Mission, and fed us on some rather dubious mutton which had been hastily purchased from the local market.

On the morning when we were to leave Oron by launch for Jamestown near the mouth of the Cross River, Usip was greeted by an excited Mallam who told him that the District Clerk had just rung up from Eket to say that Usip's wife had decamped, taking a lot of his property with her. While Usip went to the Post Office to ring up the Police Sergeant in Eket, I parked my car in one of the Government garages near the waterside of which Mallam was the custodian. It was evident that the garage in question was being used by him or someone as a store for yams, bags of flour and other merchandise. However, sufficient space had been cleared to accommodate my car. While we waited to board the launch, a young man called Umoh, who was helping me with the arrangements for the Eket local Government elections, gave me a report about repairs to a number of ballot boxes which he had put in hand. A police constable from Lagos produced a juvenile delinquent, whom he was in the process of escorting back to his home in Eket Division. Reuben, a contractor who had undertaken to mend leaks in the roof of the Court, made excuses for having failed to do so, and Mallam informed me at length of the great repairs and improvements which he and his two labourers had recently undertaken at the Rest-House. I noticed that his own house boasted a new matting wall around it; and I was ungenerous enough to suspect that some of the mats intended for the repair of the Rest-House roof had been diverted. Usip returned fairly soon from his telephoning, not looking in any way despondent. He told me that it was not his wife who had left but his sister — an odd confusion of relationships!

A few minutes later we were all aboard the *Snipe* and were heading south for Jamestown. On arrival a couple of hours later we anchored off shore, and during our two days' stay we used the launch as our "Rest-House". From it we had a wonderful view across the wide estuary of the Cross River to Cameroon Mountain some eighty miles to the east, and to the north we could see the Oban hills in the far distance.

We went ashore by means of the dinghy, paddled by a member of the crew. On landing for the first time we were greeted by a dancer wearing a grass Ekpo costume who pranced around in what appeared to be a menacing manner. Evidently it was not intended to be so, however, because on finishing his capering he shook hands with both of us. Jamestown was a quiet, friendly little fishing settlement, and we much enjoyed our restful couple of days there. While I sat in Court, Angela spent some time in the little whitewashed dispensary building opposite.

One Saturday evening after our return home we had seven American Lutheran missionaries and my A.D.O., Robert, to supper. After eating we walked across the station to the African Club, where a "Ball" dance was being held. The large single room was lit by six Tilley lamps, which contributed appreciably to the heat already engendered by the press of bodies. A brass band was tucked away in a corner, and we were given seats behind a table laden with bottles situated close to it. The noise effectively drowned all attempts at conversation. A wide variety of garb was to be seen. The dress of the ladies varied from long pink satin evening gowns to short cotton frocks. Some wore brightly coloured head-ties, and some did not. There were men in tight suits, others in white dinner jackets and some in low-hanging spiv coats. One man wore long trousers which ended half way up his shins; and three wore navy blue berets. Essien, my office boy, was dressed in long trousers and native-style shirt. He had a thick pullover hoisted up around his neck and a slouch cap on his head. Mallam was present, looking very distinguished in his flowing Hausa robes. Usip had a permanent grin on his face and a foot-long pipe in his mouth. The dances were "High Lifes"; all sounded exactly the same, and it was immaterial whether one had a partner or not. I saw my District Clerk drunkenly pirouetting on his own in a corner; other men moved around the floor in various stances and positions suggestive of clutching invisible female forms. Dances lasted for half an hour at a stretch, and no sooner did one finally come to an end than the indefatigable band started up its rhythmic pounding once again. Our activities caused great interest to a large number of Eket's younger generation who thronged each window and applauded vigorously. One small boy with a white towel wound round his head, whom I saw peering in, made me think of Kim.

The first phase of the local election programme was concluded at the end of October. On the 31st of that month I informed Enugu by telegram that in all 55,000 persons had registered as electors. The next task was to produce six copies of the lists of voters. I engaged two or three extra typists for this purpose, and accommodated them in my own office in order to ensure that they wasted no time. Compilation of the six lists involved 10–11,000 sheets of typing paper.

I had a great many other things to think about, however, apart from local Government elections. Shell was increasing its oil exploration activities in the Division, and on November 1st I had a joint discussion with two representatives of the Company and the Secretary of Eket County Council about the use of roads. The heavy Shell vehicles very quickly ploughed up the County Council's earth roads and rendered them impassable to normal traffic. On my return from the County Council headquarters at Ikot Ubo, just beside a place where the main road degenerated into a particularly horrible patch of quag, I saw a Headman watching two of his labourers trimming grass on the sides of the road! I stopped and briefly told the Headman to attend to first things first. Partly because of the dreadful state of the road I did not reach home for lunch until 4.15 p.m. After a swift meal Angela and I went to the nearby Lutheran Hospital to meet the American Vice-Consul from Lagos, who was paying a brief visit. Later that evening on returning home we had a look at our Boys' quarters. Our purpose in doing so was partly to greet Bonniface's newly wed wife, to whom Angela gave a handbag, and partly to inspect the state of the rooms. All were neat, tidy and reasonably well equipped — except for Desmond's, which had nothing in it except a sleeping mat and a couple of broken ballot boxes. We gave him a chair and various bits and pieces which pleased him greatly.

A few days later great indignation was expressed by the Boys, who had been served with Tax and Rates demands. The minimum flat rate level of tax and rates amounted to £2. 3s. 6d., which in the case of Desmond represented more than one month's wages.

On our way to Ikot Ubo to prepare ballot boxes for the Eket County Council elections we witnessed the end of an Emergence from Fattening Chamber ceremony. The ceremony took place in a playground and a great number were present, women being dressed in all their finery. Those who had just come out from Fattening wore heavy bangles on their legs and had reddish-orange powder on their faces and were scantily clad in gaily coloured cloths and head-ties. These ceremonies were usually shared by about twenty girls and included dancing and the presentation of gifts to parents and Chiefs. After the ceremony, provided all customary marriage formalities had been observed, the nearly naked girls were borne at a trot shoulder high by groups of catcalling naked men through the bush to their husbands. The men were naked because of the exercise involved in carting the well-built maidens for distances up to six or seven miles. Having been delivered to the husband he was at liberty to do what he liked with his bride. However, so Umoh my informant told me, he had often by that time drunk so much that he was incapable of doing anything for two or three nights. Depending upon the wealth of her parents a girl might remain in the Fattening Chamber for as long as three years, during which time she did nothing but eat, sleep and wash. The purpose of this incarceration was to increase the girl's physical charms, fat women being much admired by men. It was also thought that a fat woman was better able to bear childbirth than a thin one. The amount of dowry paid for a girl from a Fattening Chamber varied between £40 and £50.

A week or two later a few miles from Oron I passed a girl from a Fattening Chamber on her way to her husband. She was being carried on the shoulders of a young man, who was sweating profusely under the strain. Her body was partially covered with a few silk scarves. Her back was bare; and her face, arms and legs were covered with the same sort of powder as I had previously seen. On her head she wore an elaborate, brightly coloured, cone-shaped head-dress in the tip of which was stuck an electric light bulb. I felt the effect would have been complete if this had intermittently flashed on and off! The pair were accompanied by a small cortège of children and two or three young men whose duty it was to take turns in carrying the burden of beauty.

On November 11th, the eve of County Council Election day, I had a spate of visitors. These included Bishop Jackson of Liberia, a Mr. Lightbody who was concerned with Pioneer Oil Mills for the processing of palm oil, our local U.A.C. Manager, two senior employees of Shell, and a Mr. and Mrs. Smith. This couple arrived at Eket on a pole-propelled barge, which was followed by a second barge similarly manoeuvred. Mr. Smith, we discovered, was a Marine Department Officer and was at that time employed as a "Snagger". For six continuous months during the drier part of the year his job was systematically to tour navigable coastal creeks and to dispose of all snags, e.g. fallen down trees, which he came across. His usual way of getting rid of a snag was to blow it up. This method was expeditious, and it also ensured that neither he, Mrs. Smith nor his accompanying staff ever lacked for fresh fish.

During the day I received a complaint that the Secretary of one of the District Councils to suit his own purposes had shifted the registration of certain voters from one ward in his area to another. If there were truth in this allegation I feared that trouble was likely to result. At 7.30 p.m. one of my assistants came to report that three of his six Presiding Officers had failed to turn up to collect their equipment for the following day's Election. I refreshed him with a bottle of beer, and sent him off to recruit three more.

I was up by 6.45 a.m. the next day in order to interview, briefly instruct and formally appoint the three replacement Presiding Officers produced by Inyang. As I had anticipated the day proved to be a very gruelling one. At 7.30 a.m., accompanied by Angela, Usip and two Constables I set off in a police Landrover to inspect polling in as many polling stations as I had time to visit. Going towards one of them I was taken aback to see the Presiding Officer, followed by the P.C. attached to him for the day, cycling hell for leather in the direction of Eket. I stopped them and was told that rioting had broken out at their station. I took them on board and drove quickly to the school in which the polling station in question was located. On arrival I found the classroom building invaded by hundreds of milling men and women (in their Sunday best) and one man stabbed. The only way of getting rid of the mob was to lash out with batons; and after about twenty minutes with the help of two or three polling staff, three constables and Usip I succeeded in clearing the place. We barricaded all but one door, and voting was then resumed, voters' lists, ballot papers, etc., having miraculously survived the free-for-all.

In half of the polling stations I visited during the day confusion reigned to a greater or lesser extent. I had not been able to obtain any police reinforcements for the occasion; and it caused me no surprise that Presiding Officers with the support of only a single constable and a couple of Court Messengers were unable to maintain order. In one polling station I found two rival Presiding Officers, each claiming to be the properly appointed one! At another one I found the candidates' agents, in complete disregard of the instructions given regarding the absolute need for voting to be carried out secretly, comfortably ensconced in armchairs inside the polling booth in full view of the ballot boxes! Elsewhere I saw half a dozen or more voters clutching their ballot papers all inside the polling booth at the same time. I saw ballot papers left on tops of boxes or dropped onto the floor of booths; and in some cases registration receipts were placed inside the boxes instead of ballot papers. There were roll calls of voters outside polling stations; and children were sent into vote and were given ballot papers. I dreaded to think how many infringements of electoral regulations must have taken place during the course of the day. I did what I could to remedy all the malpractices which came to my notice; but as I could only be in one place at a time I could not do much to control the proceedings.

We returned home at 4.30 p.m. for a breather. No sooner had we seated ourselves than we were visited by a blustering gentleman, who called himself Prince Issong, and who complained about discrimination on the part of polling staff at the station to which he had gone to vote.

"I have lived in U.S.A. for twenty years and in U.K. for ten," he said, "and I never saw such a thing there."

He parted with a promise that he would file an election petition.

Counting of votes began in the Magistrate's Court in Eket at 6.00 p.m. In response to popular demand this was done by Angela, my A.D.O. Robert and myself. The last of the boxes brought to this centre arrived at 9.00 p.m., and we completed counting by the light of three Tilley lamps at 10.00 p.m. We then drove thirty miles to the other collection centre at Oyubia. We began counting soon after midnight, finished at 3.00 a.m., and were in bed by 5.30 a.m.

Two weeks later we were back in Oyubia, organising the Oyubia-Oron Rural District Council elections. These passed off reasonably satisfactorily, except that one Presiding Officer ran out of ballot papers. This was surprising in view of the fact that he had been issued with slightly more ballot papers than there were registered voters!

Shortly before Election day a very bold robbery had taken place at Oyubia. A gang of thieves arrived on a lorry at 1.00 a.m. They remained for two hours during which they blew open six safes belonging to the District Council. They successfully intimidated everyone living in the neighbourhood by randomly discharging their firearms from time to time. It seemed that no attempt had been made either to hamper or to identify them in any way; and they had vanished into the night with a haul of £1,100.

During our stay at Oyubia I disposed of a land case which had been dragging on for six years. It concerned a piece of swamp to which the villages of Isa and Eweme both laid claim. The dispute arose in 1949, and the first hearing of the case ended in 1951. On appeal a re-hearing was ordered, and this lasted from July 1952 until February 1955! It seemed to me that it was high time that the issue was settled. Accompanied by a sizeable group of people, which included parties to the case, witnesses, hangers-on and Court Messengers, I walked to the swamp — following a convenient Shell seismic exploration line — and then as far as it was possible to do so I circled the disputed area. On returning to Isa village we all sat down in someone's compound thereby putting to flight a number of dwarf cattle which were ruminating within it at the time of our arrival. Fortified with a swig from a fresh coconut, I then proceeded to write my judgment. I pronounced in favour of Isa; and as we left we heard the local inhabitants rejoicing.

We attended Sports Day at the Salvation Army School in Akai, where we were introduced to a great number of Captains and Majors, male and female, and to a visiting Brigadier from Lagos. Major Squibb, the local commander (who came from Newfoundland but found Eket sufficiently cold during the rainy season to make it necessary for him to wear ankle-length woollen pants!), shewed me a recently completed dormitory block, built of fourteen parts mud to one part cement. Later I met Mr. Akpan, one of Eket's two House of Assembly members. He took much pride in this school, the establishment of which was due in part to the encouragement he had given.

My mother-in-law sent us a cutting from *The Times* which read as follows: "The marriage took place on October 8th at St. James's, Piccadilly, between Mr. Sunday Prince Akpabio, son of Chief Prince Akpabio of Eket, Calabar, Nigeria, and Miss Thelma Ann Hopwood of London. Mr. and Mrs. Akpabio have just returned from the French Riviera, where they have been spending their honeymoon." I was interested to make the acquaintance of Chief Akpabio a day or two later. He was a dignified old man, and was dressed in traditional manner in a lapper of cloth and a flannel nightgown-like garment. On his head he had a somewhat battered sun helmet. He was on his way barefooted to the Lutheran Hospital, and suspended by a string from his wrist he carried an empty bottle. He called in at the District Office as he was passing, and I had a short chat with him. He told me that his son was studying medicine and that he had supported him in England for the past seven years. He said that he was pleased he had married a white woman, because it was his father who had first welcomed the white man to the Mkpok area of Eket.

One Sunday at the beginning of December when there was a touch of Harmattan in the air we went to the seaside with Robert and Eric, Dorothy and Beatrice from the Lutheran Hospital. We drove seven or eight miles to Ibeno at the mouth of the Qua Iboe river, and parked our cars in the Rest-House compound. A canoe was waiting for us on the foreshore in front of the Rest-House. In boarding this Dorothy had the misfortune to put her foot into a lump of human excreta, the local people being regrettably casual in matters of hygiene and sanitation. Thanks to a strongly ebbing tide it took only half an hour to reach the long sandy beach fronting onto the open sea. On our way to it we passed Big Town and saw the large two-storey Qua Iboe Mission house built in the days of the founder, Samuel Bill. Next to the house there was a fine Church with a lofty spire painted white. This served as a useful leading mark for the *Joseph Flint* and other small coasters when crossing the bar of the river on their way up to Eket. The spire was topped with a weathercock, the first I had seen in Nigeria, and it also boasted a clock which shewed the right time and chimed every quarter of an hour.

The sand was firm and white and untrodden. Behind the sand there was a tangle of low bushes and grass, and behind that the forest reared thick and high. From time to time bicyclists passed by with loads of dried fish. They came from fishing villages further along the coast and were bound for inland markets. The sea was calm and warm; the sun shone and a gentle breeze blew all day.

At the end of the Christmas term Angela and I were invited to the Eket Government School. The Headmaster introduced us to the assembled staff and pupils, and the infants sang a song of welcome. I was then asked to read out the end of term class orders. To begin with the children clapped everyone irrespective of whether

133

their position was first or thirtieth; but as time went on their enthusiasm for applauding waned. Angela presented the prizes to the Captains of the three best Houses: a stack of paper exercise books for the first, a boxful of pencils for the second, and a packet of cabin biscuits for the third. Miss Eyo, one of the teachers, thanked Angela for coming and handed her a table-cloth embroidered by some of her girls. After various further expressions of thanks the Vacation song was sung lustily and the ceremony came to an end. We inspected handiwork displayed in the domestic science classroom, signed the Visitors' Book and then left.

My assistance was required by Shell in connection with the conclusion of a lease of a certain area in the Western part of the Division. I travelled by canoe, then on the carrier of a bicycle and then seated on a camp chair in the back of a kit-car to the drilling site at Ikot Eko Ibon. Accompanied by a representative of the Company I went to the nearby village hall, where sundry Chiefs and others had already gathered. After much talk they finally agreed to sign the lease documents. We then returned to the drilling camp, and I had a wash in one of the staff caravans. These were air-conditioned and were equipped with electricity, running water and W.C.s. We lunched, and then had a look at the towering rig. Drilling had reached a depth of 6,000 feet. I was shewn some worn-out bits; and it was explained that whenever a bit needed changing the whole issue had to be pulled up, dismantled and re-assembled. Next we drove to a nearby school compound where a small helicopter was parked. I was given a trip in this; and then the Company's representative at the village discussion took my place, and the machine headed back to Shell headquarters at Owerri.

Visits to the various Council Treasuries had revealed that local Government finances were in a parlous state. Further insight into them, gathered as time went on, confirmed all too forcibly my first impressions. One day I held a meeting with the Finance Committee of the Ubium Rural District Council for the purpose of discussing the 1956–1957 draft Estimates. When I arrived three Councillors were present, and after half an hour two more appeared. This was considered sufficient to make a quorum and we got down to business. As drafted the Estimates, instead of observing the requirement that revenue should exceed expenditure by at least five per cent, revealed an appreciable excess of expenditure over income. To comply with the Ministry's instructions the Council ought, I calculated, to end the financial year with a reserve of about £3,500; but it became apparent that it would be fortunate if it were to have a reserve of as much as £1. In the current 1955/1956 Estimates provision had been made for the levying of an eight-shilling General Rate. However, without authority the Council had arbitrarily reduced this to three shillings and the Council's revenue was destined therefore to be considerably less than had been envisaged. Its financial position was even worse than it would have been because not only had this cut been made, but in addition the Council had made little effort to collect its dues. I discovered that less than twenty-five per cent of taxpayers had paid their tax and rates demands! And when I checked the books I found that the Council was insolvent. It had cash assets of only £500 and its liabilities exceeded £3,500. Not a wit daunted by this state of affairs the Council had nevertheless provided in the coming year's Estimates for an increase of 100 per cent in the rate of remuneration to be paid to Councillors and for a fifty per cent increase in the Chairman's allowance. There were also various other items of increased expenditure. No increase in the level of tax or rates was, however, proposed to meet the cost of the heavier commitments; and when I enquired how it was intended to balance the budget the Councillors merely broke into childish tittering. It proved to be one of my more abortive mornings.

Elections in the various Rural District Council areas were held at weekly intervals, always on Saturdays. When it was the turn of the Council situated on the western side of the Qua Iboe river we were handicapped by the difficulty of road access. Although the Council Headquarters was only a few miles from Eket as the crow flew, to drive to it by road involved a journey of forty to fifty miles. On the day of the election we travelled by the direct route, which necessitated beginning with a canoe trip. On board in addition to Usip we had his motorcycle; and on arrival at Ikot Ebidang Usip first ferried Angela on his pillion to the Council Headquarters at Abat and then returned for me. Angela remained at Abat while Usip and I visited various polling stations. Considering the load it had to support his small machine managed admirably, and I was impressed by the way in which Usip was able to operate it without the use of a clutch, the cable being broken. We returned to Abat to eat our picnic lunch. However, before doing this, the Council offices lacking certain necessary facilities, Angela decided to walk down the road a little way and I accompanied her. At the very moment that she entered a leafy cassava plot the one and only vehicle of the day bowled along the road, came to a stop where I was standing, and two oil drillers got out and greeted me.

Counting of votes, carried out as usual by Angela, Robert and myself, began at 5.00 p.m. in the Native Court. We found that supporters of two of the candidates had made considerable use of forged ballot papers. These were of such a poor standard, however, that they were readily distinguishable. The paper was of a different texture; the size did not correspond; the perforated edge was not in the right place; and for the most part they all bore the same number.

At the end of the count Chief Imo kindly provided his ancient lorry and the services of a driver to take us to Ikot Ebidang where our canoe was waiting. It was a dark night, and the lorry, which left a merry trail of sparks in its wake, had no lights. Nothing daunted the driver kept his foot hard down; and it was a relief a short while later to find ourselves being gently paddled up the river to Eket by the light of a thin crescent moon.

Our series of elections came to an end shortly before Christmas much to the relief of Angela, Robert and myself. On December 23rd we gave a party in our house, which Angela had decorated with pieces of casuarina and numerous candles, to various members of the Government staff in Eket: the District Clerk, Usip, the Postmaster, the local Government assistants, who had helped with the elections, and others. We played competitive games like guessing advertisements, working out jumbled Nigerian place names and identifying objects by touch. These they seemed to enjoy; and musical parcel and a whispering game caused much hilarity. At about 10.15 p.m. things suddenly took a formal turn. Mr. Orjih, one of my local Government assistants, called upon Mr. Ikpe, the Secretary of the Eket Rural District Council, to give a vote of thanks. This he did very nicely, saying that none of them had been to a party of that kind before and that the occasion had been an "important" one which they would remember all their lives.

Friends arrived on the 24th to spend Christmas with us. On Christmas Day we listened to a recorded programme of the King's College Carol Service, and the "Round-the-world Greetings" programme which was followed by the Queen's speech. If I remember aright in the Round-the-world programme we heard the noise of stars in collision 200 million years earlier and also sounds from 12,000 feet below the surface of the sea. The Queen made a gracious reference to her impending visit to Nigeria. During the day, having received a report from the Eket Dispensary Attendant that one of the inmates of the prison was suffering from a strangulated hernia, I went round to the Lutheran Hospital and my good friend Eric readily agreed to admit him and to do the necessary. In the evening Robert and a friend, Tony, who was staying with him, joined us for Christmas Dinner. In the course of the meal many toasts were drunk, but the one which met with most acclaim was undoubtedly that to Mr. Gorsuch, the author of the recent Government Salaries' Revision Report! On Boxing Day we joined up with our American neighbours and drove down to Ibeno in the Lutheran Hospital Chevrolet. On our arrival we met a party of eight or nine Salvation Army missionaries embarking in a canoe in order to be ferried to the beach. Our party of nine embarked in another and we travelled in convoy. On reaching the seashore we were surprised to see in the distance a flock of great white birds, but the sun and the sand were so bright that we were unable to identify them. However, on approaching more closely we discovered that the "birds" were in fact a dozen white-clad Nuns who were paddling in the sea.

Our friends left us on the 27th, and I spent the last few days of the year writing the Divisional Annual Report and also a report on the recently concluded County Council and Rural District Council elections. The Harmattan was blowing hard and on the morning of the 30th the temperature in our house was down to an all time low of 68 °F. On that day amongst the official mail I received a letter which ran: "Find enclosed for your information copies of telegrams forwarded to irrelevant authorities . . ."! The "irrelevant authorities" appeared to be the Governor General, the Governor of the Eastern Region, the Minister of Lands Enugu, the Resident Calabar, and the Manager of "Pamol" Calabar. Each of these gentlemen had been sent a telegram which read somewhat obscurely as follows —

"PAMOL RUBBER PLANTATION EKET CAUSED TROUBLE LAND LORDS UNWHOLLY DECLARED PROBE SURRENDERING ISSUE PROTEST FOLLOWS

ODUOK ESHETT INYANG OTHERS"

On December 31st we drove from Eket to Oron and on the way passed two Fattening Chamber ladies. In addition to the usual coloured scarves, gay headdress and orange powder they carried curious walking sticks each ornamented with a fringe of brightly coloured raffia about six inches long halfway down the shaft. It was market day at Oruko, and many sinister looking Ekpo dancers were out and about. Their bodies were blackened, and they wore huge black masks topped with hair of grass which stretched to their waists. Some were able to raise and lower the bottom jaws of their snout-like mouths. Two of them had ropes tied to their legs, and were led along by attendants as if they were performing bears. I took photos of a couple who posed for me, and then placed coins in two greasy fists, which were stuck through the window of the car.

We travelled by ferry from Oron to Calabar, where that night we saw the new year in at the Club. Driving through Oron we found the main road littered with glass from countless broken bottles, unwelcome evidence of an over-hearty Christmas. It still had its carpeting of glass when we passed through on our way back to Eket on January 2nd.

Chapter 13

"And I will not accept any bribe"

Vincent, our gardener, returned from leave in his home town somewhat crestfallen because he had failed to bring back a wife with him. "Marriage business no good," he told us. However, he had found a girl who "appreciated" him; he had paid a £20 dowry deposit for her and intended to pay the balance of £10 by instalments over the next six months.

We drove to Port Harcourt, 120 miles away, taking our small-boy, Desmond, with us. He was rather apprehensive at being taken to this city, but cheered up when he saw the market. I stopped the car, and he disappeared for a few minutes and returned the proud possessor of a pink singlet.

Early in the new year I forwarded to Enugu the draft Estimates for 1956–1957 of the County Council and the four Rural District Councils. Apart from normal duties I was busy hearing tax appeals and making arrangements for Eket Division's participation in the forthcoming Royal visit to Calabar. I held a meeting in the Rest House at Oron at which agreement was reached regarding the hundred school-children and ten teachers to go from Eket for the occasion. While at Oron I also dealt with tax appeals. The appellants wore their most tattered garments and indulged in much coughing, spitting and blowing of nose through forefinger and thumb. A great many displayed hernias, and I saw one the size of a rugger ball. Some suffered from elephantiasis; some were blind; and many had ulcers or "cough" (i.e. T.B.). I noticed that many names had been removed from the tax rolls because of individuals having died or gone to Fernando Poo. While staying at Oron, Robert rang me up from the District Office to report on a clash between certain villages in Opobo Division and some in Eket over a land dispute. Four hundred men were involved and attempts by the police to arrest ringleaders had been resisted. I told him to go to the area the following day and sort things out. We had a minor domestic disaster to deal with in Oron. We awoke one morning to find that the kitchen had been burgled. Sundry saucepans, kettles, other utensils and food supplies had been taken together with Philip and Bonniface's cooking pots and chop, which had been stowed in a couple of ballot boxes. Mallam believed the caretaker of a neighbouring house to be the thief. "Hungry worry him too much," he said, and explained that this poor fellow had visited the Rest-House the previous day with a request that he be allowed to pick a pawpaw in order to stave off his pangs. However, a visit to his quarters by Mallam and a police constable brought nothing to light.

From Oron we went to Jamestown, travelling on the *Snipe*. As we approached our destination we passed clouds of butterflies flying over the translucent water. It was a lovely evening. The shore was lightly swathed in a Harmattan haze; blue smoke circled upwards from the rooves of huts; the sun, a golden globe, sank down behind the palm trees; and wafted by the light breeze canoes with tattered sails went slipping past.

Next morning while seated in Court I saw a party of women dancers with hoop skirts, raffia headdresses and orange-powdered faces pass along the road, accompanied by a man in masquerade dress. The carving on his head resembled a crocodile, and its jaws could be made to open and shut. Some attendant children carried a banner and a cloth awning. I was told that they were on their way to an island to "play". On leaving the Court at 2.00 p.m. and returning to the *Snipe* I saw them seated in a canoe at the waterside. After some lunch I went ashore again and was taken by Usip on his motorcycle to Ukontigha Creek, where the local inhabitants were engaged on a community development project of building an embankment through the swamp. On our return journey a man on foot coming towards us threw his hat onto the road as a sign of begging to be allowed to speak, so we stopped, and he proceeded to make a lengthy complaint about one of the Jamestown Court members. We were in the forest, and in a moment tsetse flies were feasting on us. We had to walk the last part of the journey home because the motorcycle suddenly "quenched".

Back at Eket I rose one morning at 6.00 a.m. while it was still dark. Half an hour later I walked down to the Government Beach and found Usip and his motorcycle already in a canoe. I climbed on board and was followed by Mr. Ikpe, Secretary of the Eket Rural District Council. Half a dozen chanting paddlers propelled us rapidly up-river to Okat. We made our way through an old abandoned rubber plantation, and after a mile or two we reached the junction with the new "community development" road which the people of Mkpok Clan had recently begun to build. This new road was intended to reach a point on the west bank of the Qua Iboe river opposite the U.A.C. "factory" at Eket. We cycled one and a half miles along a track cleared through cassava farms. Then *terra firma* came to an end, and we found ourselves in thick bush standing in swampy ooze. Many villagers were at work felling trees and preparing the foundations for a roadway. We inspected the rest of the route as far as the river's edge. For the first mile we made our way along tree trunks which had been laid lengthways to mark the edge of the "road". For the second mile the the route was largely uncleared, and we had to wade and claw our way through muddy ooze and tangled roots. On our return journey we saw many more people at work. The men had been joined by their womenfolk, who, armed with pangas, were hacking away at branches and undergrowth. I was greeted effusively by all, who were no doubt hopeful that as a result of my inspection I would help them by providing tools, cement, and culvert rings.

We reached the parked motorcycle at 9.40 a.m., and Usip drove the two of us to the Qua Iboe Mission School and partially completed Teacher Training College at Ndon Eyo. I cleaned myself on the verandah of the Headmaster's house, first standing in one basin of water and then in another while washing the mud off my canvas shoes in the first. I felt like abandoning my repellent stockings, but the Headmaster's wife very kindly rinsed them out for me. I sat in the Headmaster's little study for a few minutes and was interested to see that among his books there were copies of *She, Pickwick Papers, The World that Works* and *Vanity Fair.* I was then taken to one of the upstairs rooms in the T.T.C. block for breakfast, and we sat round a table covered with American cloth. The room was clean and airy, and we had a good view across the surrounding bush. We were provided with egg sandwiches and coffee, and there was beer or Scotch for those who wanted it. After eating, Usip and I went to the nearby District Council headquarters at Abat, where I first swore in the newly elected Councillors (the oath ended with the words: ". . . and I will not accept any bride, or any unlawful recompense, reward or benefit whatsoever — so help me God"), and then heard tax appeals in the course of which I again had to look at a terrifying selection of hernias and other disabilities. The worst sight was an unfortunate young man, whose skin on his back, chest and arms was all puffed up into one enormous blister.

During the morning of February 7th I supervised the transportation of school-children from Eket to Oron and their departure by ferry for Calabar, and Angela and I left on the *Snipe* in the afternoon. On arrival we were taken to the District Officer's house, which was originally the old Consulate — a large two-storeyed timber house with spacious verandahs upstairs. We were accommodated in the wing said to be haunted by Roger Casement.

We were meant to be in our places at the Rally Ground the following day by 8.00 a.m., but at that time I was stranded on the Royal Route in a colleague's car which I could not get to go. Some constables pushed the car into the compound of a nearby police station; and Angela, a friend and I walked from there to the Ground. It was a hot sticky morning, and by the time we arrived we were in a pretty moist state. We took our seats in an enclosure close to the royal stand; and there followed a long, hot wait in the sun.

Immediately in front of us were seated the Natural Rulers and County Council Chairmen who were to be presented. The former were clad in a variety of exotic garments. One Chief wore ankle-length golden robes; another wore leopard skins on top of a red toga. All had something on their heads. One of them had a woollen cap through which a mass of twigs, twelve inches or so long, had been stuck, the effect being like an untidy bird's nest. The cap of another was adorned with cowry shells; and the brim of another was studded with leopards' teeth. One Chief was distinguished by a crown. Another one, dressed in colourful robes, wore a black top hat. They all sported long silver-topped maces. A spectator seated near me was wearing a red striped blazer, and a single peacock's feather sprouted from his trilby hat.

In the centre of the playing field, which served as the Rally Ground, hundreds of schoolchildren, Girl Guides and Boy Scouts were massed; and around the perimeter there were a number of enclosures for the general public. At about 9.00 a.m. the Press arrived and occupied a nearby stand. While we waited for the royal visitors we enjoyed a preview of the entertainment to which they were to be treated. Ntimi women dancers, brilliantly attired, danced their slow rhythmical dance. Afterwards Abak puppets danced and pirouetted above the top of a sort of Punch-and-Judy stand to the music of a drum band; and then two live "puppets" were hoisted by ropes to a height of about twenty feet above the ground. They twirled round and round, wriggled their arms in time with the drumming and were finally lowered at speed in an obviously erotic embrace. Similar performances were repeated at intervals. I later learned that the play performed by the Abak puppets had a juju association, it being believed that a pregnant woman who might happen to see it would herself give birth to something like a puppet.

From where we were seated we saw the royal plane coming in to land. After their arrival at the Airport the Queen and the Duke drove through the town to the little cemetery on Mission Hill, where the Queen laid a wreath on the grave of Mary Slessor, the famous Church of Scotland missionary. A visit to the Residency for light refreshment followed. At about 10.45 a.m. our patience was rewarded, and the Royal Couple arrived inside the Rally Ground standing up in a specially prepared

Landrover. The children cheered and waved their flags; the Landrover drove one and a half times around the field and came to a halt in front of the royal stand; the Queen and Duke mounted the dais, and a bouquet was presented by a small girl called Stella Inyang. A Loyal Address was read by a local notable, and the Queen replied briefly. There followed presentations (District Officers not included); then the puppet display, and then the Ntimi dancers. It was all over by 11.15 a.m., and a little later the Queen and Duke were again airborne and on their way to Port Harcourt.

In the evening there was a cocktail party in the garden of the District Officer's house, while down by the river's edge Mr. Brock in person fired off £500 worth of rockets. The day ended for us with dance at the Calabar Club.

The following Saturday we held at Eket our local Divisional celebration in honour of the Queen's visit. In the early hours of the morning I was awakened by the sound of people singing in canoes, and at 6.00 a.m. drumming started up on the golf course close to our house. It continued more or less continuously for the ensuing twelve hours. Different clans sent their own drummers and dancing groups. Activity proper was not scheduled to begin until the afternoon; and after lunch I donned my white uniform and Eric's white buckskin shoes, worn by him when operating, which I had borrowed for the occasion. Angela wore a white broderie anglaise dress and looked lovely. At 2.30 p.m. we drove to the Magistrate's Court. On our arrival the Union Jack was broken, and Williway's orchestra, especially brought from Calabar for the festivities, played the National Anthem. After this, accompanied by Angela, I inspected a troop of Scouts, and then we toured the golf course looking at the various drumming and dancing groups in turn.

The team from Awa, which had been the first to arrive, was the most impressive. One of the dancers was apparently a giant — in fact it was a man, completely concealed beneath draperies, with a masked child balanced on top of his head. Another group had a masked dancer on stilts, who unfortunately lost his balance and fell headlong. In this group all the dancers were men or youths. They were festooned with bright silk handkerchiefs and scarves, and carried a variety of odd articles such as combs, mirrors and electric torches. Some had whistles in their mouths, which they blew shrilly as they pranced about. One of the groups had only a single dancer, a man dressed in a bright hooped skirt which made him look rather like a woman. On his head he wore a sort of grey woollen stocking, attached to which was a curious and brightly coloured headdress made of wicker, tassles and feathers. This contraption kept flopping over, and two attendants were constantly tugging at it to get it straight. Another group consisted entirely of women, who circled round and round in a crouching position waggling their bottoms. A male team from Oron, which included the Chairman and the Secretary of the District Council, did a rather inspired dance which was enlivened by the participation of an Ekpo man. He was a freakish sight, being dressed from head to toe in a clinging black knitted garment. Except for his hands and feet there was not an inch of flesh visible. Around his neck he wore a huge ruff of brown raffia and on his head a wide-brimmed straw hat. Dangling somewhat like an elephant's trunk from the wool covering his face was a length of red raffia, and suspended above his backside by a white cloth there was a handbell. The clapper of this he held with one hand, in which he also clutched a bundle of leaves, and from time to time he clanked the bell as he capered around. With his other hand he flourished a long wicked-looking whip.

After making the round of the dancers we went to the African Club which was already packed with people. I made a brief speech, and half a dozen Chiefs from different parts of the Division were formally presented. After this bottles and glasses were produced, and various toasts were drunk.

We gave tea to a number of people in our house; and soon after 5.00 p.m. Angela kicked off at a football match at the Government School. At half time we adjourned to the African Club tennis court and I joined in a game. The day ended with a Ball-dance; and as we lay in bed we could hear Williway's orchestra beating out the ceaseless Highlife rhythm.

Aba, about eighty miles by road from Eket, was the nearest place where I could get my car serviced. Thither we drove one Saturday, leaving at 5.30 a.m. and arriving at 8.00 a.m. While the car was being attended to we did some shopping. We had been told that one could buy fresh vegetables from Jos at the Aggrey Hotel. This was a two-storey structure situated beside the main road and within a stone's throw of the market. Humanity in the shape of motor repairers, bicycle repairers, truck pushers, hawkers and the inevitable swarms of children seethed around it. We went up an outside flight of concrete steps and entered a small room which contained potatoes lying in heaps upon the floor and cabbages, carrots, leeks and other vegetables on some shelves. We bought an assortment, and on leaving our salesman gave me a card on one side of which I was amused to read "For quiet lodging and friendly hospitality come to Aggrey Hotel . . ." and on the other an advertisement for the sale of various vegetables including: "Cauliflwers, leecks, beetoots and lettiuces".

On leaving Aba we drove to Owerri where we spent the night in the V.I.P. Rest-House in the large Shell D'Arcy base camp. I played a game of squash. After dining out of doors we listened to bawdy French records and then went to the Camp Club, where we sat on padded chromium-plated stools beside a lengthy bar and danced on a polished wooden floor.

It was down to earth again the following week with a visit by the Resident, an Inquest (at a recent feast eighteen persons had been taken sick and two had died; poisoning was suspected) and an inspection of the County Council Treasury. For the latter the two Councillors who were keyholders of the strongroom were in attendance. When the appropriate moment arrived each produced his key and unlocked a lock in the strongroom door; then the Treasurer produced the key held by him and unlocked the remaining lock. With difficulty he swung open the massive iron door, and we entered the Council's treasure trove. The entire place was completely bare except for a single small bundle on one of the shelves. This contained two £5 notes and eight ten-shilling notes — £14 in all! The Council's financial position was even more precarious than I had imagined.

A colleague from Enugu visited us in order to see the community development work which the people of Mkpok were undertaking. We crossed by canoe to the end of the new "road" opposite the U.A.C. factory. We then floundered along the route of the road, and I was interested to see that considerable progress had been made since my inspection three weeks earlier. On emerging from the mire onto dry land after a two-mile walk we were greeted by a Mr. Ninedays, a native of Mkpok. He asked us to line up, and then took a photograph of the mud-stained band with an expensive camera mounted on a tripod. Mr. Ninedays was evidently a man of substance, because parked nearby he had a Vauxhall car in which he kindly drove us for the remainder of our journeyings.

We looked at the site of the Mkpok-Awa bridge and the gaunt pile-driver which had stood there unused for the past twelve months because of funds having run out. Then we visited the unopened Mkpok Maternity Home, after which we drove to the still uncompleted Teacher Training College. Once again I found myself seated in one of the upstairs rooms; and on this occasion we were regaled with beer, whisky, coffee, cornbeef sandwiches, rice and chicken stewed in palm oil. After the meal a few speeches followed, and Prince Akpabio, the Chief of Mkpok, shook hands with us as we left. We returned to Eket by canoe from Ikot Ebidang where we saw Chief Imo's men hard at work on their rival road.

The pressure of work in the District Office was always unremitting, and virtually every day Essien carted stacks of files across to the house for me to deal with at my leisure in the evening. One morning I started by interviewing would-be recruits for the Army. Then I heard charges against a number of Tax and Rates defaulters who had been arrested in different parts of the Division and brought to Eket. Thereafter I was visited in succession by two Apostolic missionaries, a German engineer who

144

was building an oil mill, Eric from the Lutheran Hospital, the Eket Court clerk, the new Senior Warder, the Police Sergeant and many others. During the morning a report arrived from the Secretary of the Ubium Rural District Council that in a village in his area some of the local inhabitants had prevented Court Messengers from arresting a defaulting tax collector. In the afternoon therefore I took a Corporal and two constables in my car to arrest the five ringleaders.

The time arrived to go off on tour once again, on this occasion to the area on the western side of the Qua Iboe river. After we had packed up and I had attended to a few files, Angela and I prepared to set off down the grassy slope in front of our house to the Government beach, station labourers having already carried our loads down to the waterside. Just as we were about to leave, a little boy aged about ten, wearing a white shirt outside his shorts and clutching an old cap, came up to where we were standing. He had a "complaint" to make, and the Headman of a P.W.D. termite gang who was nearby kindly interpreted. The boy said that his father and brothers did not care for him, and that they did not feed him because they wanted him to die. However, he did not wish to die, so he had got a lift on someone's bicycle in order to come and see me. The child certainly looked as though he were just out of Belsen. It was a bad moment, however, for attempting to plan his future, so I gave him some money for food and told Desmond to look after him until our return.

Angela and I and the loads travelled in one canoe, and Usip, Philip and Bonniface followed in another. On our way down river we passed close to the *Joseph Flint* (313 tons) moored at the G.B. Ollivant's Wharf, which was taking on drums of palm oil and bags of palm kernels. Having disembarked at Ikot Ebidang, considerable confusion reigned for at least twenty minutes.. A gang of road labourers was present to act as carriers, but the Headman appeared quite powerless to control them. All wanted to find the smallest possible load to carry. The situation was not helped by the many interested onlookers who kept getting in the light, and by the steady stream of persons making their way along the road to the canoes at the river's edge, amongst them women with towering stacks of earthenware pots balanced on their heads bound for market. Finally the carriers started off, escorted by Philip and Bonniface. Angela and I seated ourselves on the carriers of two bicycles, and after a half-hour's ride we were delivered at the Teacher Training College, where we were given the use of a long, airy and completely empty upstairs room. After a time carriers began to arrive with our belongings.

I cycled to the nearby District Council headquarters where I spent the next three hours checking the cash and accounts, as a result of which I discovered that the Council was as insolvent as I had feared it would be. I cycled back to the T.T.C. for lunch which we finished at 3.45 p.m. I drafted a report on my Treasury inspection; and we then went for a short walk. On return I collected four concrete blocks from a pile outside the T.T.C. building, which was still under construction, and bore them aloft. With these and two pieces of bamboo I rigged up a tolerable lavatory seat — fortunately we had thought to bring a bucket with us!

The following day, accompanied by Usip and a Court Messenger, I cycled about twenty-five miles. We went first to a place called Ikpe, and *en route* we had to cross a number of streams. I was carried across two, and negotiated several others by balancing on felled palm tree trunks. Fallen trees along the route were evidence of the severe storm we had had the previous night. Arrived at Ikwe I was given a seat in the village shed, and a small table covered with a cloth was placed in front of me. The shed had no walls, but its matting roof extended to about three feet above the ground. The roof was supported on two massive iron wood "pillars". On both sides within the shed there were long low seats made of palm frond ribs, which were polished by much usage. At the far end there was a rough native-style bed, which was also used as a seat. A conical fish trap and a net were suspended from the roof; and two empty bottles placed at the base of one of the vast wooden pillars suggested a juju significance. Talk concerned the building of a motor road with concrete bridges to link Ikwe with the outside world; and at the close of the meeting I was presented with six bottles of beer. From Ikpe we cycled to Odio, where a somewhat similar meeting took place. This village was situated within a mile or two of the open sea, and during our discussion I could hear clearly the sound of waves breaking on the shore. At the end of our discussion, a young man chipped off the outer husk of a coconut as easily as if he were sharpening a pencil. Then he sliced off the very tip of the nut, placed it to his lips and took a single mouthful. He then passed it to me, and I drank a long swig. I did not know why he had taken a mouthful first, but I saw him do so again before handing Usip a coconut.

In walking around Odio I saw some yam-like plants, the tendrils of which had thorns. I was told that these were known as white yams, and were very tasty and expensive. On our return journey we passed many women making their way to Ikot Akpatek market. They carried their wares on their heads: dried fish, piassava, bananas, gari, cooking pots and so on. The majority also carried a small stool for squatting on.

A week or so later we visited Oron in order to attend a meeting of the Board of Governors of the Methodist Girls' Elementary Training Centre. I was the only Governor who was not only not a member of the Methodist Mission but also not a Methodist. One of the members of the board was a Nigerian Methodist Minister, who as a result of leprosy had been left with a twisted mouth. We listened to the

Principal's report, considered arrangements for the holding of entrance examinations, and discussed a proposal to move the E.T.C. to another site.

On returning home we found that P.W.D. carpenters had made some modest efforts to shore up the floor of our house in those places where the supporting beams had been practically demolished by white ants. We were also pleased to see that Vincent's wife had arrived, notwithstanding that dowry had not yet been paid in full. Using beer bottle caps as counters she and Mrs. Bonniface were happily playing draughts together, while Vincent looked on and Bonniface was seated nearby writing a letter.

One Sunday morning I was aroused at 7.15 a.m. by Philip banging on our bedroom door, and saying something about a sick woman. On entering the sitting-room I was surprised to see a young woman in native dress seated in one of the armchairs with Philip and a police constable standing over her. Apparently when Philip had opened up the house she had installed herself and had refused to budge. I put some questions to her, which she answered quite sensibly, and after some minutes' talk with Vincent acting as a very inadequate interpreter I was able to persuade her to leave of her own accord by giving her a note to take to the Sergeant. When she had left Philip informed me that she was "small mad now" and that in three or four days' time she would be completely mad unless she received suitable treatment from a doctor. I went round to the hospital, and Eric readily agreed to accompany me to the police station, where we found the woman sitting quietly. We succeeded in inducing her to talk, and, punctuated with dramatic gestures, she told a garbled tale of sleeping with a Mr. Bata, a penknife under the pillow, a vision of angels, the stabbing of two children, her expulsion from the house, and an injury to her legs. Eric felt her pulse and examined her pupils and was somewhat at a loss. He decided, however, that there were no grounds for supposing that she would turn violent. I told the Sergeant to be patient with her and to send someone to Mr. Bata to investigate her story.

Eket Division was by Eastern Nigerian standards somewhat remote, and to keep the local people in touch with the outside world we were visited — possibly once a year — by a Government public relations mobile Cinema Unit. On 1st March I received completely unexpected notice of the arrival of a Cinema Unit on the 5th. I hastily made out a programme and sent word to the villages concerned. Instead of arriving on the 5th the Unit in fact arrived on the 6th (we were on tour at the time), thereby upsetting the entire programme prepared for it. Worse was to come, however. Barely had the cinema van reached Eket than it was discovered that some essential item had been left behind. The Unit therefore returned to Enugu, 250 miles away, to get it. It arrived back in Eket on the 7th, and that evening went to

147

Ibeno to give a show. After two reels there was a total breakdown. When I returned to Eket on the 10th I found the members of the Unit slumbering peacefully. I had some terse talk with the man in charge, and a few minutes later the Unit left Eket for Enugu — its mission unaccomplished.

The time arrived to pay Jamestown another visit, and once again we travelled on the *Snipe*. I spent a morning in the little Court and devoted a couple of hours to a protracted land case which had first begun in 1953. When I adjourned for lunch the Court Clerk walked back to the waterside with me. *En route* we passed a blind man, and he told me that there were many blind persons in the area. I enquired the reason for this, and he replied that it was because of the people's wickedness and belief in juju. I asked what juju had to do with it, and he made some garbled remarks about people being taken into the water when juju was being invoked and having a pin stuck into the eyeballs.

Outside a shop in the market place I saw three palm oil drums each with a square shaped cemented opening in its side. These drums were used, I was told, for transporting illicit gin from the mainland. It sold for seventeen and sixpence a kerosene tin (four gallons).

After tea Angela and I went for a walk along the only road leading in and out of Jamestown, accompanied by the Court Clerk and a little yellow-coloured man who was only four and a half feet tall. We passed a tumbledown Church of the African Church of Christ Mission and a mud and thatch Methodist Church. We saw one house built of concrete blocks with a corrugated-iron roof. It was clearly unoccupied, and the Court Clerk said that the owner, a rich man, had been killed by juju. Since then no one had been prepared to live in the house nor had anyone else risked building a concrete block house.

On our return to the *Snipe* we passed a mad woman standing by the roadside completely naked. She was believed to have become insane after imbibing a love potion. Apparently she was a familiar sight about the place, and lived by begging daily in the market. Just after her we passed a young woman vividly dressed in royal blue, with a bright red hat, bag and shoes. I imagined that she must have recently returned from a rewarding stay in Calabar or Fernando Poo, but was told that she had in fact just left the Fattening Room. A bell tolled as we neared the waterside, which proved to be a call not to prayer but to a village meeting.

That evening the sky looked very threatening. Ominously dark clouds piled up over the vast expanse of water at the mouth of the Cross river, and, fearing a tornado, we weighed anchor and sought shelter up a side creek.

There was no semblance of a garage nor even a petrol filling station anywhere in Eket Division, and when in the direst straits I invoked the assistance of one Isong, more commonly known as "Mechanicy". In fact I think he knew less about cars than I did, but his moral support helped to sustain me when having a particularly fractious servicing or repair session. The garage attached to the District Officer's house boasted a deep and murky pit, and once a month I used to clamber down into this beneath my car. The first time I did so, I clambered out again pretty smartly, because, by the light of my torch, I found it already occupied by one live rat and one dead one.

One Saturday morning Mechanicy appeared at my office with another man whom he introduced as the leader of Williway's Orchestra. Williway and his music makers were due to play at a dance to be held that night in the African Club; and the leader of the band wished to know whether I would agree to prisoners erecting a temporary screen around the Club premises. I did so, but required him to insert a ten shilling note into my collecting tin for the British Empire Society for the Blind (as it was then styled). The band possessed the attraction of an electric guitar, and with the help of a portable generating plant it was hoped that it would be possible to make use of it.

Later in the morning a bail bond in the sum of £500 was put in front of me to sign. Surprised by the magnitude of the security I made enquiries and discovered that the accused was a former Eket Postmaster who was alleged to have defrauded a Post Office Savings Bank subscriber of £700. There were also other charges of fraud and theft against him. I refused bail; and the ex-postmaster was lodged in Eket Prison. Earlier in the week nineteen County Councillors, the Secretary, the Treasurer and one Road Overseer had been brought before me charged with corruption. Their numerical strength appeared to give them confidence, because they seemed to be in buoyant spirits and not a wit cast down. As local Government Commissioner for Eket Division it was not to my mind the most happy of situations in which to be confronted by half my County Council and its two most senior officers! In their case I had allowed bail.

In checking my Vote Book I noticed that monthly expenditure on conservancy services had increased; and I was told that this was due to the fact that the number of lavatory pails at the Government School had risen by eleven. I asked my District Clerk to obtain particulars about these extra pails. He referred to the Headmaster, who wrote an inexplicit reply. The District Clerk thereupon wrote back to him, and the Headmaster's second reply, which was no more informative than his first, read as follows: "Vide your letter of the 16th instant and my reply, you could see that the pails have been in use as from last month. And, if the D.O. refers to you, my reply to yours affords reply to your present letter through bearer the contractor."

At this time various ambitious ideas were emanating from Enugu. I had already borne the brunt of one of them, namely, the holding of universal adult suffrage local Government elections by secret ballot. Two others also involved me in considerable additional work. One of these was the introduction from 1st April, 1956, of a P.A.Y.E. tax collection system in respect of all salaried persons; and the other was free universal primary education. Implementation of the former involved the engagement and training of additional staff, and with a population scattered over an area of 2,500 square miles its operation presented many difficulties. The latter necessitated the urgent conclusion of contracts for the construction of innumerable additional schools and classrooms, with considerable resulting contention between the many and varied denominational organisations which vied with each other in the educational field.

Apart from these high priority preoccupations there was all the usual run of the mill stuff also to deal with. A Treasury Query was referred to me, which required me to produce the receipt I had received when paying an Enugu Catering Rest-House bill for a two-night stay one year and eleven months earlier! A murder was reported, in which the victim's throat and private parts had been removed — possibly for some juju purpose. This reminded me of a case concerning a native doctor who had required some persons wanting to obtain a special medicine from him to provide him first with a woman's breast. I attended a meeting of the Oron Methodist Hospital Advisory Board, and learnt that the former Nigerian Doctor-in-charge had paid out the whole of the agreed sum for the construction of a new theatre before the contractor had even begun to start the work; and as one might in the circumstances have expected he had failed to complete the building. Furthermore, the concrete ceiling of the new theatre, presumably insufficiently reinforced, had collapsed — fortunately when no one was inside. In censoring some prisoners' letters the following extract from one of them caught my eye: "Extend my sinful greetings to my Brother Anwa. Mine trouble is that my mistress reported me to the Police telling that I have committed ripe with her daughter which I have not done so."

The Police Sergeant brought before me a young man from Ibeno who had visited him in the middle of the previous night in order to accuse a certain person of having strangled with a towel a man whose corpse had been brought to Eket some hours earlier. We doubted his story because he appeared to be an unreliable individual. Furthermore, whereas in a written statement he had said that he had been drinking palm wine with others in Ibeno on the night before the death of the man in question, in the course of some oral remarks he mentioned that he had spent that night with a harlot in Eket. However, since he swore an affidavit to the truth of the charge, there was nothing for it but to have the body exhumed. Eric very reluctantly performed a post-mortem as a result of which he discovered nothing to suggest that the deceased had died other than from natural causes.

I had noticed in the Eastern Region's Estimates for 1956–1957 that there was provision for a Ministry of Transport. This interested me because until then I had not appreciated that such a Ministry existed in Enugu. I idly wondered what services for the benefit of the community this Ministry performed; and a few days later one contribution made by it to the common weal was brought to the notice of a great number of persons including myself. I received a circular from the M.O.T. addressed to every conceivable Department, District Office and Local Government Council in the Region, in which it was announced that life buoys could be supplied at a cost of £6. 5s. 5¼d. each . . .

Within the space of a day or two I set eyes on two strikingly different Eket maidens who between them contrastingly represented the New and the Old. I gave permission for a procession to be held in Eket town to welcome home a local girl who had just returned from Britain where she had qualified as a nursing sister. She was neatly dressed, had straightened hair, wore fly-away spectacles and carried an umbrella. Driving between Ikot Oquot and Uyo a couple of days later I passed a playground, gay with brightly coloured awnings, and saw nonchalantly walking towards it a buxom young woman completely naked except for some beads on her body and thick brass bangles on her legs.

Visitors to the District Office were many and varied. A newly engaged office messenger of one of the Rural District Council offices came to tell me that the Council Secretary had demanded £3 from him for having given him the job. Because he had not paid, first some of his wages had been withheld and then he had been terminated. A District Councillor expressed misgivings to me about the state of affairs at his Council headquarters. He said that the Chairman, the Secretary and the Chairman of the Finance and Staff Committee were hand in glove, that the three of them held the keys of the Treasury strongroom and that they did what they liked with the Council's money. He made allegations of bogus payment vouchers, forged signatures and phoney deposits with the bank. A Mr. Seeborne of the Apostolic Mission informed me that some of his flock had been sued in Oyubia Native Court by their Village Chief for refusing to contribute towards the cost of a certain sacrifice. The Secretaries and Treasurers of the County Council and of the four Rural District Councils converged on the District Office for instruction in the newly devised procedure for assessing, collecting and accounting for tax. I did my best to explain to them the contents of a spate of circulars which had issued thick and fast from Enugu on this subject. Our session was interrupted by the appearance of

Major Squibb of the Salvation Army, who had a problem on which he wanted some advice. Having finished with the Secretaries and Treasurers I found that there was a visiting Fisheries Officer waiting to see me about obtaining a site at Oron for a boatyard.

Some weeks earlier Mrs. Bonniface had returned to Owerri, where she had subsequently given birth to a daughter. Bonniface went to visit mother and child, and on his return reported that all was not well with his wife. He said that she had been "touched by a spirit", and was receiving treatment. He attributed her trouble to the fact that the Second Burial ceremonies of someone who had died in her village had been overlooked. Arrangements having, however, by then been made for the second burial he was confident that all would be well. Unfortunately all did not become well, and his wife's condition in fact deteriorated. Her parents then did what they should have done at the outset and took her to the Roman Catholic hospital at Emekuku. Bonniface paid his family another visit and discovered that his parents-in-law had against medical advice removed his wife from the hospital after three days because fees had already totalled more than £4. Bonniface had her readmitted, and then returned to Eket. *En route* the lorry, on which he was travelling, crashed. Five persons were killed and seven injured, but he escaped without a scratch.

Desmond appeared with a swollen left cheek which was clearly causing him some pain. This affliction was due to the fact that he had been to a show given by a visiting magician an evening or two earlier in the course of which he had allowed himself to be hypnotised and had had a pin stuck into his cheek. Desmond went to the magician and demanded money for an injection. He was offered three shillings; but he refused this and insisted on seven shillings. The magician told him to return that evening, and when Desmond did so he found that the magician had left. Philip was not sympathetic. He disapproved of the fact that Desmond had been to the show in the first place, and considered him foolish not to have taken the three shillings. The next day both Desmond's cheeks were swollen! This was because instead of going to the hospital he had visited a quack who had administered an illegal injection in his other cheek.

As a result of visiting the farming plot of a Temporary Occupation Licence holder in Eket I discovered by chance the little European cemetery, which was in a very neglected and overgrown state. I had it tidied up and fenced. The cemetery contained four quite elaborate gravestones and one stone or concrete cross. I was able to make out the names of four of those buried there. One was a Mr. Roche, a native of Freetown, who had been District Clerk. His date of death was indecipherable. One was a Frederick Ernest Keates. His stone recorded that he had died at Qua

Iboe on 4th March, 1910. Another was Edward Elwell Potter, Assistant District Officer, who died on 3rd December, 1918, aged thirty. He, poor fellow, succumbed to the influenza epidemic which swept through Eket Division during 1918. No doubt his resistance was lowered by the exacting existence he had been leading, because during that year up to the time of his death he had been on tour for a total of 178 days! The largest of the gravestones bore the following inscription: "Capt. Reginald Walsingham Farmar Cotgrave, Political Officer, born 1883 and died 6.3.22". Cotgrave, a former D.O. Eket, was shot by a police constable while seated at his desk in the District Office. Another former District Officer had died in Eket, allegedly from poisoning, but in his case at his own specific request he had been buried elsewhere.

One morning I fell out with men of Usung Inyang village. I found several of them hacking away at the river bank in the middle of the Government station and only 200 yards from our house. No prior reference had been made to me, and I was most annoyed. This sudden activity on their part was due to an inter-village dispute as to the points on the east and west banks of the Qua Iboe river between which a projected new pontoon ferry should ply. I stopped the Usung Inyang men from working and they left in some dudgeon. Later in the day Chief Amah came to see me in the hope of pouring oil on troubled waters. He said that hot-heads were proposing to send off telegrams to all and sundry at Enugu and were contemplating suing me for using abusive language, and he urged me to agree to meet the Chiefs of Usung Inyang the following day. In the hope of bettering relations I consented to do this.

Next morning, accompanied by Usip, I went to Usung Inyang, and about thirty of us seated ourselves in the village Ekpuk shed. The mat roof was supported on iroko wood pillars, two to three feet thick, which I was told were 100 years old. On this occasion the tables were turned, and I was in the position of being the man in the "dock". Chief Sam, at whom I had let off steam the previous day, said in the course of his statement that I had been abusive and had called them mad and foolish. In reply I rebutted the charge of having been abusive by explaining that unfortunately I did not at the time have my District Interpreter with me and had made use of the services of a Road Overseer. I had since discovered that this individual was not on good terms with Usung Inyang, and it was therefore possible that he had distorted my words. All I had in fact said was that it was foolish to attempt to make a road through a perpendicular river bank when it was possible a few yards away to make it up a gently rising slope. After I had finished speaking a dozen or more Chiefs removed themselves to the shade of a nearby tree where they deliberated for a time.

On their return Chief Amah announced that they were satisfied with the explanation I had given; and Chief Sam asked me if there was anything I would like to say in conclusion. I told them that in public affairs it was impossible to please everybody all the time; and pointed out that had they thought to come and see me first before beginning the road work the misunderstanding would probably not have arisen. On leaving I gave Chief Sam a salute and we shook hands, much to the delight of all; and I returned to Eket feeling that a sudden and possibly dangerous breach had been healed.

Certain burial customs were strictly observed by the Ibibios. Chiefs were buried in their bedrooms, usually before the death was announced — a coffin displayed being in fact an empty one. This was done in order to minimise the risk of the corpse being mutilated, it being believed that by obtaining the tongue, hand, etc., of a dead man one could thereby acquire his skill, learning and so on for oneself. It was most important that a corpse should not be mutilated, lest the deceased should take offence; and a mutilated corpse or a wrongly buried corpse would result in a deformed or handicapped child being born into the family. Senior men were permitted to be buried in their compounds. An old widow or an old woman living on her own (provided not the mother of twins) might also be buried in her compound. Everyone else was buried in thick bush, men in one place, women and children in another, and pregnant women in another. If a pregnant woman were not buried in the place for pregnant women, then another woman in the family on becoming pregnant would have a miscarriage or would die in childbirth.

The Ibibios liked to erect memorial "effigies" after the death of distinguished persons. These concrete structures were costly. Usip told me that the memorial to his father-in-law which was in the shape of a man had cost £96 and apart from this while the "sculptor" was on the job he expected to be fed daily with yams and a fowl. Memorial "effigies" were usually erected by the roadside so that they could be seen, and they did not mark the place where the bodies were actually buried. The figures seen on these memorial structures were not necessarily intended to resemble the deceased, and in fact they often represented the Ekpo Society of which the deceased person had been a member during his life.

When enquiring about juju I was told that each village still had its own shrine, and that different societies in a village had in addition their own particular shrines. There were also certain Clan juju shrines. In Eket there was one known as "Abasi-Ibeno", and when it was wished to invoke it the Priest had to come from Ibeno. Ubium Clan had a powerful juju known as "Ibritam", which, it was said, was an offshoot of the Arochuku Long Juju.

Some people firmly believed that witchcraft societies still operated; and I was told of a case in which three women charged with witchcraft had not only admitted having bewitched another woman but had in addition confessed to having eaten various parts of her anatomy including her eyes. Usip said that an innocent man might have the misfortune to be bewitched and find himself initiated into a witchcraft society. If that happened, whether he liked it or not, he was fated to remain a witch. Ordinary people did not know who was a witch and who was not; but one witch instinctively recognised another.

With regard to trial by ordeal I heard of an unpleasant custom believed at one time to have been practised in Eket, namely the pouring of boiling palm oil over the hands of a suspect in the belief that if innocent the oil would not burn him.

A case which bore a similarity to trial by ordeal was reviewed by me at Okobo Native Court. A young woman charged five men with "unlawfully giving the complainant juju to drink on oath at Nang Atai Odobo on 12.7.56". It appeared that she had fallen out with her husband, the first accused. In settling the palavar the juju priest, second accused, had been asked to produce juju for the woman to swear on. However, in addition to swearing on the juju she had been compelled by her husband, the juju priest, his assistant and two other men present at the time to drink the juju fluid. The accused hoped that I would reverse the Native Court judgement which had found them guilty; but far from doing that I in fact increased their sentences.

The people of Eket Division were very keen on belonging to clubs known as Osusu clubs. Each village had at least one Osusu club; and all men and many women belonged to one if not more clubs. Each club had its fixed contribution, which varied between about five shillings and £1, payable either weekly or monthly. Every week or month as the case might be one member received his share, this being all the contributions for that week or month paid by his fellow members. Having acquired his share a member naturally had to continue paying contributions until all members of the club had been paid out. Membership of a club gave two advantages: it helped to look after savings and it provided members with a lump sum of capital when wanted.

A visiting auditor drew my attention to the fact that the Treasurer of one of my Rural District Councils had failed to balance his Cash Books for the past one year and eight months, and that he had lied to me when he said that his 1954/1955 Cash Book was with the Audit Department. A couple of days later I received a circular letter from the Ministry of Internal Affairs bearing the uninspiring title "Resignations by Councillors under Section 33, Eastern Region Local Government Law 1955". It clarified the procedure by which a Councillor might validly resign his seat, and went on to explain what the Law Officers interpreted "notice of resignation delivered to the Chairman" as meaning. It seemed to me remarkable that the Ministry was prepared to engage in academic antics of that kind when the very structure of local Government — at any rate in Calabar Province where it had been in existence longest — was crumbling.

The following day a telegram from the Ministry of Internal Affairs arrived. This said that the Union of Local Government Employees had declared its intention of striking at midnight on June 6th, six days later, and that I was required to visit Councils and Council staffs and warn them that striking would be regarded as breach of contract, and that subsequent re-employment would be regarded as new employment and would be subject to the Minister's approval. At the same time I was enjoined not to "give any impression of coercing them to remain at work". On an occasion such as this I would have expected the telegram to be in code but it was sent in clear.

The next time we were on tour at Jamestown I received an invitation from an old Chief, who had come to Jamestown from Calabar some sixty years earlier, to visit him. Usip led me to his mud house situated near the market and introduced me. The Chief had extremely light-coloured skin and unusual grey eyes. I seated myself in an old wicker chair beside him on the verandah, which faced onto the street. Through an inner doorway I was able to look through a central room into another room behind it which gave onto the backyard. All the floors and walls were made of mud, which was almost the colour of the old man's complexion. The interior of the house was very bare. There was a table in the central room, and on the lintel of the inner doorway were chalked the words: "God is the head of this house". Squatting in the sunlight on a stool in the backroom was a young woman, who was facing my way. She had a pleasing appearance and a generous smile, and seemed to be wearing nothing except a yellow shift which exposed to advantage her brown thighs and revealed the deep cleft between her breasts as she leaned forward while pounding fufu. A chicken or two pecked around the floor beside her. A black goat emerged onto the verandah from the central room; it picked its way past our chairs and stepped out into the street. No one paid any attention to it.

The old Chief wished to seek my advice as to the Court action he should take in respect of one of his young wives who had gone off with another man. This young woman had none of her family living from whom he could claim refund of dowry, assuming it were possible to prove what dowry, if any, had been paid by him twenty years earlier when he had "married" this wife who at that time was a small girl. In lieu of any kith or kin the old Chief was contemplating claiming refund of dowry

156

from the man with whom his wife was then living. I suggested that in the circumstances it would be more appropriate to claim payment of dowry rather than refund of dowry from this man. He seemed very pleased with this modest advice, thanked me heartily and shook my hand.

After leaving, Usip told me that this Chief was the head of a certain Calabar Ekpo society, and anyone wishing to be initiated into this society had to come to him in Jamestown for the necessary ceremonies. Two weeks previously a well-known Calabar barrister had been to him for initiation.

At about this time I received an invitation card from the Okon Improvement Union to "A Reception to be held at Okon Group School on 16th June, 1956, at 10.00 a.m. in honour of their illustrious son, Mr. V. D. Uwemedimo, B.A. Hons. (Lond.), Barrister-at-Law, and their beloved daughter Mrs. Rosemary Uwemedimo B.A. Hons (Lond.)". At the bottom of the card there was printed somewhat ominously: "Donation £ : : d.".

I was detained in the office on the 16th and was unable to reach Okon Group School until 12.30 p.m. I found the long classroom building decorated with pieces of greenery and full of children; but there was no sign of the guests of honour. The only other white person present was a Roman Catholic Father, who told me that he had been there since 11.00 a.m. Rather than remain inside the building with the din we paced together up and down in front of it. This involved an element of risk because from time to time a group of cheerful and excited ruffians loosed off ear-shattering *feus-de-joie* from their ancient muzzle-loading guns. One volley was fired in the immediate vicinity of my car, which I then removed to a safer distance.

At 1.30 p.m. there was the sound of drumming, and a procession consisting of a band, a troupe of dancers, a crocodile of school girls in yellow dresses, a posse of gun-bearers, one large American car and one shooting-brake entered the school compound. Space inside the building was severely limited, and I was wedged between a Nigerian woman and Father Deegan. We literally had our backs to the wall, and faced a crowded scene. The long room was packed with people sitting on benches and on the floor, and a great number more, who had failed to get inside, pressed round the doors and windows which stretched down both sides of the classroom block. The chanting, which had been going on non-stop since my arrival, continued; and the noise of this plus the general hubbub was deafening.

In front of Mr. and Mrs. Uwemedimo there was a table which was covered with a felt cloth. In the middle of the table there was a large silver cup, resembling a sporting trophy, into which a bunch of red hibiscus flowers had been stuffed. This somewhat obscured one's view of the guests of honour; however, from where I was seated nearby I could see them quite clearly. Mr. Uwemedimo was smartly dressed

157

in an elegant grey suit and white shirt. Throughout the proceedings he dandled a pretty little girl wearing a pinafore made of the same green material as his wife's dress.

At 2.00 p.m., four hours after the scheduled time, the function began. The Chairman made an opening speech, and other speeches followed. Then a Welcome Address was read and presented. From this I gathered that, in addition to being a B.A., Mrs. Uwemedimo also possessed a Diploma in Education, and that the Okon Improvement Union evidently looked forward to her doing great things for them.

I was surprised to see Rosemary Uwemedimo rise to reply to the Welcome Address and not her husband. Rosemary was an Englishwoman aged about twenty-six. She wore a simple cotton frock. Her long light-coloured hair was held back by a green ribbon. She was tallish, freckled and wore glasses. She seemed remarkably self-possessed and, in spite of intermittent gunshots outside, spoke without hesitation in English for about five minutes. It was evident that she was imbued with zeal and had a sincere wish to help the people amongst whom she had come to live. She assured those present that she welcomed the opportunity which had been given to her to make use of such talents and qualifications as she possessed in Nigeria where the need was so great. She said she was happy to be a member of the Clan of Okon (cheers); and then to my surprise and admiration she broke into the vernacular, speaking without notes.

For some reason, which was not clear to me, the people present grew restive and had to be called to order twice by the Chairman. Then, while Mrs. Uwemedimo was still on her feet and speaking, there came a more abrupt interruption. A large, self-important man in European clothes rose to his feet, barged across to the table, and with much ostentation thumped a £1 note onto it. Turning his back on Mrs. Uwemedimo he said something loudly in Ibibio and stalked back to his seat. This resulted in general hurly-burly, and a stream of people began to come up to the table and to place shillings on it. At this point the brass band at the back of the hall struck up, and Father Deegan and I decided that this was a good moment to quit. We shook hands with the Uwemedimos and the Chairman, and I invited Mrs. Uwemedimo to visit us when in Eket, but doubted whether she heard me because of the noise.

Chapter 14

"Black is White and Green is Black"

In the Lagos *Daily Times* of 21st April mention was made of the motion directed against Dr. Azikiwe, which had been filed by Mr. E. O. Eyo, the recently sacked N.C.N.C. Chief Whip, in the Eastern House of Assembly. The motion in question read: "That this House regrets that Dr. Azikiwe, Premier of the Region, grossly abused his office by allowing public funds totalling nearly £200,000 to be invested or deposited in the African Continental Bank Limited, in which Dr. Azikiwe has substantial interest at a time when he knew the said bank was operating at a substantial loss and deposited money was being used to finance the premises of the bank . . .".

This motion was in due course ruled out of order by the Speaker. One of his reasons for doing this was because the matter was *sub judice*, Dr. Azikiwe having announced his intention of suing two publications for alleged libel in their treatment of the motion.

This affair led to a breach between Dr. Azikiwe and Sir Clement Pleass, Premier and Governor of the Eastern Region respectively. The *Daily Times* of 17th July summarised the position in the following words: "A disagreement between the Premier and the Governor of the Region, Sir Clement Pleass, is believed to have brought about this new crisis in the East. The dispute is in connection with the request of the Opposition that the Eastern House should be recalled in order to debate Mr. Eyo's motion. This motion, which accused the Premier of financial abuses, was ruled out by the Speaker two weeks ago on the ground that this matter was *sub judice*. The Governor is understood to have declined the advice of the Executive Council that the request of the Opposition should be refused".

The following day the *Daily Times* referred as follows to a cable sent by Dr. Azikiwe to the Secretary of State: "Dr. Azikiwe's cable says that Sir Clement

159

cannot adapt himself to contemporary British Colonial policy and should not be allowed to continue. It asks Mr. Lennox Boyd: 'Why must you blindly take sides against the Government always?' It continues: 'In view of your prejudice and unwarranted antagonism against the N.C.N.C. Government I am requesting my colleagues to resign their offices following my impending resignation in protest against your insulting high-handedness and complete disregard of elementary courtesy in handling matters relating to the affairs of Eastern Nigeria . . . If your continued attitude of antagonism against Eastern Nigeria is a pretext for stultifying the forthcoming constitution conference then you have misfired because there is no force on earth to impede our march towards political as well as economic freedom. We must decide where our money must be banked and you cannot properly interfere in order to protect British banking monopoly. Because of your pronounced partiality I have instructed all N.C.N.C. Ministers and Parliamentary Secretaries in the Federal Government as well as in the Regional Government to be ready to tender their resignations so that you can have the full scope to rule arbitrarily 4,000 miles away on secret information from obdurate and old-fashioned Governors . . .''

The Secretary of one of my Rural District Councils regarded this sudden turn of events as divine intervention to delay or prevent the granting of self-Government to the Eastern Region. It was not, however, to have this effect.

Neither Zik nor any N.C.N.C. Ministers or Parliamentary Secretaries did in fact resign as a result of the Enugu crisis, notwithstanding that the Secretary of State announced his intention of appointing a Commission of Enquiry to investigate into the affairs of the African and Continental Bank. The *Daily Times* of 28th July carried the headline: "Zik (In Tears): We Will Not Surrender". The paper contained a report of the address given by Dr. Azikiwe at a Special Conference of the N.C.N.C. called to discuss the crisis over the Enquiry ordered by Mr. Lennox Boyd. Dr. Azikiwe's closing remarks were quoted by the *Daily Times* as follows: "What are we waiting for when we have millions of people supporting us and itching for direction? Why should we not mobilise our forces, and make demonstrations all over the country in a constitutional manner in order to assert our rights to exist and enjoy a constitutional form of Government? . . . If you would stomach this challenge to our manhood as a people then let us fold up as a militant nationalist party, otherwise let us strike the blow for freedom constitutionally and damn the consequences. We are now passing through the crucible of British imperialism but I have no doubt that we shall emerge a final breed worth all the fruits of freedom. I am prepared to face the Commission.''

Relations remained very strained in Enugu. Regional Ministers refrained from meeting or speaking to the Governor except at Executive Council meetings. The *Daily Times* of 26th October included the following news item: "Members of the Enugu Urban District Council are not attending the cocktail party arranged by the Governor of the East, Sir Clement Pleass, in honour of the Governor General, Sir James Robertson, now touring the Region. The reason for the boycott is because the N.C.N.C. which controls the Council decided not to fraternise with Sir Clement."

In due course the Commission of Enquiry, known as the Foster-Sutton Tribunal, published its findings. Notwithstanding its unfavourable conclusions the Eastern Regional Government decided to close all Government accounts with the Bank of British West Africa from 1st December and to transfer funds to the African Continental Bank.

Sir Clement Pleass left on retirement in November after many years of devoted work. The *Daily Times* of the 21st reported that the Eastern Working Committee of the N.C.N.C. in a statement marking the occasion had said that Sir Clem's administration had been "abhorred" by the people and that he had "succeeded in inflicting a lasting wound on the sacred shrine of democracy"!

A new Governor of the Eastern Region was sworn in before Christmas. No Administrative Officer from my part of the Region was invited to witness this event, but House of Assembly members and their wives of course received invitations to attend. Honourable Akpan, one of the members for Eket, intended to go to the ceremony until he learnt that he would not be permitted to draw travelling allowance for the journey to and from Enugu. Eartha Kitt, on location in Enugu at the time, was apparently given a place of honour.

At the same time as this "Sturm und Drang" was taking place in Enugu I was faced with somewhat similar difficulties at my local level. The Eket County Council passed a vote of no confidence in me as Local Government Commissioner and requested the Ministry of Internal Affairs to have me replaced. Opposition from this quarter was primarily due, I think, to a mistaken belief that I had been responsible for getting eighteen County Councillors and three members of the staff charged with corruption.

After a year in Eket I felt the need to escape from its somewhat claustrophobic and by no means entirely congenial atmosphere and it was therefore a great relief to be granted some leave during August and to be able to enjoy a change of scenery and climate at a place called Vom, situated not far from Jos in the Plateau Province of the Northern Region.

The journey from Eket was more than 650 miles. At Nine Mile Corner to the West of Enugu we branched off onto the main road north. We ate some sandwiches parked in the shade of some mango trees outside the District Office at Oturkpo, and then drove on to Mikurdi where we spent the night in the Catering Rest-House. After tea we strolled round the residential area and had a good view of the Benue river and the bridge spanning it; and we watched an old stern-wheeler, emitting clouds of dirty smoke, slide downstream. We passed a bright red Bishop bird clinging to a stalk of elephant grass, and in one of the gardens saw a tiny bird with a soft blue breast. Back in our comfortable chalet we bathed in brown Benue water, two hot bucketfuls of which were emptied into our bath. We dined by the light of two Tilley lamps, and went to bed early. In the distance we could hear a railway engine shunting and nearby the honking of a fruit bat.

The next morning after crossing the half-mile-long bridge over the Benue we headed north for Lafia. All along the road P.W.D. labourers were in evidence, and thanks to their efforts the earth surface was not too bad. The countryside undulated gently, and the scrub on either side of the road appeared for the most part to be uninhabited. As we approached Lafia we passed a man riding a horse — the first horse we had ever seen in Nigeria — and in the town we saw three donkeys. After leaving Lafia we could see hills ahead of us, and before long we were threading our way through them. We skirted Wamba, and lunched just off the main road. During the course of our picnic only one lorry and one car passed by. Some time after we had resumed our drive the cloud-capped mass of the Plateau began to loom up on our right; and for fifty miles or more we seemed to be skirting it.

Meantime it had begun to rain and the condition of the road deteriorated. We ploughed through red slushy mud and bounced in and out of potholes. Eventually we came to a gate across the road the purpose of which was to prevent lorries from proceeding further until twelve hours after the rain had stopped. Fortunately cars were allowed through. A few miles beyond the junction with the Kafanchan road we finally began to climb the Plateau escarpment. After a mile or two to our great joy we came onto a tarred surface, and sailed to the top with no trouble at all; and, to our amazement, the tar continued and we bowled merrily along a straight flat road on top of the plateau. Through the mist and rain we saw strange tor-like hills and outcroppings of rock on either side. From time to time we passed Pagans* crouching underneath tent-like hoods of matting, which they fondly imagined kept them from getting wet. Twenty miles before Jos we turned left off the main road where a signboard pointed to Vom. A bare two miles from our destination our luck gave out — we became completely and utterly stuck in a morass of mud. However, for a

---

*The name by which the local tribe was known.

162

small consideration a crowd of willing helpers lifted the car bodily out of the quag. That evening after a bath and a good meal it was bliss to relax in front of a log fire.

Vom was a large veterinary research station. The buildings nestled against a low hill, which was encircled by a road flanked with eucalyptus trees. On one side, screened from each other by fir trees, there were delightful stone-built houses set in gardens which were a mass of dahlias, roses, cannas and nasturtiums and of such flowering shrubs as oleandar, hibiscus and jasmine. On the other side of the road there was ploughed land, and beyond that miles and miles of flat green plain stretching to a skyline of low rocky crags. The scene was profoundly quiet and peaceful. There was a smell of cows in the air; bright red Bishop birds darted here and there; swallows flitted hither and thither; parson birds made abortive attacks on smaller birds; and from time to time we saw crown birds flapping overhead or standing daintily poised on their thin legs on the ploughed earth.

One day we went for a drive to Mbiango. The road weaved in between countless rock outcrops, and there was a wonderful and constantly changing panorama at which to gaze. After the confining bush of southern Nigeria it was exhilarating to be in open country, to enjoy extensive views on all sides and to look up and see a huge expanse of sky overhead. We passed several herds of cattle grazing near the road, and I was amused to see one herdsman wearing in addition to the customary bunch of leaves fore and aft a blue plastic mackintosh. Everywhere we saw men and women working on their farms, ploughing by hand and planting seeds by stabbing a hole in the ploughed soil with a large toe and dropping a seed inside. We passed a man chipping roots out of the earth with a pickaxe, which were collected by a woman balancing a headpan on her head. The road skirted two old volcanic craters, the slopes of which were heavily cultivated. On entering Mbiango we passed the Sudan Interior Mission compound with its "Welcome" signboard. Some of the streets in the village were lined with walls of sharp cactus plants. The local inhabitants appeared to be shy, and retreated when they observed us. For the most part they wore only leaves; and we saw one woman with sticks through her ear lobes and another with a stick through her cheeks.

On another day we motored in a different direction to Barikin Ladi and Ropp and saw many signs of tin-mining operations. To enquire the way to Kurra Falls I stopped at a small and isolated house. I was greeted by a Scotsman and his three baying mastiffs, the only desire of which at that moment was clearly to tear me to pieces. The Scotsman was very friendly and invited us into his small stone dwelling (which we later heard he had bought for a mere £60 from one of the tin-mining Companies) for a cup of tea or a glass of gin. We sat down in easy chairs in front of a large open fireplace where some logs were burning. The walls of the room were royal blue. There was no ceiling and we looked up at rafters supporting a white painted corrugated-iron roof. Our host, who looked no more than 55, told us that he was 69 and had first come to Nigeria in 1921. He had not been home for eleven years. He was a chartered accountant by profession, but for some years had been tin mining on his own. He invited us to drop in any time we were passing, and we told him to do the same when in the vicinity of Eket!

On several occasions we drove to Jos, seventeen miles away. To us, coming from the steamy south where we were perpetually encompassed by oil palms and rank vegetation, this seemed a beautiful town, and we marvelled at the delightful houses in their boulder-strewn gardens. A notice near the Plateau Club announced that the altitude was 4,000 feet above sea level — and what a difference to life living at that height made! We had twice as much energy as we had in Eket. Jos was a small town. Kingsway Stores and Chellaram's were the best shops. There was also the S.I.M. Bookshop, a Lennard's shoe shop and various other stores. There was a Cinema, which unlike those in the Eastern Region was an enclosed and roofed building. We went to morning service in St. Piran's Church, and admired the rich blue carpeting and the timber panelling erected in memory of the famous missionary, Dr. Miller. There were three stained glass windows at the east end, one of which depicted St. Piran the patron Saint of Cornish tin miners. After church we had a drink with the District Officer, and admired (and secretly were rather envious of) his lovely house and garden full of beds overflowing with flowers of all kinds and trim lawn on which a tethered pony was lazily grazing. We enjoyed a couple of visits to Jos's hotel known as Hill Station. We dined in the panelled dining-room, on one wall of which were hung large signed photographs of the Queen and the Duke of Edinburgh. On another occasion we lunched there and strolled around the garden in which dahlias, balsam, roses, salvia, chrysanthemums, hollyhocks, Michaelmas daisies and much else besides were growing in profusion. In Jos's little Museum we saw Stone Age implements, masks and terracotta heads, and in the nearby "zoo" a desert tortoise believed to be 250 years old.

On my birthday I visited the Government dentist in Jos, a Mr. Black, as the Eastern Region dentist, Mr. Green, had not been available during the two days we spent in Enugu. ("BLACK IS WHITE AND GREEN IS BLACK" was reputedly the reply sent by telegram to an officer in the bush who wished to know which of the two dentists was British and which Nigerian.)

We departed from Vom on a bright sunny day, and apart from knocking two more dents in the sump of the M.G. Magnette on the way to Makurdi we suffered no mishaps on the return journey, and we arrived back in Eket much refreshed as a result of our visit to the North.

Chapter 15

"Order in Court!"

Six months of my tour still remained, and those last months in Eastern Nigeria proved to be as busy as any I had ever had. Apart from the normal day to day work there was a new system of tax collection to be implemented, arrangements to be made for the introduction of free universal primary education at the beginning of 1957, and as I was later to discover preparations to be made for a Governor's visit and the holding of House of Assembly elections early in the new year.

For interest I noted my doings during the course of an ordinary day's work in the District Office. They were as follows:

Before Breakfast — signed various letters drafted by me the previous day. Also signed some payment vouchers.

Looked through the incoming mail and glanced at a couple of local newspapers.

Drafted a letter about obtaining Dobbin Barrows for road construction purposes, and began a lengthy circular to District Council Secretaries about the new taxation procedure.

After Breakfast — the clerical warder was waiting to see me with one prisoner for discharge. I signed him off and saw him given the fivepence which he had had with him on admission. Signed the Daily State Book — strength 149. Checked the warrant of a newly admitted prisoner; and signed a payment voucher for prisoners' rations supplied during the preceding month.

Next to appear was a Court Messenger bringing me the Criminal Judgement Book from Ibeno Native Court to inspect. Looked through cases heard during preceding month and endorsed the Judgement Book.

As it was raining heavily I had none of the usual daily host of complainants — only one person who wanted permission to visit a prisoner.

The Secretary of Eket Rural District Council came to speak about an application made by his Council for a grant to buy an ambulance. I speedily drafted a short letter supporting this application. Next he enquired about tax arrangements, and wanted to know whether I would support a project to build a Council Hall near the Council Offices.

On the Secretary's departure, a P.C. brought me a Witness Summons to sign; and an Agricultural Assistant popped in briefly.

During the ensuing pause I signed letters on a variety of subjects. Then my District Clerk came in to speak about gun licences. I signed one, and vetted a couple of letters he had drafted.

A new Vauxhall stopped outside the office, and the Honourable Akpan wreathed in smiles entered. He had enquiries on the following subjects: a rubber plot belonging to him, the introduction of Customary Courts, the Uquo road, a bridge for Odoro Atasung and the pontoon ferry across the Qua Iboe river.

No sooner had Mr. Akpan left than a P.C. came to say that a call for me from Enugu had been put through to the Police Station. It was Dr. Azikiwe's Parliamentary Secretary who wished me to pass on a message to Mr. Akpan. Fortunately I was able to catch him before he left Eket.

Back in my office I was visited by five members of the Eket Helping Society, who wished to have the name of their Society registered as a business name.

Assisted by the District Clerk and my Orderly I opened and counted the contents of some Red Cross Flag Day tins — £5.0s.10d. all told.

A Forest Guard asked me for some solignum for his house, and a Court Messenger from Opobo brought me a warrant of arrest to endorse for execution in Eket Division. An office messenger brought me ten shillings and ninepence, being my petrol rebate for the previous month, and I receipted the payment voucher.

Mr. Usip then appeared bringing a file on which I had minuted "please speak". It concerned a village road, and we studied a map together.

Peace followed and I completed the circular about the new taxation procedure. I also drafted a letter about taxation stationery.

Opened registered mail, and recorded details in the special register.

Signed further letters. Finally went quickly through about twenty files, minuting on them and putting them in my "out" tray.

Lunch — 3.00 p.m.

Evening — Dealt with a box of files which Essien brought across to the house.

About this time my A.D.O., Robert, went on leave and in his place I was sent a newly appointed Nigerian Administrative Officer, called Achike. He was 26. He came from Bende Division where his father, like his father before him, was a native

166

doctor, with a forte for curing madness. Achike told me that his father had all together twenty-eight children, many of whom had done well for themselves. Three or four of his brothers, however, had not distinguished themselves at school and they had in their turn become native doctors. Achike won a scholarship to the Hope Waddell Boys' School in Calabar, and after leaving there his village supported him for five years at Ibadan University, where he read Latin and Greek. He graduated in 1954, after which he taught for a year at Hope Waddell. Then he joined the Administrative Service, and worked for a year in Enugu first as Private Secretary to the Minister of Welfare and then as an Assistant Secretary in the Ministry of Health before joining me in Eket.

Soon after his arrival I gave him a test job. We had recently received a pamphlet giving the procedure to be followed in dealing with persons charged with murder. I asked Achike to summarise its contents to enable us to see at a glance the action to be taken by the various officers concerned, i.e. D.O., O.C. Police, Medical Officer, etc. In due course he presented me with five pages of typescript, almost more than the pamphlet itself!

One evening Angela and I strolled round to the A.D.O.'s house to pay a call. As we entered the compound we saw a small boy nip into the back of the house. We walked round to the front which was all shut up, but after some minutes the front door was partially opened and a servant told us that the A.D.O. had gone out. We asked him to tell his master that we had called, and left. We both suspected that the Shadow — that being our nickname for him — was in fact recumbent upon his bed. Be that as it may, within ten minutes of returning home he appeared. In the course of conversation it came out that he was a chess player; so we had a game, which to his great delight he won.

The Shadow shewed real keenness to learn the job of an Assistant District Officer. He worked hard; and as time went on I found him to be a useful colleague.

Angela and I went to the re-opening service of the English-speaking Qua Iboe Mission Church in Eket — its roof had been blown off in a storm some months previously. I was sorry to see that no efforts to improve its surroundings had been made in honour of the occasion — cassava still grew right up to the walls of the small building. About half the congregation consisted of students from the Qua Iboe Mission Elementary Training Centre, who were smartly dressed in white shirts and long white trousers and carried rolled up plastic mackintoshes. The sermon was given by a little Nigerian in a tightly fitting, double-breasted grey suit. He preached on the theme "Thou shalt have none other gods but Me", and urged the congregation to have done with juju, sorcerers and the like. On our way home through Eket after the Service we first passed a board which said "Herbal Home" and advertised certain "elixirs" and "talismans", and a little later a banner advertising a native doctor's establishment. In addition to some Ibibio words it bore a picture of a man sacrificing a cook before a spreading tree.

Life in Eket had a distinctly ecumenical flavour. In the course of one week, for example, we had supper with the Flemings of the Salvation Army one evening, and played canasta with the American Sisters at the Lutheran Hospital on another. Sister Holgate from the Methodist Hospital at Oron came to stay with us for four days. Angela, in her capacity as District Commissioner, went one afternoon to the Convent School at Ikot Oquot to supervise Girl Guides; and on Saturday afternoon we had tea with the Nicholsons of the Qua Iboe Mission.

Mrs. Nicholson told us of an experience she had had as a missionary in Eket before she was married. In the course of some village visiting she was taken into a house where a pregnant woman was lying seriously ill. A female native doctor had tried to do all she could for the recovery of the woman but without success, and the parents wished to see whether the white woman would be more successful. They asked her to pray to her God. Mrs. Nicholson said that she could see that the woman was about to die, and for five minutes she wrestled in her mind as to what she should do. Should she pray, although certain the woman would die? Or should she not pray and so avoid giving the people a chance to say either that her God had not heard her or was powerless to do anything? Albeit with little faith, she decided to pray and did so with the native doctor standing beside her. Within minutes of her prayer the woman's condition improved and she lived.

Later in the year I stayed with Mr. Smith, for many years the General Manager of Methodist Schools in the area, and Mrs. Smith in Ikot Ekpene. I went with them to the local Methodist Church for a choral Harvest Thanksgiving Service. Between the pillars of the Church, which were decorated with oil-palm leaves, some strings of faded Union Jacks were tied; and here and there piles of fruit and vegetables were heaped upon the concrete floor. The Service took the form of congregational singing, interspersed with solos. In spite of the singing and periodic applause a small boy who lay flat on his tummy across three chairs in a side aisle remained asleep throughout the proceedings. The District Officer, Ikot Ekpene, was introduced as Chairman of the Service, and several notabilities sat at the same table with him. After the solos members of the congregation wishing to show their appreciation of the singing walked up to the Chairman's table and put a contribution in an alms plate. The "Service" continued interminably, and eventually we left before it had come to an end.

About this time I attended the Anniversary Service at the English-speaking Church in Eket. Fortunately there was no suggestion that I should be Chairman!

However, I was privileged to the extent of being given a seat to myself close to the pulpit. Members of the Atabong Qua Iboe Mission Church choir sat opposite me. In front in the body of the kirk there were several rows of white-clad boys from the Elementary Training Centre, and behind them sat the rest of the congregation. The Reverend Norman Shiels entered the pulpit, which resembled an enormous wooden pen. He told me afterwards that the first thing he noticed was that white ants had attacked the floor and he hoped that he would not go through it! During the reading of the lesson the boys of the E.T.C. zealously followed the words in their Bibles, some even taking their pens out and marking the text. Opposite me the Atabong choir also had their Bibles out; and in the front row I saw a minute boy, who looked no more than five years old, seated between two older girls, all three of whom were craning over one copy.

Later in the Service the choir sang an anthem. Men stood at the back, women in the middle, and children in the front. Each had a sheet with the words and music on it. The five-year-old tot held a sheet like the others and sang merrily. It was difficult to make out the words, but the effect of the singing was quite melodious. The leader of the choir, who was a very little man, faced his choristers and tapped the time with the thick crêpe sole of his right shoe. Almost before the last note had ended the music sheets had been passed along to the end of each row and collected up. At the back of the choir I saw my friend, Mechanicy. I barely recognised him because he looked so neat and trim in white shirt and long navy blue trousers; and he was wearing spectacles — the first time I had ever seen him do so.

Having learnt some months earlier that Angela was due to have a baby in February 1957, I decided that it would be best for her to fly home in October and to spend the intervening period in the care of her parents while I completed on my own my final tour of duty in Nigeria. When the time for Angela's departure approached we gave a small farewell party in our house for Usip, the District Clerk and various other members of my staff. The former appeared resplendent for the occasion. Wrapped around his body and stretching to his ankles he had a mighty length of patterned purple brocade, one end of which was hoisted over his right shoulder. He also wore a transparent yellow shirt which revealed his vest underneath. On his head he had a light-coloured cap of mackintosh material; and he carried a wooden staff. Before leaving at the end of the evening each guest made a short speech in turn in order of seniority, in which hearty thanks for our modest entertainment, hopes for Angela's safe journey home and assurances of support for me until I followed her were expressed.

A day or two later Angela arrived safely in England, and I was back in Eket after seeing her off at Enugu with four months still to serve.

169

Angela was not the only one to leave Eket at this time, because Mrs. Ajoku, Philip's wife, also returned home — in her case because the farming season had come round again. Philip asked permission to go with her to the mammy waggon station to see her off on the start of her journey back to Owerri. In due course I saw them setting off: in front little Philip, wearing shorts and a white shirt, with a small tin box balanced on his head — from a distance looking very like a schoolboy — and fifteen yards behind him his wife, bearing an enormous load in a vast enamel basin on her head on the very top of which there was a single white pillow.

That evening while I was writing to my spouse Mechanicy appeared at the house. In Nigerian fashion he was wearing a woollen pullover around his neck like a muffler. He was anxious about the application he had submitted through me to the Provincial superintendent of Police for a job as a driver; and he was very keen to have this fixed up before the time came for me to leave Eket. He was optimistic about his application succeeding since he had promised, I gathered, "six quids" to a constable in the Calabar police office if he did what he could to get it pushed through.

The pressure of work during my final months in Nigeria was intense, and I am left with a jumbled assortment of recollections of that period. The Universal Primary Education plan involved building ninety-eight new "schools" or classroom buildings throughout the Division; and in addition leases for the sites had to be negotiated, and staff had to be selected. The new taxation procedure necessitated the opening of a new central Tax Office in Eket under my direct control. For want of any more suitable premises this was located in an empty garage close to the District Office. I spent hours in this pitifully ill-equipped building with my new and inexperienced tax staff; and one Saturday as I was pouring over various ledgers cheek by jowl with Obot, the senior tax clerk, I noticed that he was suffering from a skin complaint which I took to be craw-craw. It was, however, something more serious. First thing on Monday morning Usip came across to my house and told me that Obot was down with smallpox; and this was subsequently confirmed by Eric.

A few days later, while on tour on the *Snipe*, Philip was stricken with fever. I found him forlornly squatting on his mat in the microscopic pantry, which he regarded as his funk-hole on board. I looked at his head and arms — no spots. He pulled up his shirt — no spots on his front; but on his back — horrors — a number of bumps! Fearing that these might be an early manifestation of smallpox I decided to return immediately to Oron. I installed Philip in the Rest-House, and brought Sister Holgate to have a look at him. She diagnosed nothing more serious than a touch of malaria, and said that the bumps on his back were due to the fresh fish he had been eating! When on the Sister's departure I told Philip how thankful I was that he did not have the bad sickness, smallpox, he grinned one of his rare grins and said that I need not have been worried. He went on to explain that no one from his village would ever catch this sickness because special medicine to prevent it had been buried in the middle of the village — and for good measure he had in the past had a special protective ointment rubbed all over his body.

I spent several hours with the County Council discussing arrangements for the new Governor's forthcoming brief visit to the Division on 4th February, 1957. At their request I drafted for them an Address of Welcome, which incorporated all the points they wished to include. It was a fine and loyal tribute with agreeable references to the Crown and the benign influence of the British Government; and it was gratifying to hear H.E. in due course congratulate the Council on their thoughtful and well-expressed Address.

The gubernatorial visit was, I suppose, a success. At any rate nothing went disastrously wrong as far as the arrangements were concerned. I met H.E. and Lady Stapledon at the waterside at Oron on their arrival from Calabar. They first spent a moment or two looking around the small Museum. When they emerged from this low mat-roofed building, a wonderfully attired Mallam prostrated himself before the distinguished visitors. His appearance was unexpected, or perhaps I should say "unscheduled". Anyhow he clearly made a good impression, and I introduced him with a flourish as the Serikin Hausa (not as my Head Station labourer!). The first port of call was the Oron Boys' High School, where we attended an assembly of staff and pupils, at the end of which the boys sang a lugubrious refrain about hoping to meet again.

Lady Stapledon then parted company and went straight from Oron to Uyo, while H.E. and I drove to the County Council Headquarters at Ikot Ubo. The Rolls Royce purred to a halt between two ranks of Court Messengers drawn up outside the Council Hall, and we alighted. I had warned the Governor that on our arrival a cannon was to be fired, and that this was to be followed by the playing of the National Anthem by a local band. However, there was no cannon blast, nor was there any National Anthem. After an embarrassing pause a man with a trumpet came to life and unexpectedly blew "Come to the Cookhouse Door"! And then to my relief this was followed by "God Save the Queen". The rest of the proceedings went without hitch. At 1.15 p.m. H.E. re-entered his Rolls. I did so too, and accompanied him as far as the Eket-Uyo boundary. There I changed from the sublime to the ridiculous, and was driven home in a noisy and diminutive Volkswagen.

At the end of January came the news of the dissolution of the Eastern House of Assembly and an eight-page telegram outlined the timetable and procedure for the

171

ensuing General Election. I selected from amongst an abundance of applicants seventy persons to be Registration Officers, and thereafter instructed them in their duties. My stock of 58,000 forms for application for registration as an elector became suspiciously quickly exhausted; and it was evident that some person or persons had succeeded in cornering a large part of my initial issue. I obtained a further supply of about 30,000 forms, which I issued in bulk to the three contesting parties (N.C.N.C., Action Group and U.N.I.P.) hoping to ensure that thereby all would get a reasonable look-in. This appeared to have the desired effect for during the remainder of the registration period I was less harassed than previously by constant reports of shortages of forms. I did, however, receive complaints that many under the age of twenty-one were being registered; and as registrations were in due course found to total the huge figure of 91,000 out of a total population of 240,000 it seemed likely that there was truth in these allegations.

It fell to my successor to make arrangements for polling — on Election Day I was at sea somewhere between Lagos and Liverpool.

I paid one more visit to Jamestown, this time accompanied by my friend Eric. All the usual touring paraphernalia was loaded onto the lorry which was to take it to Oron. This included camp bed, tin bath, the Boys' sleeping-mat bundles, a tin office box full of files and touring books, a few chickens and my hockey stick, which Philip always insisted on taking — possibly in the absence of any more lethal weapon. Anyhow, it proved useful at times in slaying scorpions and various unattractive rodents and insects.

We anchored as usual about 100 yards off shore, and apart from an invasion by flying ants spent a very pleasant evening on the *Snipe*. The next morning we both went ashore — in my case to the Native Court. It was a hot day, and we all began to feel somewhat drowsy. Suddenly there was quite a commotion caused by the scuffling of some lizards on top of the matting ceiling, and the Head Court Messenger rudely roused from his slumbers vigorously shouted "Order in Court!" Eric visited the Dispensary where during the course of the morning he was greeted by a score of people who had at one time or another been his patients in the Lutheran Hospital at Eket. As we were returning together through the village we saw a young man with a small bag hanging from his shoulder. For some reason we enquired what he had in this bag, and to our surprise he produced a "Viewmaster" and a collection of cards offering a variety of views. His selection included: "Nativity Scenes", "Dover", "Windsor Castle" and "Adventures of Tarzan"; and he charged viewers a penny for a card. I had a pennyworth and saw Tarzan grappling with apes and crocodiles.

As Christmas approached a young clerk asked me for leave from December 24th to 28th. When I asked why he could not return on the 27th, he said that he needed the extra day because he hoped to get married. I congratulated him, but it was apparently necessity rather than love which was causing him to wed. He explained to me that the new Finance Law made it imperative for him to marry in order to become eligible for a lower rate of income tax!

I gave a Christmas party for some of the Government staff, and sadly missed Angela's assistance. As each person arrived I pinned a piece of paper on his back, and by asking questions he had to find his partner. Somewhat incongruously the burly Police Sergeant, Rufus Nwanebo, was "LOVE" and his partner was the Senior Warder, who was "KISSES".

I spent the end of the year at the Rest House in Ibeno, and two friends from Enugu came and stayed with me. I noticed that the people of Ibeno intended to see in the new year in appropriate fashion because there were advertisements about the town for a Ball-dance to be held in the Co-operative Hall. Prices of admission were displayed on a blackboard in the market-place: gentlemen three shillings, women sixpence, children threepence, and "men" one shilling!

Shortly before midnight we lit a bonfire in the Rest-House compound. I switched on my wireless just in time for the end of "Auld Lang Syne", and then the New Year 1957 was announced. Almost on the dot the bells of Ibeno's stately Qua Iboe Mission Church began to peal, and from the town the noise of drumming grew louder and livelier. We sat beside our fire, drank a bottle of wine and speculated about the coming year.

After we had gone to bed I was disturbed by the intermittent singing of some revellers in a bar close to the Rest-House. To end the nuisance I got up and walked across to the hut in my pyjamas. In a small mud-walled room I saw by the light of a single tallow lamp four or five bodies grouped around a table on which several empty palm wine bottles were littered. I wished them a happy New Year, and they replied cordially. I then asked them either to continue their celebrations rather more quietly or else to go elsewhere. I returned to bed, and there was no more singing. After a few minutes, however, a native band approached the Rest-House, but possibly one of the revellers intercepted it because the drumming came to an abrupt end. Later it began again in the distance, and slowly faded away.

After he had washed up the supper things one evening Desmond came to me and suggested that as the end of the tour was near at hand we ought to have a photograph taken. I agreed and spoke to Philip about it; and so a day or two later Desmond, Vincent, Bonniface, Philip and I posed for a photographer behind the D.O.'s house. Desmond wore a very bright yellow shirt, new shorts, socks which were formerly mine and sandals. The others, including even Philip, wore long trousers; and Bonniface and Vincent sported ties.

The last official business I did as District Officer, Eket, was to enquire into an application for a lease made by the Salvation Army. For the purpose of this I stopped for half an hour at Ikot Ubo Native Court on my way to Oron, from where I was taking the ferry to Calabar in order to spend a night with friends there (my successor having arrived in Eket). Nine Family Heads declared their right and willingness to lease the land in question; and Major Squibb who was seated at the back of the Court sighed with relief as they made their thumb impressions on the necessary forms.

On reaching my friends' house in Calabar I was given a message to telephone Oron Post Office. This I did, and the nice little Postmaster, with whom Angela and I had often played tennis in the past, gave me the wonderful news that I was the father of a son. The cable from my mother-in-law had passed through his office on its way to Eket, and knowing that I was staying at Calabar he had very kindly decided to get in touch with me there.

The next day, February 13th, I returned to Eket, saying goodbye to good friends in Oron on the way and being congratulated by them in return. That evening I had one final alarm. At 6.00 p.m., the owner of the lorry, which I had engaged to transport my crates to Port Harcourt the following morning, came to tell me that this lorry, which was only one month old, had "done spoil" . . . In moments of stress it had been my wont to appeal to Usip, my able and willing Interpreter. I did so once again, and he rose nobly to the occasion. Within an hour he was back at my house to let me know that he had arranged another lorry for the morrow.

That evening I had a last meal with my close American friends at the Lutheran Hospital. They were in a sentimental mood, and we reminisced about the time we had spent together in that somewhat remote part of Eastern Nigeria a few miles inland from the Bight of Biafra. Before I left they insisted on playing a record of "Home Sweet Home". Later I walked slowly back to the D.O.'s residence which for the past eighteen months had been home. I stood for a few minutes in the bright moonlight near the lofty flagpole, and took a lingering last look at the river, the rubber trees and the silent house.

I was up early the next morning, and by 7.30 a.m. my twenty six crates had been brought out of the Prison Store and loaded onto the lorry. Three-quarters of an hour later the lorry with Philip on board left, followed by me in my faithful MG Magnette. The gang of station labourers gathered round my car and sped me on my way with greetings to "Ma". The last Eket person to whom I said goodbye was Mechanicy. I stopped outside his "workshop", and he came and grinned into the car. He grinned yet more widely when I told him that Madam had delivered a male child — he was highly delighted.

Chapter 16

"It is much in little"

Letters, newspaper cuttings, programmes and a pile of miscellaneous pieces of paper revive memories of days past and of places and people once known so well and now seen no more. The people of Eastern Nigeria were enthusiastic letter writers; and in my possession I still have many letters written to me by a wide variety of people. They do much to recall to mind the endearing qualities and characteristics of those amongst whom I used to live.

Joseph was a friendly young schoolteacher whose acquaintance I made during my first tour. In sending me a photograph he had taken of me he wrote: "May you receive it whole heartedly. By then I was a learner and you know the sun was too intensive . . . .. It is much in little."

The first letter Philip wrote to me was during my first leave. It began: "I hereby to ask about your present feelings and situation. How are you now, my dear Sir? As to my own self I am hole, only last week I suffered headache of which I nearly died but now I am all right". Our ex-small-boy John, who obtained a job as a driver after I had taught him to drive, said in a letter: "My salary now is not too poor but expensive is too much, much expensive makes my salary very poor."

Godwin was an amiable and somewhat rascally ex-serviceman, blessed with plenty of blarney, who constantly sought my help in getting him employment. He began one of his many letters as follows: "This my humble petition may once more appear like 'a bolt in the blue' to you, particularly due to my delatory attitude in penmanship. However, in this vein, I am still sedulous, and being optimistic, I'm sure that my assiduity would not incur your displeasure by my requests." Godwin deduced that I must have got married. "It appears to me," he wrote, "that you are now coupled. Why? Because I often see you a far off in your car PH4 in company of a lady; if thus extend my best wishes to her, please."

When in Ogoja we gave the Head Warder a kitten of which he became very fond. While he was on leave he wrote us a long rambling letter from his home town, in the course of which he said "My pussy is very well with me here at Udi busy with the mouse and rats in my father's compound, and funs with my dogs. As I love the cat, I took it along with me on leave." He was a dear old man and much too kind-hearted to be a gaoler.

Finally a farewell greeting from just an ordinary person — a man in the bush. It does much to remind me of the good nature, the warmth of feeling and kindliness of those amongst whom I lived and worked in different parts of the Eastern Region of Nigeria for eight years:

"I lack words to express my feelings over your departure.

It shall soon come to the time when you will say goodbye to our shores on your departure to England to meet your dear wife, and I pray may Heavens pitch their tents around you. I wish that you may convey my sincere greetings to Ma and say me well to her.

I enclose herein my portrait for Ma to refresh your memory of me while at home.

Fare you well my dear Mr. K. V. Arrowsmith. God bless you till we meet again."